D1518438

The Politics of Race and International Sport

The Politics of Race and International Sport

The Case of South Africa

RICHARD EDWARD LAPCHICK

Center on International Race Relations
University of Denver
Studies in Human Rights No.1

GREENWOOD PRESS

Westport, Connecticut • London, England

Library of Congress Cataloging in Publication Data

Lapchick, Richard Edward.
The politics of race and international sport.

(Studies in human rights ; no. 1)
Bibliography: p.
Includes index.
1. Sports–Africa, South. 2. Segregation in sports–African, South.
I. Title. II. Series.
GV667.L3 796′.0968 74-11705
ISBN 0-8371-7691-3

Library of Congress Catalog Card Number: 74-11705
ISBN: 0-8371-7691-3

First published in 1975

Greenwood Press, a division of Williamhouse-Regency Inc.
51 Riverside Avenue, Westport, Connecticut 06880

Manufactured in the United States of America

To Sandy and to my students at Virginia Wesleyan College, who have helped me to increase my capacity to grow, love, and understand.

Contents

Foreword

The importance of sport in society is still imperfectly understood and inadequately studied. Thousands of books are written about sport—mainly for sports fans—but few are written on the important part played by sport in the thinking and activity of a community.[1] The intriguing degree to which sport is a microcosm of the issues fought out in the larger political arena has hardly been considered.

A specific area of the sports scene, the extent to which political ideology influences sports policy, has received even less attention. This has been the case despite the general recognition that it was in the area of sport (together with other forms of entertainment) that blacks in the United States achieved some of their earliest breakthroughs in the general racist structure.

An especially interesting area of study is that of South African racism and the application of the apartheid policy to sport—a study whose interest is heightened by the long and complex story of largely successful opposition to this policy. That the South African ambassador at the United Nations, Mr. Roelof Botha, should have adverted specifically to the concessions[2] made in sport, when attempting recently to defend his country from expulsion at the Security Council, is sufficient proof.

This scholarly and extensively documented study by Dr. Richard Lapchick, the first full-length study of its kind, is therefore of considerable importance and is performing a valuable service. It is the first major examination of some of the general issues, political and otherwise, which affect international sport, and focuses in great detail on the specific issue of apartheid sport.

Lapchick's meticulous account of events in South Africa over the past ten years (the period over which the campaign against apartheid sport developed) and careful analysis of the forces that operated to bring about certain changes are the most valuable part of the book and an indispensable addition to the limited literature on the subject. There are, of course, other less complete writings on the subject. Richard Thompson's *Race and Sport*[3] was a pioneering work dealing specifically with South African-New Zealand sports relations and is still the best of its kind. Thompson's work is shortly to be supplemented by a study by another New Zealander, Tom Newnham. Muriel Horrell's *Sport and Race in South Africa* was a useful and exact account; it carefully withheld judgment or comment since the South African Institute of Race Relations, which published it, survives under government pressure by resolutely insisting that it is a "non-political fact-finding body." Chris de Broglio's pamphlet *Racism in Sport*[4] is to date the best concise statement of the facts. Lapchick's book is more comprehensive than any of these.

Racism in sport and society is as old as South Africa itself and predates the establishment of the Union of South Africa in 1910. After a rapid survey of earlier conditions, Lapchick concentrates on the most eventful and significant years: the period from the 1950s to the present. At all times, as he demonstrates, the problem had the same elements: to establish that the South African body was racist and excluded blacks; to establish that the international bodies forbade racial discrimination in sports; to document the practice of racial discrimination in South African sport; and finally, and most difficult, to secure action by the international authorities against the racist South African bodies, first by constitutional means and, then, if need be, by protest and direct action.[5]

Some day a South African who was intimately involved in the campaigns against racism in sport will, hopefully, write the inside account of what was an absorbing and exacting—and often hazardous—struggle. George Singh, lawyer and former secretary of the South African Soccer Federation—the largest nonracial sports body and one of the first to fight for international recognition—might do it; but he was long ago banned, detained in prison without trial, and forbidden to associate with any sports organization. Morgan Naidoo, former secretary of the Non-Racial South African Swimming Federation, might do it; but he too has been banned, forbidden to associate with sports bodies or to write anything for publication under penalty of criminal prosecution. Don Mattera, the young poet and journalist who set up the recent encounter between Arthur Ashe and the nonracial sports officials who accused him of Uncle Tomism, might do it; but he too has been banned (on the eve of the Ashe meeting he had arranged) and has been deprived of the right to earn his living as a journalist. These are only some of the many who have felt, in different ways, the pressures of the South African police state because of their opposition to racism in sport. All would have an interesting story to tell if they were permitted to do so.

Many of the courageous sportsmen have been silenced, but they have the satisfaction of knowing that there has been steady and increasing success in the fight. Indeed, since the formation of the South African Sports Association at the Milner Hotel, East London, in October 1958, there has been a long list of successes. The three most important and satisfying are probably the exclusion of South Africa from the 1968 Olympic games (Mexico City), the expulsion of South Africa from the International Olympic Committee in 1970 (Amsterdam), and the related exclusion of Rhodesia from the 1972 Olympics, an event which evoked worldwide attention until it was overshadowed by tragic events at Munich. Of almost equal importance has been the recent success in expelling racist South Africa from the World Football Federation (FIFA) at its Frankfurt congress in July 1974.

All these events (with the exception of the last, which came too late) are fully chronicled and carefully analyzed by Lapchick.

There are many other useful discussions in the book: the comparison of South African sports policies with those of Nazi Germany, the political factors influencing international voting patterns, and the role of the black sportsman in the United States. And much more.

Two questions need to be asked: why has the struggle been so long and arduous? And what is the future of this endeavor? From Lapchick's study an answer to the first emerges: it is that racist South Africa has powerful friends. They are her trading partners and allies in the "free" world. These Western countries, which have a stake in South African stability and in the South African economy to insure the continued profitable exploitation of South Africa's resources and manpower, have consistently acted in the realm of sport, as they have in international politics, to defend their racist friend. What of the future? The South Africans will press on, in sport as in all other areas, with their demands for social justice and human equality, and will no doubt march on to a successful conclusion. The apartheid gamble, to persuade the world to accept the notion of multinations and of multinational sport, will fail. But much will depend on allies in other countries; on those who share their commitment to the eradication of racism from all spheres of human activity. There is much that opponents of racism can do to support those fighting racism in sport. Far too little is being done—though this is not to minimize the splendid efforts made in Australia, Britain, New Zealand, and, of course, Africa.

Even as this is being written, Walter Elcott (U.S.A.) and Basil Reay (Britain), the president and secretary of the ILTF respectively, are defending South Africa's membership in the Davis cup tennis competition after India had refused to play South Africa in the finals because of apartheid in tennis. And protests are taking place in Australia, against Gary Player participating in a golf tour, and in France, against the apartheid Springbok Rugby team touring there. The struggle continues.

I am glad to take this opportunity to pay tribute to our many friends and allies; I am pleased to have had some share in the preparation of this study; and grateful that I was able, with many thousands of others, to have some part in the fight against racism in sport in my country and elsewhere.

Richard Lapchick's study is the fullest record available at the present time. It has a significance far beyond the boundaries of sport: it is instructive both on the nature of racism and on the methods which can be used to challenge and overcome it. It is an important document and a valuable achievement which must, itself, contribute to the ongoing struggle.

Dennis Brutus, Visiting Professor,
University of Texas, Austin

NOTES

1. *The Revolt of the Black Athlete* by Harry Edwards (New York: Free Press, 1969), *Rip Off the Big Game* by Paul Hoch (New York: Anchor, 1972), and essays by Jack Scott of the Institute for the Study of Sport and Society (Oberlin) are valuable contributions.
2. In a recent speech before the Special Political Committee of the General Assembly of the United Nations (September 1974), I stressed that the "concessions" made in sport by the Vorster government, while they were inadequate "window-dressing" designed to save apartheid sport from total isolation, nevertheless represented a retreat for the "granite" policy of the past and an erosion of the apartheid position in sport.
3. London: Oxford University Press, 1964.
4. London: International Defence and Aid Fund, 1970.
5. Peter Hain's *Don't Play with Apartheid* (Allen and Unwin) is an excellent account of direct action protests against racism in sport in Britain. A parallel book on the Australian protests is *Political Football.*

Preface

This series will focus on the ways in which human rights in various parts of the world are affected by racial and ethnic variables, interacting with strategic, economic, and class factors. A few years ago the problems of secession, separation, and racial/ethnic conflict seemed confined largely to the newer nations emerging from the constraints of colonialism. Now, however, it is clear that these are problems which cut across the traditional national and geographic boundaries. The industrialized and the socialist as well as the agrarian and capitalist societies are all subject to the forces of irredentism and the aspirations of new groupings. Each in its own setting raises special problems.

The series will not focus exclusively upon the black-white problem, though this is of major importance in our first works. Nor will the African area be the only region considered. The approach is fully comparative and transnational, and will present analyses which illuminate theory as well as provide substantive factual information. The focus in our first studies is human rights because this provides a point of policy relevance. Human rights need to be considered from more than the international legal dimension. Sociological and cultural views of systemic bases of discrimination can provide us with additional insights into the problem. We expect that greater awareness of group identity will lead us to a deeper appreciation of the humanity of all peoples.

George W. Shepherd, Director
Center on International Race Relations

Introduction

> The aims of the Olympic Movement are to promote the development of those fine physical and moral qualities which are the basis of amateur sport and to bring together the athletes of the world in a great quadrennial festival of sports thereby creating international respect and goodwill and thus helping to construct a better and more peaceful world.
>
> Pierre de Coubertin, 1894[1]

> It is bound up with hatred, jealousy, boastfulness, disregard for all rules and sadistic pleasure in witnessing violence—in other words, it is war minus the shooting.
>
> George Orwell[2]

These contrasting and irreconcilable views of international sport represent the extremes of attitude on the subject of the Olympic movement. When Le Baron Pierre de Coubertin helped to rekindle the Olympic flame in 1896, he was unquestionably moved by the noble thought that international sporting competition would help to bring together men and nations—otherwise kept apart by political entanglements—where a common understanding might be reached.

To achieve that end, it was recognized from the outset that international sport must be free from all governmental pressures, and this was incorporated into rule 25 of the Olympic principles. Furthermore, it was ruled that participation could never be determined by race, religion, or politics. The recently retired president of the International Olympic Committee (IOC), Avery Brundage, summed up the need for this principle:

> Were this fundamental principle [Number 1] not followed scrupulously, the Olympic Movement would surely founder. It is essential to the success and even to the existence of any truly international body that there are no restrictions of this kind. . . . As it is,

> the Olympic Movement furnishes a conspicuous example that when fair play and good sportsmanship prevail men can agree, regardless of race, religion, or political convictions.[3]

Indeed, sportsmen have chosen to believe in these principles ever since de Coubertin. On the level of individual competition, it has long been argued that sport is an area where there is equal opportunity for all, based purely on the ability of the athlete, with no reference to the athlete's personal background and/or beliefs; and, on the level of international competition, it has been said that nations compete with each other for the sake of sport only. (As the coach for the Soviet basketball team on its 1973 tour of the United States said, the team was in the United States to give his players a chance to compete, not to win.)[4] Avery Brundage has said, "We must never forget that the most important thing in the Olympic Games is not to win but to take part."[5] In essence, "sport, like the fine arts, transcends politics."[6]

These are the ideals of sport in general and of the Olympic movement in particular. The reality has been something less than the ideal. On the international level, the 1936 Berlin Olympic games were an early example of the politics of international sport. Prior to their opening, these games aroused the greatest worldwide protest in the history of sport to that time. The protest began early in 1933 as the growing oppression of German Jews became more and more apparent. Various segments of the populations of the United States and Western European nations threatened to withdraw their national teams if the games were staged in Berlin.

Adolph Hitler lulled sports leaders, especially Avery Brundage (then president of the United States Olympic Committee), into believing in his integrity with words that would have made de Coubertin proud:

> An honorable and fair struggle awakens the best virtues in man. It does not separate; on the contrary, it binds the contestants together in mutual understanding and equal respect. It serves to strengthen the bonds of freedom between nations. For this reason, may the Olympic flame never die out.[7]

Led by the United States and Brundage, all the doubtful teams participated in Hitler's propaganda festival. After the conclusion of the games, Brundage addressed twenty thousand members of the pro-Nazi American-

German Bund in New York City's old Madison Square Garden:

> We can learn much from Germany. We, too, if we wish to preserve our institutions, must stamp out communism. We, too, must take steps to arrest the decline of patriotism. Germany has progressed as a nation out of her discouragement of five years ago into a new spirit of confidence in herself. Everywhere I found Germans friendly, courteous, and obliging. The question was whether a vociferous minority, highly organized and highly financed, could impose its will on 120,000,000 people.[8]

Perhaps it was possible for Brundage to believe this was a triumph for idealism in sport at that early date, before the Nazi crimes against humanity were committed. However, this claim was repeated by Brundage in 1963 at the sixtieth IOC session in Baden-Baden in full light of Hitler's use of the games as a propaganda vehicle.[9]

Another example of the politics of international sport was the case of the "two Chinas" and the IOC. In May 1959, the IOC ruled that Nationalist China "no longer represents sports in the entire country of China" and must reapply as Taiwan.[10] This ruling was immediately followed by an official statement of position by the United States Department of State:

> It is evident that Communist pressures have been directed to obtaining the expulsion of the Chinese Nationalists. . . . We trust that public and sports organs, both here and abroad, will recognize the Communist threats for what they are.[11]

On the same day, Congressman Francis E. Dorn of New York introduced a resolution condemning the IOC, and Congressman Melvin Laird (later to become the Secretary of Defense) introduced an amendment to it prohibiting the use of any U.S. Army equipment or personnel in the 1960 winter Olympic games, to be held in Squaw Valley, California, if any "free nation" was banned.[12] When President Eisenhower himself condemned the IOC action, Avery Brundage suddenly became an advocate of readmitting Nationalist China as the "Republic of China," a complete about-face in Mr. Brundage's position.[13]

In retaliation for "communist pressures," the United States refused visas to East Germans to compete in the upcoming modern pentathalon world championships in Harrisburg, Pennsylvania.[14] In February 1960, the Department of State refused visas to the East German press and members of their Olympic staff to attend the winter Olympics on the grounds that "admission was not in the best interests of the United States."[15]

This brand of sport, unknown to de Coubertin, has proven to be the rule rather than the exception in the 1960s and 1970s. International sport has been a reflection of international tensions in general and of the cold war in particular.

The Olympic committee of the Soviet Union has fought for the inclusion of communist nations such as East Germany, North Korea, and the People's Republic of China. The United States Olympic committee has, dutifully, opposed the same.[16] Both France and the United States refused visas to East Germans as recently as 1962.[17]

Later in 1960, the fourth Asian games were marred by President Sukarno's refusal to admit teams from Nationalist China and Israel. When India implied that the games became "unofficial" as a result, Indonesian Trade Minister Suharto broke off trade relations, and four thousand Indonesians vandalized the Indian embassy in Jakarta. Prime Minister Nehru accused the Chinese communists of playing up anti-Indian feelings in Indonesia.[18] Demonstrating its pro-Western bias, the IOC chose to ban the Indonesian team from the 1964 Tokyo games for not admitting Nationalist China and Israel; however, it barely mentioned the actions of France, the United States, or the Philippines (which had barred Yugoslavians).[19] The entire Arab League then threatened to boycott the Tokyo games unless the ban on Indonesia was lifted.[20]

President Sukarno left no room for doubt about his intentions for the use of sport, saying, "Indonesia proposes now to mix sports with politics and we are thus establishing 'the Games of the Newly Emerging Forces.' "[21] All of this in the name of sport.

In the United States, Edward Hébert, chairman of the House Armed Services Subcommittee, said that a two million dollar bill for athletes was designed "to make the United States the most powerful nation in the world athletically."[22]

In an incredible statement for a man of his position, then Vice President Hubert Humphrey said: "What the Soviets are doing is a challenge to us, just like Sputnik was a challenge. We are going to be humiliated as a great nation unless we buckle down to the task of giving our young people a chance to compete."[23] This was in reference to the unofficial team defeat (although nations are not supposed to keep a national count of victories, most nations do) of the United States Olympic team at the hands of the Soviet team in Tokyo. Humphrey concluded by saying that the United States must prove conclusively that a free society produces better athletes than a socialist society.

Such events and statements have drawn their share of criticism from the idealist, Avery Brundage. He, too, however, has frequently viewed the role of sports in international politics as somewhat more important than it is in reality. In his own unique historical perspective, Brundage largely attributed the downfall of ancient Greece and Rome to an improper sports outlook:

> Twenty-five hundred years ago the Greeks made a breach in the city walls to receive their home-coming Olympic champions. A city with such heroes for citizens needed no fortifications. When they began to give large special awards and prizes, however, they created a class of athletic loafers instead of heroes. The Games were finally abolished and the glory of Greece departed.[24]

> The Romans did not descend into the arena, which was left to professionals, gladiators, grooms, etc. They were spectators, not partipants, and lacked the discipline of sports training. Eventually a victim of her own prosperity, Rome fell to the barbarians, the hard and tough Goths and Vandals, invaders from the North.[25]

The lofty role that Brundage projects for sports today, led by the IOC, was revealed in his speech to the Sixty-second IOC session in Tokyo in 1962:

> The Olympic movement is a 20th Century religion, a religion with universal appeal which incorporates all the basic values of other religions, a modern, exciting, virile, dynamic religion, attractive to Youth, and we of the International Olympic Committee are its disciples.[26]

One can readily conclude that international sports competition by the 1970s had become a self-important sphere, filled with politics as much as sport. And, yet, all the examples cited above do not touch the most flagrant post-World War II example of the politics of international sport. The case of South African participation in sport, both domestically and internationally, is the most spectacular example. This case marked the shift of major concern in the politics of international sport from ideology (as seen in the cold war aspect already discussed above) to a new factor: race and racism. This shift was, to a large extent, influenced by the rise of non-Western nationalism in general and African nationalism in particular.

The adamant refusal of the South African government to permit integrated teams to represent the country—which is, of course, the extension of apartheid into sports—has led to intensive global pressures and protests. Despite those protests, South Africa was permitted to continue its international competition for nearly two decades until 1970, when the South Africans were dismissed from almost all of the international sports federations, including, most notably, the Olympic movement itself.

Apartheid as the official government policy was introduced by the National Party after its victory in the 1948 election. New laws were gradually introduced to affirm the social system that had already evolved in South Africa since the Union of South Africa was formed in 1910. Apartheid in sport became official almost simultaneously. Before that, the sports bodies themselves had affirmed the social system of segregation in sport. After 1948, the government gradually took control of the sports policy until the 1960s, when the pretense of independent sports bodies was dropped and policies emanated from the highest governmental offices, including that of the prime minister. Indeed, even a ministry of sport was created to handle sports issues as they became increasingly more complex.

South African teams, that is, white South African teams, regularly received front-page coverage in the South African press. (When South Africa is referred to in this text, the reference will be to white South Africa, for it is the whites who control all sports and, of course, the government in South Africa. When the reference is to nonwhite South Africans, this will be so noted.) When Prime Minister John Balthazzar Vorster suggested that an integrated team from New Zealand might be permitted to enter South Africa as part of his "outward policy"—which broke down several segregation barriers on the international level—a national election had to be called for 1970—the issue was that important in South Africa.[27]

Although most observers of South African life were aware of the obvious racial discrimination in South African sport, the international sports decision-making bodies chose to allow South African teams to continue to participate in international games. The decisions of these bodies in general, and of individual nations in particular, at times have seemingly been motivated by some means other than strictly sports criteria. In fact, these decisions, as well as internal sports decisions in South Africa, often seem as motivated by racial, economic, and political factors as by sports factors.

It is clear that politics has become an integral and growing, if unwelcome, part of sports, with significant repercussions for both the future of international sport and the relations of the nations involved. The question of race and international sport is no small part of this politics.

Perhaps it is, after all, more honest to look to George Orwell than to Avery Brundage or Baron de Coubertin for the reality of international sport; perhaps it is "war minus the shooting."[28]

The general purpose of this study will be to analyze both racial discrimination in South African sport and South African participation in international games as it is affected by such discrimination. The method will be a historical study of how the policy of apartheid was extended into domestic and international sporting relations from 1959 through May 1970, when the South Africans were finally dismissed from the Olympic movement.

This study will analyze the South African political system only as it relates to sport. As a brief introduction to the general system, however, apartheid, officially put into practice by the National party in 1948, has three essential components: segregation, racial purity, and white domination.

The racial ideology of the dominant white minority rests largely on the concept that races are basically incompatible and that contact between them results inevitably in conflict. A key to the ideology is the belief that whites, because they are a minority, must either dominate or be dominated.[29] They have clearly chosen the former course.

The result of this ideology has been the series of laws and policies formulated by the National party that enforce the system of segregation: nonwhites (Africans, Asians, and Coloreds) have been stripped of their political rights, as well as their rights of movement, choice of property, residence, occupation, and marriage. These laws and policies render nonwhites incapable of creating a power base as competitive groups. Hence, white domination is assured as long as apartheid remains in force.

A racial group is defined as a group distinguished according to its physical characteristics (such as skin color). The South African government defined four such groups in the Population Registration Act of 1950: white, African (Africans are also referred to as Bantu and Native), Asian, and colored (the Coloreds are a mixed racial group resulting from early miscegenation between Europeans and Africans).

One of the most striking aspects of the case of South Africa as an example of the politics of international sport is the degree to which parallels can be drawn between South Africa's sports policy and that of Nazi Germany up to the Berlin Olympics. This will be discussed in chapter 1.[30]

Chapters 3-5 will deal with several other substantive issues. They are:

1. A study of the importance of pressure groups within those nations that have competed most regularly with South Africa (the United States, Great Britain, and New Zealand). Also included is a study of the more broadly based groups, SAN-ROC (the South African Non-Racial Open Committee) and the Supreme Council for Sport in Africa. The latter group is viewed particularly as it reflects the growth of non-Western, and especially, African nationalism and how this, in turn, affected South African participation in international sport.
2. A study of the reactions of both white and nonwhite nations to the continuance of South African participation in international sport.[31] This covers the period from February 1968, when the IOC readmitted South Africa to the 1968 Games, through May of 1970 when South Africa was eliminated from the Olympic movement itself. A survey of the various national Olympic committees was made in respect to this issue.

3. An analysis of the special relationship between Britain and South Africa in sports and its international repercussions for Britain.

This study is significant for several reasons. The first concerns a survey conducted in the United States in summer 1972, which indicated that the racial factor in sport is not nearly as recognized as the more general political factors. Sixty-seven percent of the total population (black and white) thought that politics and sport were thoroughly mixed at the national level, while 68 percent felt the same about the international level; however, only 45 percent thought that race was a factor in sport (blacks tended to view it as more important than whites; 54 percent of the blacks thought it was a factor, while only 42 percent of the whites questioned did).[32] The case of South Africa may show that the racial factor—not the more general political one—has become the most important theme in international sport in the 1960s and 1970s.

Second, although there have been several books written on some aspects of South African sport and/or sports relations with other countries, there has been no comprehensive, documented, in-depth study of exactly how apartheid was extended into sport and how this affected South Africa's overall international sports relations. With the exception of Richard Thompson's *Race and Sport,* which only went up to 1964 and dealt primarily with South Africa's sports relations with New Zealand, the other books are, more or less, accounts of personal involvement in a specific issue.[33] Furthermore, the general issue dealt with in this study is one that is of wide interest to laymen and scholars alike and, thus, merits a scholarly treatment.

Finally, the growing importance of sport itself makes the study all the more relevant. In the United States, for example, there are many reflections of this growing significance. There has been a proliferation of professional leagues, as well as of teams within those leagues. New professional sports have been created—track and field, for example. Salaries of athletes have become astronomical. The television time devoted to sports has become vast, not to mention the coverage by the press, both in sports sections and as news items. Sports stories frequently appear on page one of the daily newspaper.

Athletes have become heroes as well as anti-heroes (depending on the hero-worshiper's life-style and/or political views): witness Joe Namath,

Mark Spitz, Muhammad Ali, and George Foreman. Athletes are sought out by political candidates and themselves become political candidates.

President Nixon made a habit of calling coaches on the night before a game to give them advice on tactics. When Mr. Nixon made a personal request to the head of the National Football League to end local television blackouts, Commissioner Pete Rozelle refused his request. The President then threatened to investigate the "monopoly" of professional sports.

Internationally, the use of sport can be seen at its best in the cases of Chinese ping-pong relations with the United States and the 1973 tour of Soviet gymnasts, particularly Olga Korbut. It can be seen at its worst in the 1972 tour of the Soviet basketball team in which players had many near fights and the United States fans were hardly polite to the visitors. On the larger scale, the 1972 Munich Olympics clearly demonstrated the danger in making sport too important and too much of a focus of attention. The 1968 Mexico Olympics, with their student riots, should have been, but were not, an indicator that political groups were ready to use the spotlight of international sport to publicize their causes.

The masters of the use of international sport for political purposes were the Nazis in the 1930s and the South Africans in the 1960s, due partially to the great importance of sport in those countries.

The leaders of protest groups also recognize this and have freely relied on this importance in their own countries to make people of their countries look at the issue of apartheid in sport as a reflection of the nature of apartheid for the entire society on all levels.

There are three main hypotheses to this study. These are more for the purpose of understanding the role of race in sport than for actually testing. They are not meant to be quantified or field tested in this study. The hypotheses are:

1. Sport in South Africa functions as a supportive and integral part of the apartheid system. Domestically, when whites and nonwhites compete within the framework of apartheid sport, they, in effect, give their approval of that system. Internationally, when other nations compete with South Africa, South Africans view it as an approval of the political system.

2. South Africa is the recipient of more domestic and international pressure than other nations that have used sport for political purposes and/or introduced politics into sport because the factor dealt with in the case of South Africa is not ideological but racial. This increased pressure is also directly related to the spread of non-Western nationalism, especially in Africa.
3. South Africa is more susceptible to such domestic and international pressure because of the importance of sport in that country. When nonwhites refuse to compete within the framework of apartheid sport, it is viewed as a rejection of that system. Similarly, when other nations refuse to compete with South Africa, South Africans view it as a rejection of their political system.

For purposes of organization, the main body of this book will be divided into four chapters.

Chapter 1 will set out the eight main themes in the history of South African sport. This will serve as an introduction to the chronological study that will follow. The chronological study itself is divided into three parts, a division that has been drawn to reflect the characteristics of the three basic approaches to the extension of apartheid into sport during the period under examination.

Chapter 2 covers 1959 through 1963, with background material from 1946 through 1958 as an introduction. In terms of approaches to the extension of apartheid into sport during this period, nearly all white sportsmen and administrators accepted it. At the same time, it was the period of the growth of the nonwhite protest movement against the extension of apartheid into sport.

Chapter 3 deals with the years 1964 through 1968, when the compromises were made by white sports administrators and accepted by a significant portion of the nonwhite administrators and sportsmen amid a growing international protest against South African sports policy. The question of whether these compromises actually changed apartheid sport will be thoroughly discussed.

Chapter 4 is an examination of the period beginning in 1969 and extending through May 1970, which was characterized by a rapidly growing militant international opposition to the extension of apartheid into sport. During this time, there was also an escalation of demands resulting in calls for complete equality for whites and nonwhites to compete together both inside and outside of South Africa. The culmination was the expulsion of South Africa from the Olympic movement and the cancellation of the South African cricket tour of England, resulting in the almost total isolation of South Africa in international sport.

The concluding chapter will contain an analysis of the hypotheses, as well as a summary of the complex and fascinating story of South African sport and sporting relationships. It will be followed by an epilogue bringing the story of apartheid sport up to 1974.

List of Abbreviations

AOC	American Olympic Committee
IOC	International Olympic Committee
NOC	National Olympic Committee
SAOC	South African Olympic Committee
SANOC	South African National Olympic Committee
SAOGA	South African Olympic Games Association
SAONGA	South African Olympic and National Games Association (the latter four names have all been used for what is, in effect, the Olympic Committee of South Africa)
SCSA	Supreme Council for Sport in Africa
USOC	United States Olympic Committee (same as AOC)

Pressure Groups

AAM	Anti-Apartheid Movement (in this study, the British and Irish AAMs were examined)
ACOA	American Committee on Africa (New York)
ANC	African National Congress (South African, in exile)
CARDS	Campaign Against Race Discrimination in Sport (England in late 1950s)
CABTA	Citizens All-Blacks Tour Association (New Zealand in the late 1950s, 1960)
CARE	Citizens Association for Racial Equality (New Zealand, 1960s, 1970s)
CARIS	Campaign Against Racialism in Sport (Australia, late 1960s, 1970s)
CCIRS	Coordinating Committee for International Relations in Sport (South Africa, 1955)
FCC	Fair Cricket Campaign (England, 1970)
HART	Halt All Racialist Tours (New Zealand, 1969-1970s)
OCHR	Olympic Committee for Human Rights (United States, 1967-1968)

SAN-ROC South African Non-Racial Olympic Committee–became SAN-R Open Committee in 1967 (begun in South Africa in the early 1960s, now in exile in London)

SASA South Africa Sports Association (South Africa, 1958-1962–preceded SAN-ROC)

SONREIS Support Only Non-Racial Events In Sport (South Africa, early 1960s)

STST Stop The Seventy Tour (England, 1969-1970)

Individual Sports

Athletics

IAAF International Amateur Athletics Federation

SAAAU South African Amateur Athletic Union (all-white)

AAU Amateur Athletic Union–United States

Boxing

IABA International Amateur Boxing Association

SAABA South African Amateur Boxing Association (white)

SAN-EABA South African Non-European Amateur Boxing Associations (affiliated to the white body)

Cricket

ICC Imperial Cricket Conference

MCC Marleybone Cricket Club (governing body for English cricket)

SACA South African Cricket Association (white)

SACBC South African Cricket Board of Control (nonwhite)

Football (Soccer)

AFA African Football Association

CFA Coloured Football Association

FASA Football Association of South Africa (white)

FIFA	International Football Federation
IFA	Indian Football Association
NFL	National Football League (white, professional)
SABFA	South African Bantu Football Association
SABSF	South African Bantu Soccer Federation (affiliated with FASA)
SASF	South African Soccer Federation (nonracial)
SASL	South African Soccer League (nonracial, professional)

Golf

SAGU	South African Golf Union (white)

Rugby

IRUB	International Rugby Union Board
SARB	South African Rugby Board (white)
SARU	South African Rugby Union (nonwhite, affiliated with SARB)
SARF	South African Rugby Federation (nonracial)

Swimming

FINA	International Swimming Federation
SAASU	South African Amateur Swimming Union (white)

Table Tennis

ITTF	International Table Tennis Federation
SATTU	South African Table Tennis Union (white)
SATTB	South African Table Tennis Board (nonracial)

Tennis

ILTF	International Lawn Tennis Federation
SALTU	South African Lawn Tennis Union (white)

Weightlifting

FIHC	International Weightlifting Federation
SAAWF	South African Amateur Weightlifting Federation (nonracial)
SAAWLU	South African Amateur Weightlifting Union (white)

The Politics of Race and International Sport

1

Themes in the History of South African Sport

"German sports are for Aryans. German Youth Leadership is only for Aryans and not for Jews." Athletes will not be judged by ability alone, "but also by their general and moral fitness for representing Germany."

Reichssportfuher Hans Von Tschammer-Osten[1]

I, therefore, want to make it quite clear that from South Africa's point of view no mixed sport between whites and non-whites will be practiced locally, irrespective of the standard of proficiency of the participants. . . . We do not apply that as a criterion because our policy has nothing to do with proficiency or lack of proficiency.

Prime Minister B. J. Vorster[2]

Contained in these two quotes, one by the Nazi sports leader in 1933 and the other by the South African prime minister in 1967, are the seeds of the debate that has dragged politics inexorably into sport.

The basic policies seem very simple: In Germany, no Jew could represent Germany internationally or compete with Aryans internally; in South Africa, no nonwhite could compete with white South Africans inside South Africa. In addition, both countries used their influence to keep "undesirable" foreign players from competing in their countries. In the 1936 Berlin Olympic games, two American Jews, Marty Glickman and Sam Stoller, were mysteriously dropped from the four-hundred-meter relay team on the very day of the event.[3]

This chapter deals with the eight main themes in South African sport and compares them to what existed in Nazi Germany. The eight themes are: why is South Africa singled out?; sport in South African life; tradition and law as they affect sport in South Africa; a policy defense; protest of sport inside South Africa; nonwhite opinion in South Africa; protest against sports apartheid outside South Africa; international protest and the resulting change in South Africa's sports policy.

Why single out South Africa when the world is ridden with nations that exercise domestic political repression? In 1959, Avery Brundage, president of the International Olympic Committee, said: "In an imperfect world, if participation in sport is to be stopped every time the laws of humanity are violated, there will never be any international contests."[4] In fact, Brundage said this at the very IOC session during which he knew that the Soviet Union was going to raise the question of South African discrimination in sports for the first time.[5]

Brundage had used the exact words in 1956 to defend the staging of the Melbourne games in the face of the crises in Hungary and the Suez Canal. However, he failed to note the essential differences in the case of South Africa (as well as that of Nazi Germany). In South Africa (and Nazi Germany), the sports policy was intricately linked to the political system, a political system that had institutionalized racism (and ethnocentrism) as part of the sports structure.

In other nations where political repression is a fact of life (South Africa's defenders invariably point to the Soviet Union), there is no evidence that an entire racial or ethnic group has been excluded from participation in sport. If an athlete has been banned from a nation's competition because of his political convictions, he has the ability to change those convictions. In South Africa, a black cannot become white just as a Jew in Germany could not become Aryan.

A great deal of time passed before the South Africans themselves were able to realize how their own form of repression differed from others and why they were the targets of such massive international protest. The first acknowledgment of such a realization was an editorial in the *Rand Daily Mail* [Johannesburg] following South Africa's exclusion from the 1970 Davis cup:

> Nothing could have illustrated more sharply the fact that it is racialism, not politics, that is causing our isolation in sport than the decision of the International Lawn Tennis Federation to ex-

clude South Africa from the Davis cup competition while allowing Rhodesia to go on participating. . . . The point is that there is an essential difference between politics and racialism. The one concerns the general manner in which a country orders its political affairs; the other amounts specifically to a denigration of a portion of the human race.[6]

SPORTS IN SOUTH AFRICAN LIFE

When the IOC commission to South Africa was in the process of completing its investigation into charges of racial discrimination in South African sport in 1967, Lord Killanin, the head of the commission (and now IOC president), said he was amazed at the extent to which South Africans go out for sports: "South Africa is obviously a very sports minded country."[7]

According to Dennis Brutus, Chris de Broglio, Omar Cassem, and Peter Hain, sports approaches the status of a national religion in South Africa.[8] Brutus, de Broglio, Cassem, and Hain are the primary leaders in the movement for integrated sport in South Africa. All four were born in South Africa and now operate in exile in London. In surveying the press of South Africa, especially after 1964, sports stories were as likely to be found on the front page as in the sports sections of the newspaper.

Another indication of the importance of sports in South African life can be demonstrated by the number of times that cabinet ministers, as well as the prime minister himself, have spoken out detailing apartheid sports policy. The best known example of this to America is how Vorster personally banned black American tennis star Arthur Ashe from entering South Africa to compete in the 1970 South African Open.

Sport is perhaps even more important in the international context than domestically, for it is with international sports competition that South Africa is able to measure itself against the rest of the world. Many government proclamations have been made to regulate international sports. In fact, it was one of the key factors in Prime Minister Vorster's calling of the 1970 national election as many disputed his "liberal" international sports policy.[9] South Africans view these international events as having importance far beyond the sports field. *Die Volksblad* [Bloemfontein] on October 28, 1969, said, "Every international success of

South Africa is a blow against our sport and political enemies."[10] *Die Burger* [Cape Town], at the time of South Africa's sports controversy with England over the 1969-1970 Rugby tour and the 1970 Cricket tour (see chapter 5), said that South African players had an extraordinary responsibility to influence the British public opinion in favor of South Africa.[11]

This recalls a statement by the German Press *(Der Angriff)* after the German soccer team played in London in December 1935 amid widespread British protests: "For Germany, it was an unrestrained political, psychological and, also, sporting success. . . . It is hardly a secret in well-informed circles that a resumption of closer contact with Great Britain is earnestly desired."[12] As early as 1933, the Reichssportfuher Hans Von Tschammer-Osten had said, "Sports are something to conjure with in international relations and it is my duty to improve these relations."[13]

Later, when the American Olympic Committee voted to participate in the Berlin Olympics despite the controversy then raging in the United States, Reichssportfuher Osten said that the decision marked "a turn in the international campaign of hate against Germany."[14]

At the opening of the games neared, the official Nazi party newspaper, *Volkischer Beobachter,* revealed the propaganda value of the games and the national exhibit, Germany: "The exhibition will present a concrete demonstration of the National Socialist principles and program."[15]

Despite Brundage's assurances, both before and after the Berlin games (he was then president of the American Olympic Committee and his "investigation" of the conditions in Germany with respect to the Jewish people convinced the AOC to go to the games) that the Olympic games were run solely by the German Olympic committee and the IOC, the German government actually paid for all the sports facilities, and the army paid for the Olympic village, which was later to become an army facility.[16]

The use of the games as blatant propaganda was highlighted by the dedication: "Germany's thousands of years of history find their ultimate meaning in Adolf Hitler. Adolf Hitler fulfills a thousand year old German dream."[17] The official Olympic poster had a map of Europe that included German-speaking sections of Southeast and Central Europe within Germany's borders.[18]

When the Austrian team arrived in Berlin, the members were greeted by the German national anthem.[19] The opening ceremonies showcased the British and French teams giving the Nazi salute to Hitler. The 100,000 spectators cheered them wildly. When the American team refused to salute Hitler, the crowd showed tremendous displeasure.[20]

When black American athletes began to roll up victories, *Der Angriff* attacked the AOC for bringing "black auxiliaries" to the games.[21] The victories by these blacks caused a huge storm in Berlin. An English report charging that the blacks had leg operations to increase their speed was circulated. The Germans claimed they were effective because of their peculiar bone structure, while the South Africans openly deprecated their achievements.[22]

But the Germans had their sports propaganda success as they rolled to an impressive athletic triumph. Thus, Nazi Germany utilized its sports and sports festivals as tools of propaganda so effectively that it was able to lull sportsmen and diplomats alike into believing that Germany was a fine nation in the family of nations. Richard D. Mandell in his study, *The Nazi Olympics,* maintains that this was a major turning point for Hitler, giving him tremendous self-confidence in the international spectrum.

The lesson was not lost, for other nations have used sports ever since as a vehicle for national prestige. That the South Africans have used this vehicle most effectively is attested to by the fact that they were able to continue competing in international events for so long.

As will be described in detail in the next chapters, many whites in South Africa would like to see nonwhites banned as sports spectators as well as participants. Could it be that the overriding reason for this desire is that perhaps it is only as spectators that nonwhite South Africans may express their true feelings about apartheid in sports? While numerous nonwhites are hauled out of segregated sports associations to defend apartheid in sports to international sports bodies, nonwhite South Africans at matches invariably cheer wildly for the opposing team and boo the South Africans.[23] Nonwhites have also mounted several successful boycotts of apartheid events that have meant the difference between a profit or a loss for the promoters.[24] Thus, in more than one way, sport is a vehicle by which nonwhites are able to express their frustrations against apartheid.

The important point made in this study is not that sport is important to white South Africans but that nonwhites began to view international sport as being important for themselves. This awareness began slowly in the late 1940s and did not get off the ground until the late 1950s. Once these nonwhite sportsmen got together, the course of South Africa's international sporting relations was challenged time and again, leading eventually to its virtual isolation in international sport.

TRADITION AND LAW IN SOUTH AFRICA

In South Africa, a combination of traditional policy and law regulates sport. There are no laws per se banning mixed sports participation in South Africa. In fact, until 1956 there were no major government policy statements on sports. One reason for this was that the national sports organizations themselves enforced a color bar and, thus, there was no need for a specific government policy. It was not until 1956 when the international federation withdrew recognition of the white South African table tennis body that any meaningful challenge to apartheid in sports had been raised. Dr. T. E. Donges, the minister of the interior, jumped in at this point to spell out the traditional policy.

Basically, Donges affirmed the principle that white and nonwhite sport must be completely separate, both on the competitive and administrative levels. This principle applied to both domestic and international competition. Donges threatened that there would be repercussions for anyone who attempted to change South Africa's traditional racial divisions in sport. He labeled such attempts "subversive."[25] The seven specific points of Donges' statement will be detailed in the next chapter. With few modifications between 1956 and 1970, these became the major tenets of South Africa's extension of apartheid into sports.

In an interview, Omar Cassem, an exiled leader of SAN-ROC living in London, revealed how these policies affected nonwhite sports proficiency in South Africa:

> In strictly sporting terms, we had no control of good facilities as these were all controlled by the white sports organizations. Even the facilities we had were not adequate because so many of us wanted to play. I know some great cricket and soccer players who only played three weeks because of the lack of facilities. It was amazing that they were as good as they were.

> By not being able to compete against whites or international teams, we were not able to develop the subtle points of our game or compare styles with the white stars. In my time, it was the sports organizations that kept us out. Now it is primarily the Government.
>
> Another factor was that we had to obtain permits to play outside our home areas. How many of us could bother to do that? Too few!
>
> When we were finally banned as spectators in so many areas—my god—we could not even watch the bastards play to see their technique without getting a permit from the Government.
>
> In non-sporting terms, we had nowhere near as much leisure time to practice—even if we had the facilities. That went with economic self-sufficiency, and damned few of us fit that bill.[26]

Again, parallels to Nazi Germany come to mind. In June 1933, Osten approved the anti-Semitic resolutions in German sports clubs, which, taken with the municipalities, controlled most of the sports facilities in Germany. Therefore, German Jews were not able to train properly.[27]

In November 1933, Osten ruled that Jews could not be members of athletic governing boards, thus effectively cutting them out of sports administration.[28]

In August 1935, Osten ruled that Catholic and Protestant athletes must join Nazi consolidated sports clubs, with a commitment to Nazi principles and ideals, if they were to compete for Germany.[29] Jews could not join these clubs, even if they placed their faith in National Socialism. Jews were also forbidden to compete abroad.[30]

As Cassem pointed out, mixed audiences are not allowed to view sports events in South Africa, except by government permit. This was made official in February 1965 under Government Proclamation #R26.[31] However, this policy of spectator bans had been evolving gradually since the Bloemfontein city council banned nonwhite spectators in 1955.[32]

In Nazi Germany, there were similar spectator bans. In August 1935 Jews were forbidden to attend the winter Olympic games in Germisch, and signs on the gates proclaimed, "Jews are not admitted."[34] (These signs were later taken down because of international protest.) In October, a United States swimming team swam in Berlin before an all-Aryan audience. A sign over the box office read, "Jews are not wanted."[34]

Thus segregation of sports was complete in both countries, encompassing athletes, administrators, and spectators.

Despite these handicaps for nonwhites in South Africa and for Jews in Nazi Germany, the nonwhites and Jews both produced star athletes. Frustrated by their inability to compete at home, however, many of these athletes had to leave to compete abroad.

In 1947, Ron Eland left South Africa where he had been completely unrecognized. By 1948, he was representing England at the Olympic games in weightlifting. Jake N'Tuli, who could not box for South Africa, became the British flyweight champion in 1952. David Samaai, a nonwhite tennis star who could not compete in South Africa, played at Wimbledon in 1954. Four exiles starred in soccer abroad: David Julius played in Portugal; Steve Mokone in Holland, Italy, and Spain (Mokone later worked for the American Committee on Africa in the 1968 Olympic boycott movement); Kaiser Motaung, who became the most valuable player in the United States Soccer League; and Albert Johanneson (the English champion), who starred for Leeds United. Two weightlifters left South Africa and lifted in England: Reg Hlongwane (who also helped reorganize SAN-ROC in London), and Precious McKenzie, who became the British Commonwealth weightlifting champion in 1966. In nonwhite golf, the names of two South Africans predominate: Edward Johnson-Sedibe, presently an English professional, and Sewsunker "Papwa" Sewgolum. In cricket, Owen Williams, Dik Abed, Ghulam Abed, Cec Abrahams, and John Neethling, all South Africans, played professionally in England, in addition to Basil D'Oliveira, the most controversial of all nonwhite South African athletes. Perhaps the most curious of all the South African athletes forced to compete abroad was Ronnie Van der Walt, who was moderately successful white boxer until the government decided that he was colored. He left South Africa in 1967 to box in England because he could no longer box against those he had been fighting for so many years in South Africa.[35]

Similarly, in the short reign of Reichssportfuher Osten from 1933 to 1936, several well-known Jewish athletes fled the country. Alex Natan, who was part of the four-hundred-meter relay team that held the world record, emigrated to England. Rudi Ball, Germany's top hockey player, went to France. Germany's number one tennis star, Dr. Daniel Preen, fled to England after he was banned from competition by the German Lawn Tennis Association in 1933. Helene Mayer, the German fencing champion, was competing in the United States. (Mayer was to be the center of a storm that eventually led to her being the "compromise Jew" on the German Olympic team in 1936 where she won a silver medal. At the victory ceremony, she gave the Nazi salute to Hitler.)[36]

This list of exceptional exiles from both South Africa and Nazi Germany made it more difficult for the South Africans to claim with any credibility that nonwhites would be selected for mixed national teams except that none qualified; and for the Germans to insist that there were no Jews who qualified for the Olympic team.

Another form of discrimination in South African sports relates to the segregation of sports administrators. The structure of South African sports, in simplistic terms, follows the diagram shown below.

White Sports	*Some Nonwhite Sports*	*Nonracial Sports*
South African Olympic Committee	No equivalent body	SAN-ROC
↓		↓
National Sports Federations (affiliated to international federations) ←	National nonwhite sports federations (affiliated to corresponding white body)	National nonracial sports federations (unaffiliated, but seeking international recognition)
↓	↓	↓
Provincial sports associations (affiliated to national white federations)	Provincial sports associations (affiliated to national nonwhite federations)	Provincial sports associations (affiliated to national nonracial federations)

Through 1963, when the IOC put South Africa on notice that it would have to end discrimination in sports, the middle group was nonexistent. By 1964, sports administrators of the white federations decided to offer affiliation to the nonracial bodies, including financial aid, training and coaching, the promise of international competition in separate teams, and representation on the national white body. In theory, this seemed like a major breakthrough and was hailed as such by the IOC.

In reality, "affiliation" meant that the nonwhite bodies would be represented on the national white federation as the equivalent of a provincial association. In other words, if there were ten provincial associations making up the white national federation, the nonwhite affiliate would then have one-eleventh of the vote. In addition, in most cases such representation would be through a white official chosen to represent the nonwhites. Finally, affiliated federations would agree that competition in South Africa would be carried on in strict segregation.

Therefore, for the nonracial bodies to accept affiliation would mean to accept apartheid in sport—and fighting this was the essence of their existence. The result was that no nonracial bodies affiliated, but several nonwhite groups broke away from SAN-ROC to affiliate to the white federations because of the promise of international competition. These affiliates have been robustly employed by white sports officials to show their international colleagues that they do not discriminate.

A similar tool was used by the Germans. On the same day that the German minister of the interior banned all Jews from stadiums, sports grounds, and halls, Reichssportfuher Osten recognized as legitimate sports organizations the Sports League of Jewish Front Fighter and the Zionist Maccabi League. Thus, while neither group had access to decent training facilities, Osten was still able to point to the fact of recognition as a sign of nondiscrimination.[37]

Perhaps of more symbolic than strategic importance is South Africa's use of the Springbok colors and emblem, which are awarded to athletes representing South Africa in international contests. In sports, they have apparently become the very symbol of the purist apartheid system. So coveted are they that even when South Africa agreed to send an integrated team to the 1968 Olympics, the Verkramptes, the extreme rightwing faction of the Nationalist party, insisted that a new badge be made for the entire team so that no nonwhite could wear the coveted Springbok emblem.[38]

If it were not so tragic, it would seem almost humorous that South Africa is so principled in its fight against integration that when the very rare nonwhite sportsmen from overseas do compete in South Africa against whites (some Japanese since 1963, the Iranian Davis cup team in 1969, and Sir Ade Ademola as a member of the IOC commission in 1967) they are classified as "honorary whites." Perhaps it is the acceptance of this status that is more tragic than the granting of it.

Unfortunately, South Africans cannot even claim credit for creativity; the Germans beat them to it in 1935 when they declared Helene Mayer—

who had been living and competing in the United States while retaining German citizenship—the only Jewish member of the 477-member German Olympic team,[39] to be an Aryan, with a pledge of full rights despite the laws.[40]

A POLICY DEFENSE

South African sports administrators are, generally, defensive about their policies. Their case usually rests on the following points: the national federations have no color bars in their constitutions (while it is true that these bodies struck such color bar clauses from their constitutions between 1959 and 1963, it remains a fact that their membership is all white); South African sportsmen are not responsible for and cannot change government policy (in the process of being excluded from international participation in most sports, many South African sportsmen have spoken out against apartheid in sports); players are chosen strictly on merit, that is, there are no qualified nonwhites to represent South Africa (the number of outstanding nonwhite exiles mentioned above does not support this argument).

It should be noted that the none-are-qualified argument was also used by the Germans. Dr. Theodor Lewald, former president of the German Olympic committee (he was removed because of his Jewish ancestry, then retained as an advisor for the games because of an international protest against his removal),[41] said:

> We wish more than anybody in America that we had some Jewish athletes of Olympic calibre. But we have none, and I believe no one in America would want us to put a second-rate athlete on our team just because he is Jewish. That certainly isn't the Olympic spirit.[42]

As in the case of South Africa, the outstanding Jewish athletes in exile do not support this argument.

There are other defenses the South Africans use. They point out that nonwhite bodies can affiliate to the national white bodies and that to isolate South Africa would hurt the nonwhites more than anyone else. The latter argument sounded a great deal like that of General Charles Sherrill, a leading AOC official, when he decried the proposed boycott of the Berlin games: "My second reason for opposing the threatening form of this resolution is that it will do no good for the Jews in Germany, but will accomplish the exact opposite." His first reason was that such a boycott would cause a "move of anti-Semitic resentment" among the youth of the nation as America would not be able to join the Olympic games "because of the Jews."[43]

PROTEST INSIDE SOUTH AFRICA OF SPORTS APARTHEID

South Africans basically had three ways to approach the issue of the extension of apartheid into sports.

First, they could accept this policy. Almost all white sportsmen and administrators fit into this category, particularly in the early stages of the struggle for change (1946-1963). There is no evidence that any nonwhites were totally acquiescent.

The second approach was one of compromise—the granting to (and acceptance by) nonwhite sports associations financial assistance, training facilities, the promise of international competition, and some form of representation on the white national federation if these nonwhite associations affiliated to the national white federation. Nevertheless, under this approach, the apartheid system in sport was accepted and maintained intact, save for whatever form of representation there was in the national white federation for the nonwhites. Advocates of this position included many white sportsmen and administrators in the middle period of the struggle for change (1964-1968), as well as a difficult-to-determine number of nonwhite sportsmen and administrators. The number was probably quite small but growing larger throughout the middle period.

The final approach was one of resistance—the refusal to accept the extension of apartheid into sports and an active effort to reverse this course until there was complete equality for whites and nonwhites to compete together both inside and out of South Africa. Into this category fit almost no whites in the early and middle periods, with a slight softening of opinion beginning in 1970 (after South Africa was expelled from the Olympic movement and the 1970 Cricket tour of England was canceled), and a substantial number of nonwhites, especially after the formation of the South African Sports Association (SASA) in late 1958 and the South African Non-Racial Olympic Committee (SAN-ROC) in 1962. SAN-ROC, itself in exile since 1965, became the dominant force in the nonracial movement for sports in South Africa.

NONWHITE OPINION IN SOUTH AFRICA

It is a very difficult task to determine accurately nonwhite opinion in South Africa on the question of South African sports policy. If one listens to white sports administrators of bodies affiliated to the white national federations, it would seem that nonwhites became increasingly more satisfied with the compromises worked out by the white administrators in conjunction with the South African government.[44]

However, according to SAN-ROC and protest groups outside South Africa, nonwhite South Africans are very dissatisfied with the compromises worked out. They claim these compromises are merely tokenism and are designed to avoid isolation in international sports; they are not the result of some newly found moral need to end apartheid in sports. SAN-ROC claims that it represents nonwhite opinion in South Africa since it is free to say what it believes about the situation.[45]

PROTEST OUTSIDE SOUTH AFRICA AGAINST SPORTS APARTHEID

The protest movement against apartheid sports outside South Africa has developed rapidly since the formation of SASA in South Africa. This protest has manifested itself in several forms: outspoken members of the clergy giving the movement a moral tone; many union members, especially in New Zealand, Australia, and England, threatening to cut off their services if their national team visits South Africa or if a South African team visits their country; politicians, especially in England and the United States, taking sides on the advantages and disadvantages of sports contacts with South Africa; direct action demonstrations against South African touring teams; united actions on the part of African nations in opposition to South Africa's participation in international events; threats of and actual boycotts by the socialist countries when they were scheduled to compete against South Africa, especially in tennis; representations made to the IOC concerning discrimination in

South African sport; and, finally, the formation of pressure groups concerned specifically with South Africa's participation in international sports in New Zealand, Australia, England, and the United States. SAN-ROC, so essential to the protest movement inside South Africa, has also been a catalyst for action outside South Africa, especially since it went into exile in London in 1965.

According to Chris de Broglio of SAN-ROC, the history of the movements outside South Africa can be broken into two periods. First, the protest centered on discrimination in South African sports as the only reason not to compete with South Africa. Second, as the pressure groups grew, concern began to be equally centered on the effect that such a contact would have on the domestic relations of the nations involved in competition with South Africa.[46]

In the 1930s, protests against the staging of the Olympic games in Berlin were held in Canada, Britain, Sweden, France, the Netherlands, Poland, Palestine, and, of course, the United States.[47] Despite the protests, all of these nations sent teams to Berlin, although several also sent teams to the Workers' games in Barcelona, which were organized as a protest to the Berlin games.[48] The U.S.S.R. and Spain were not represented in Berlin, but this was not as a result of pro-Jewish sentiments on the part of either nation.[49]

Two international pressure groups–the Committee for the Protection of the Olympic Ideal in Amsterdam and the French Committee for the Preservation of the Olympic Spirit in Paris–were formed with the specific goal of having the Olympics moved from Berlin.[50]

In the United States, where the Berlin boycott movement had the widest base, another special group was formed: the Fair Games Committee, which was led by many prominent public figures.[51] Other groups were involved in the American protest between June 1933 and January 1936: twenty Olympic champions; various Catholic and Protestant groups; numerous Jewish groups; six United States Senators; seven governors; forty-one university presidents; the American Federation of Labor; the Women's League for Peace; various black groups, including the NAACP; the American National Society of Mural Painters, which withdrew its Berlin exhibit; and the Amateur Athletic Union (AAU).[52] The last was particularly important: without the AAU's sanction, no American athlete could go to Berlin. In November 1933, the AAU decided it would boycott the games unless the Germans changed their policy immediately.[53]

Reichssportfuher Osten's reply clearly showed the importance which Germany attached to America's participation in Berlin:

> The protest of the AAU is a complete impossibility and represents the dirty handywork of conscienceless agitators who want systematically to undermine Germany's position abroad.[54]

The Germans knew that if the United States did boycott, many other nations would probably follow, and the games would have been a failure.

When the AAU appeared ready to finalize its decision in December 1935, Avery Brundage said that American athletes must meet this

> . . . un-American boycott offensive with historic American action. . . . To those alien agitators and their American stooges who would deny our athletes their birthright as American citizens to represent the United States in the Olympic Games of 1936 in Germany, our athletes reply in the modern vernacular, "Oh, yeah!"[55]

He went on to say that American athletes must follow "the pattern of the Boston Tea Party, the Minute Men of Concord and the troops of George Washington at Valley Forge. . . . Regardless of AAU action, we [AOC] are going to send a team abroad."[56]

The American protest against the Berlin games was clearly not the work of one particular ethnic or religious group; it represented a cross-section of society that spanned religious, economic, and political boundaries. This protest movement brought together twenty thousand people in August 1935 at Madison Square Garden to ask for the withdrawal of the American team from the 1936 games.[57] This remains the largest single group ever to come together at one time to protest a sports-related event.

INTERNATIONAL PROTEST

With regard to those who protest South African sports policy and seek South Africa's isolation in international sports, there are two schools of thought as to the results of such an aim.

The first school of thought argues that even though apartheid is a despicable policy, only through continued sports contact will South Africa be made to change its sports policy—that is, when South Africa sees that a multiracial society is a viable alternative to apartheid, it will change its apartheid policy, at least, in sports. This can be called the "bridge-building" approach. Among its advocates are many sports administrators outside of South Africa.

The second school of thought argues that nations which continue sporting contacts with South Africa are actually condoning and supporting apartheid, and that South Africa will never change its policy with the bridge-building approach. This group argues that the only way to cause meaningful change in South African sports policy is to isolate it from the international sports community. Thus, according to this argument, the white population of South Africa, for whom sports are so important, will demand that the government change the sports policy in order to avoid isolation. This is the isolationist approach. Among its advocates are SAN-ROC and the SCSA.

The case of Nazi Germany might give a clue to the effectiveness of these approaches. The original Nazi plans were to have no Jews associated with their Olympic team. Hitler had even asked for Lewald himself to resign. However, at this point, the Americans made their first threat of withdrawal from the games, and Lewald was quickly restored to an advisory capacity. As an investigation by Avery Brundage into charges of discrimination neared, the Reichssportfuher requested the Jewish federations to name fifty Jewish candidates for the Olympic team.[58] *Before* Brundage undertook his investigation, he told American athletes to prepare for the games.[59] As Brundage left Germany, Rudolf Hess, minister without portfolio in Hitler's cabinet, ordered that Nazis could not fraternize with Jews. Brundage expressed interest in the order.[60] The AOC, which met with Brundage and voted to accept Germany's invitation to participate in the games, claimed that sport was the wedge that would lead to the end of discrimination in Germany. In a setting that added irony to the situation, the AOC meeting was held in the New York Athletic Club, which barred Jewish membership.[61]

With all the major nations deciding to participate in the games, the Jewish fencing star, Helene Mayer, became the only remaining "bridge" in the summer games as she was the only Jewish member of the 477-

person team. With the threat of isolation gone, the Germans made no real compromises. In 1959, Brundage recalled the situation and analyzed it in the following manner:

> In 1936 there was an organized and well-financed attack on the Games of the XIth Olympiad, because certain individuals and groups did not approve of the German Government at that time. . . . The outcome, however, was a great victory for Olympic principles and the United States was represented by one of its largest and best teams.[62]

In 1963, he added: "the facilities were superb, the competition was keen and the Games were a huge success notwithstanding the vicious efforts made to destroy them."[63] Brundage obviously felt that one Jewish team member out of 477 was a worthwhile bridge, and all that followed for the Jewish people in Germany did not dampen his enthusiasm for the 1936 games.

It does not take a great deal of insight to see that there were certainly no lasting bridges built in terms of an end to discrimination against the Jews. One would have to decide if the month-long journey away from discrimination merits the tremendous propaganda value Hitler enjoyed as a result of the games.

This criterion will have to be applied again in the case of South Africa's proposed concessions for continued participation in international sports in general, and the Olympic movement in particular.

The example of the use of sport in Nazi Germany has been employed as an early indication of how race and ethnicity in sports affect international politics and vice-versa.

In the remaining chapters, attempts will be made to assess the merits of the bridge-building versus the isolationist approaches. There will be many examples of the concessions made and an attempt to analyze their true significance in terms of real change in South Africa's sports policy. The arguments of both approaches will be discussed thoroughly.

2

The Extension of Apartheid into South African Sport: 1959-1963

> I love South Africa. I have many friends there. Of course, I will keep going to play. It is a tragedy that politics has come into sport—but if you ask me, South Africa has the racial situation rather better organized than anyone else, certainly much better than the United States.
>
> Margaret Court, Australian tennis star[1]

Margaret Court made this statement in January 1970. She had played tennis in South Africa for many years and had adequate time to judge for herself South Africa's racial situation. Although her statement is particularly blunt, it is in no way peculiar to her; it is an attitude shared by many white athletes who have competed in South Africa and would like to continue such competition.

By examining the extension of apartheid into South African sport in detail, an attempt will be made to determine what makes Margaret Court and many of her fellow-athletes such staunch friends of South Africa and to see if, in fact, South Africa does have "the racial situation rather better organized than anyone else."

ESTABLISHING PATTERNS FOR APARTHEID: 1946-1958

According to Chris de Broglio, a leading figure in the nonracial movement for sports for almost fifteen years, the first challenge to South Africa's policy of racial discrimination in sport was made in 1946. T. Rangasamy, a leader of nonwhite weightlifters in South Africa, asked the British Amateur Weightlifters' Association for some form of official recognition for nonwhite lifters in South Africa. At that time, the internationally recognized body was the South African Weightlifting Federation, which was all white.[2]

Oscar State, then secretary of the British body and now secretary-general of the International Weightlifting Federation, wrote to Rangasamy in 1946:

> We cannot bring any pressure on the South African Weightlifting Federation to force them to recognize you. Their rules, as with all national sporting associations in South Africa, will not permit of mixed contests between white and coloured athletes. This is also a condition of the South African Olympic Council, therefore no coloured man could be chosen to represent South Africa in the international contests.[3]

Thus, there can be no doubt that it was the national sporting associations themselves, including the Olympic council, that enforced the color bar, even before the Nationalist party took over in 1948. This was to become a crucial issue in the debate with the IOC.

State also suggested that the nonwhites form their own association so they could be recognized as an affiliated association. They would, of course, represent nonwhite South Africa and be completely separate from the white South African association.[4] Finally, State's letter demonstrates how early the international sports organizations were cooperating with white South African organizations.

The first government interference in South African sport after the Nationalists came to power in 1948 occurred in 1951. Shortly after Jake N'Tuli won the British empire fly-weight boxing title while visiting England in 1951,[5] Dr. Donges, the South African minister of the interior, announced that South Africa would not allow nonwhite boxers to enter South Africa to compete against South Africa's nonwhite boxers.[6] It would appear possible that this ruling was made because of the embarrassment South Africa suffered as a result of N'Tuli's impressive achievement. If he was banned from international competition (as he was by this ruling), perhaps his international achievements would soon be forgotten.

Between 1952 and 1954, the South African Soccer Federation (SASF), the nonwhite body in South Africa, negotiated with the white body, the

Football Association of South Africa (FASA), for a merger into one national body. SASF maintained that it represented 82 percent of the population, while FASA represented only 18 percent. However, FASA would allow SASF to join only if SASF accepted with no voting rights on the national committee. SASF did not agree; in 1954, it applied formally to the International Football Federation (FIFA) for international recognition as the governing body for football in South Africa. When FIFA told SASF to attempt to renegotiate with FASA, FASA said that the color-bar law prohibited this possibility.[7]

In 1954, the first governmental ban (in this case, by the Natal provincial council) on organized sport between whites and nonwhites was announced. The council banned mixed sport at all educational institutions controlled by the provincial administration.[8] Natal's younger sportsmen and women would otherwise have been technically free to have mixed competitions since, in most cases, they would not be members of the color-bar sports associations.

The football controversy grew in 1955 as FIFA held an emergency meeting and decided that FASA was "no real national association," since it represented such a small percentage of the total population of South Africa. FIFA proposed that both FASA and SASF join FIFA; however, neither would be allowed to represent South Africa as a whole in international matches. FASA and SASF both rejected this proposal, and the stalemate deepened.[9]

The first internationally publicized charges that South Africa was in violation of the IOC charter because of its policy of discrimination in sport were made in 1955. In July, the Reverend Trevor Huddleston said:

> The Olympic Games are open to competitors from the whole world over . . . with the exception of the non-white peoples of South Africa. South Africa teams to these Games have so far been selected only from the white population of the country although the other sections have produced men of Olympic status.

Huddleston referred to the achievements of Jake N'Tuli and Ron Eland, the Colored weightlifter who represented England in the 1948 Olympics. He continued:

> By accepting these colour-bar teams, the committees of the games have also supported the colour-bar, and made it impossible for non-white South Africans to compete as South Africans. We wish to urge that in the future both committees make it a condition of South Africa's participation that the teams be chosen without regard to race.[10]

In October 1955, Dr. Herman Santa Cruz of Chile, the head of the United Nations Commission on Apartheid, also charged the South African Olympic committee with violating the IOC charter by excluding all nonwhites.[11]

The importance of the issue of the extension of apartheid into sport was becoming internationally recognized for the first time. Nevertheless, the IOC took no note whatsoever of these charges, a luxury it would not be able to afford later.

In 1955, nonwhite spectators were banned at sports events in South Africa. The Bloemfontein City Council ruled that nonwhites were not allowed in the new stadium.[12] This ruling was tested for the first time when nonwhites could not witness the international rugby match between Britain and South Africa because "it would cause friction." (Nonwhites at previous matches had been wildly cheering the British team.)[13] That the Rugby union supported this ban showed that the sports associations were not opposing the extension of apartheid into sports.[14]

The events of 1956 presented four noteworthy breakthroughs important to this study: the first international delegation visited South Africa to try to resolve a color-bar dispute; for the first time, a nonwhite South African body was recognized as the governing body in South Africa for its code of sport, and recognition of the white body was withdrawn; the government made its first all-encompassing sports policy decree; and the first sports protest group in South Africa was formed.

FIFA sent a delegation to South Africa to attempt to break the impasse between FASA and SASF. FASA struck its color-bar clause but maintained that it would have to follow the customs of South Africa, which meant, of course, apartheid. FIFA determined that there were no laws banning mixed sport in South Africa, that is, that only custom and tradition kept the races apart in sport. It later became apparent that as sports apartheid was challenged, official government proclamations were made banning mixed sport and there were threats of legislation for the same purpose.

In the meantime, the African Football Association, the South African Bantu Football Association (SABFA), and the Indian Football Association joined together and affiliated to SASF. SASF now represented all nonwhite football in South Africa.

The FIFA congress, meeting later in the year, put off SASF's application for affiliation for two years until the 1958 congress.[15]

The major blow of the year for white South African sportsmen came when the International Table Tennis Federation (ITTF) recognized the nonwhite South African Table Tennis Board (SATTB) as the governing body of this sport in South Africa. The ITTF had originally decided to recognize both bodies, but when nonwhites were banned as spectators at matches of a tour by Israel, the ITTF completely withdrew its recognition of the white body.[16]

Dennis Brutus, who led the fight for recognition of the nonwhite body, described why the nonwhites were successful in table tennis while they failed to gain recognition in other sports:

> The table tennis struggle had already begun very curiously. This is roundabout 1950, maybe '48, '49. But just about this time, the world table tennis federation was being formed . . . under an enlightened and left-wing president, a man called Ivor Montagu. . . . It was a very fortunate position, in the sense that in many other sports the world bodies had been established for a long time before that. Here the issue was a fresh one.[17]

The success of the SATTB encouraged other nonwhite bodies to seek international recognition. The South African Cricket Board of Control (SACBC) applied, without success, to the Imperial Cricket Conference for membership.[18] The South African Weight-Lifting and Body-Building Federation applied to the IOC so that it could participate in the 1960 Olympic games. As a precautionary measure, Avery Brundage asked the manager of the South African team at the Melbourne Olympic games to assemble the facts with the South African Olympic Committee (SAOC) in case the matter was brought up at an IOC meeting. Brundage, aware of the circumstances, would not bring it up himself.[19] In cycling, the white body, the South African Amateur Cycling Federation, said that, while it could not admit nonwhites, it would be willing to assist the nonwhite bodies and would consider sending qualified nonwhite cyclists overseas to compete.[20] Thus, the pressures were bringing compromises even at this early stage.

The separate actions on the part of the nonwhite bodies, as well as the seemingly encouraging progress, led Dennis Brutus to form the Coordinating Committee for International Relations in Sport as a kind of clearinghouse committee to handle all applications of nonwhite bodies for international recognition. This group failed, according to Brutus "largely because of timidity. People feared to reply."[21] But the important thing was not really its failure. The very fact that it was formed in the first place was crucial to the subsequent formation of successful sports protest groups in South Africa. The idea had been planted.

These events of 1956 were far from unnoticed by the government. Until then, the South African sports policy had been challenged in ways that attracted little attention internationally. But in 1956, a white South African sports body was excluded from an international federation, another federation attempted to interfere in South Africa, there was a proliferation of nonwhite bodies seeking international recognition, and a sports protest group, whose strength was still unknown, had been formed. Sports apartheid was clearly being threatened. It was time for the government to step in.

In late June, Dr. Donges, the minister of the interior, noted that the government was very sympathetic toward nonwhite sports as long as they conformed with the policy of separate development. He then spelled out what separate development meant:

1. Whites and nonwhites must organize their sports separately.
2. No mixed sport would be allowed within the borders of South Africa.
3. No mixed teams should compete abroad.
4. International teams competing in South Africa against white South African teams must be all white, according to South African custom. When South African teams traveled overseas, they would respect the customs of the country where they were playing (that is, they would play against multiracial teams abroad).

5. Nonwhite sportsmen from overseas could compete against South African nonwhites in South Africa. (This apparently lifted the ban that Donges had imposed on nonwhite overseas boxers in 1951.)
6. Nonwhite organizations seeking international recognition must do this through the already recognized white organizations in their code of sports.
7. The government would not issue passports for nonwhite activities designed to change South Africa's traditional racial divisions by any process of eliminating white South Africans from international competition. Donges called such activities "subversive." He was, of course, referring to the activities of the South African Table Tennis Board.[22]

Donges' announcement quickly dashed the hopes of nonwhites that the system was changing and, no doubt, caused much of the timidity and fear that Dennis Brutus referred to with regard to the coordinating committee.

The fear was not unfounded. In January 1957, the South African police, in a raid on the Transvaal Indian Congress offices in Johannesburg, found a letter charging that the South African Olympic Council was discriminatory. The letter was used in the famous Johannesburg treason trial as further proof of "treason."[23] As stated above, Dr. Donges considered any activities toward change as "subversive." The letter was used in this context.

In November 1957, the South African Olympic Committee ruled that no mixed competition would be allowed in affiliated bodies within South Africa's borders.[24] It was unable to make a decision on the question of the possible affiliation of nonwhite bodies.[25]

As a result of this indecision, the nonracial South African Amateur Weightlifting Association was denied admission to the 1958 Cardiff Empire games. The British Empire and Commonwealth Games Federation ruled that nonwhites who were not affiliated to international federations could not compete at the Cardiff games, thus effectively eliminating all nonwhite South Africans as none were affiliated.[26]

On December 26, nonwhites booed the South African cricket team in a test match against the Australian team in Johannesburg. The Transvaal Cricket Union, emphasizing its distress at this demonstration, announced that it would do one of two things to keep out "undesirables": it would either raise the price of nonwhite admission or exclude nonwhites altogether at future matches.[27] At the end of January 1958, the Northern Transvaal Amateur Athletic Union announced that they would allow no nonwhite spectators to view meets in Pretoria.[28] The drive toward banning nonwhite spectators was fully under way.

In June, FIFA made a complete about-face and recognized the all-white FASA as the only governing body for football in South Africa. The government had refused to grant passports to representatives of SASF who had intended to present SASF's case at the FIFA congress.[29] This refusal to grant passports, was, of course, in accordance with Donges' speech of June 1956.

In July, more than five hundred people demonstrated at the Cardiff Empire games because South Africa's team was selected on the basis of color rather than merit.[30] This was the first mass demonstration against South African sports policy held outside South Africa.

But the most important event of 1958 took place in October in East London. Dennis Brutus described the scene:

> We met in October in East London to form a body which had no name, which I suggested we call SASA temporarily, South African Sports Association. This temporary name became a final one. There was some pressure from the Special Branch, intimidating people prior to the meeting and attempting to enter the meeting itself at the Milner Hotel. But, at least in 1958 we got off the ground.[31]

The formation of the South African Sports Association was an event of major importance in the history of South African sport, although surely no one could tell how important at this early date. But SASA's primary purpose was clearly to bring about non-racial sport in South Africa.

Even from this brief look at the period from 1946 through 1958, it can be seen that significant patterns were being formed: the white sports bodies began with color bars and maintained segregation in sport on their own until international pressures began to build up slowly. Token compromises were then undertaken to placate the international forces: FASA struck its color bar from the constitution; the white cycling body offered aid to nonwhites. When the white bodies began to soften their apartheid stands, even to these minor degrees, the government wasted no time intervening immediately. Huddleston and Santa Cruz challenged the IOC and a demonstration was staged at Cardiff. Two protest organizations were formed inside South Africa, one a distinct failure, the other completely untested at this stage. The police began their actions against protestors through the raid on the Indian Congress office and the intimidation at the SASA formation; the government, as Donges promised, withdrew passports from protestors. Segregation at sports events was undertaken, while nonwhite crowds were openly hostile to the white South African teams. And, finally, a combination of international pressure and protest from within South Africa resulted in a white South African body being isolated in international sport.

All these events foreshadowed the events of the next eleven years. But, at the end of 1958, no one could have imagined the magnitude of the controversy and struggle ahead. It is that story which must now be told.

1959

Four dramatic events highlighted the international aspect of South African sports apartheid in 1959: SASA's first campaign was a complete success; this led to the cancellation of two international tours of South Africa and strained relations between South Africa and three countries; the IOC discussed the matter of possible violations of its charter by the SAOC for the first time; and the South African government began to retaliate against sportsmen (as opposed to sports administrators) who were violating South Africa's apartheid customs.

SASA's FIRST CAMPAIGNS

SASA held its inaugural conference on January 10 and 11, 1959, in Durban. Alan Paton, the well-known author and liberal political leader, delivered the opening address. In this address, he said SASA's purpose was to

> coordinate non-white sport, to advance the cause of sport and the standards of sport among non-white sportsmen, and to see that they and their organizations receive proper recognition here and abroad, and to do this on a non-racial basis.[32]

Paton said that SASA was not formed to see nonwhite sport conquer white sport (an apparent reference to Donges' charges of subversion mentioned in his June 1956 policy statement) but to work for "the full recognition of non-white sportsmen abroad, and for their right to represent South Africa if they are qualified to do so, as indeed some of them are already."[33] Dennis Brutus estimated that SASA represented some seventy thousand nonwhite sportsmen in South Africa in all major sports.[34]

In March, SASA had its first chance to oppose apartheid sports openly. J. F. Naude, the South African minister of the interior, announced that a West Indian cricket team would visit South Africa and would play only against nonwhites. Naude said the tour was to be sponsored by the nonwhite Cricket Board of Control (which was not represented in SASA at this time). SASA came out against the tour.[35] It manifested its opposition by petitioning government leaders in South Africa and in the West Indies as well as by public statements by its own leaders, especially Dennis Brutus.

Brutus described what this test meant for SASA:

> In 1959 we engaged in a major campaign to stop a black cricket team coming to South Africa, led by Frank Worrell, which we felt was assisting in consolidating the racial structure in South African sports. It was the campaign in 1959 which, I think, was SASA's baptism of fire. At the same time, it established us firmly in the minds of black and white South Africans as the campaigning body on racism in sports in October 1959 when we succeeded in getting Worrell to cancel the tour.[36]

However, SASA, even at this early stage of its development, did not represent all nonwhite opinion in South Africa. Basil D'Oliveira, the Cape Colored cricket star, had quite a different view of SASA's "success" as he later wrote:

> It was the non-European politicians who called for the Tour to be cancelled. I feel particularly sad that they too should be restricting the development of sport because they insist on mixing it up with politics. . . . Their attitude still denied to the Coloured Africans contact and communicating with people from another country.[37]

(However, as shall be described later, Basil D'Oliveira is a unique figure in South African sport, and this was not to be his only disagreement with those who protested South African policies.)

Even before the West Indian tour had been cancelled, SASA had successfully appealed to Brazil to cancel a planned football match against a white South African team. The circumstances surrounding this cancellation are not totally clear. Ferreira Santos, the IOC delegate from Brazil, claimed that the Brazilian team, which had several nonwhite players, was not allowed to play in South Africa.[38] Reg Honey, the IOC delegate from South Africa, said that the match had been arranged and publicized in South Africa, and South Africa had set no conditions for the Brazilian team; it was the president of the Brazilian team who wired the cancellation at the last minute, he claimed.[39] Still another version comes from Chris de Broglio who said that the match had been arranged between a white team in Cape Town and the Brazilians on the condition that the nonwhite Brazilians remain in Mozambique, where they were touring. SASA then appealed to Brazilian President Kubitschek, who cancelled the tour.[40]

Even though it is difficult to determine the exact circumstances of the cancellation, it is clear that the Brazilians themselves believed the versions of Santos and de Broglio. In August, the Brazilian chamber of deputies studied a bill declaring that "Anyone who, in sports competitions abroad, submits himself or makes another submit himself to the rules resulting from race or colour prejudice, is liable to penal sanction."[41] This was the first time that another nation's government became involved in the issue of the extension of apartheid into sport in South Africa.

The third country to become involved in a sports controversy with South Africa in 1959 was New Zealand. In June, the New Zealand Rugby Union announced that it would not send Maoris on its tour of South Africa in 1960.[42] This announcement was followed by widespread protests in New Zealand, leading to the formation of the Citizens' All-Blacks Tour Association (CABTA). It was formed solely to protest the exclusion of the Maoris from the All-Blacks team. ("All-Blacks" was the name of the team and had no reference to race.) The controversy ultimately reached the prime minister of New Zealand, who refused to intervene in the face of several mass demonstrations in Wellington.[43]

In the meantime, the Soviet Union forced the IOC to consider possible violations of its charter by the South African Olympic Committee.[44] The Russian delegate charged that SAOC violated the Olympic charter, while Reg Honey, the white IOC delegate from South Africa, indignantly asked how South Africa could be so accused without any proof of discrimination.[45] Later, Honey assured the IOC that South Africa chose its Olympic team on merit. The reason no nonwhites had represented South Africa, he said, was that nonwhites had only developed a true sporting interest in the past two or three years and, therefore, nonwhite athletes were not yet up to Olympic standards.[46] After some debate, Avery Brundage announced that the IOC had to accept Honey's assurances that there was no discrimination.[47] From the minutes of the meeting, it appears that the documented charges SASA sent to Brundage were never introduced as evidence at these sessions.

GOVERNMENT INTERFERENCE IN THE NONRACIAL MOVEMENT

The South African government began to use its power over travel documents more and more during 1959. In February, Minister of the Interior Naude refused to grant a visa to an Indian flyweight boxer, Pancho Bathacaji, who had arranged to fight the South African nonwhite champion Sexton Mebena, in Durban before the ban.[48] In March, the government seized the passports of the nonwhite table tennis team, which was on its way to play in the world championships.[49] In December it denied visas to an Egyptian table tennis team that was coming to compete against a team sponsored by the nonwhite South African Table Tennis Board.[50]

The cases of the Indian boxer and the Egyptian team were in direct violation of the policy Donges set down in 1956 when he said that nonwhite overseas sportsmen could compete in South Africa against nonwhite South African sportsmen. Thus, the only part of this policy that would be of benefit to the nonwhites was being violated. It should also be noted that the sports singled out by the government, boxing and table tennis, were the two sports in which nonwhites had caused the South Africans the most embarrassment by having the international federations chastise apartheid sport.

1960

The struggle over the extension of apartheid into sports was expanded in 1960, with SASA continuing to test its strength and the government increasingly interfering to thwart it. Several important events pointed out the growing international concern over sports apartheid in South Africa.

SHARPEVILLE AND SPORTS POLICY

An event quite outside the realm of sport, but one which was to have a profound effect on race relations in South Africa in general and race relations in sport in particular, was what has become known as the Sharpeville massacre on March 21. On that date, between five thousand and twenty thousand people had gathered (the estimates vary) to protest South Africa's pass laws—the laws requiring non-whites to carry documents if they wanted to move about their country—in Sharpeville. The police opened first on the demonstrators, killing 69 and wounding another 178. All the victims were nonwhite. It was soon disclosed that 155 of those shot were hit in the back, indicating that they were in the process of fleeing. The government immediately declared a state of emergency throughout South Africa.[51] The result of this incident was an intensified protest against sports apartheid abroad plus increased police suppression of those protesting at home.

THE ALL-BLACKS TOUR

The controversy over the All-Blacks tour of South Africa continued in 1960. Briefly, the leaders of CABTA met with government leaders in late February, presenting them with a petition signed by 153,000 people opposed to the tour. Still the government refused to interfere.[52] After Sharpeville, the Maoris began to protest their exclusion from the New Zealand team for the first time; however, Prime Minister Nash maintained it would be cruel to send them to a country where they would be discriminated against and announced the tour would go on without the Maoris.[53] Nash, in effect, had agreed to send New Zealand's own racially selected team to play South Africa's racially selected team. All of this, of course, was done for the good of the Maoris.

The All Blacks left New Zealand in May after a state reception, returning in September to another state reception, where the prime minister thanked the team for the "great work you have all done in the cause of Commonwealth trust and friendship."[54] It was also announced, with some pride, that Maoris *would* go on tours to South Africa in the future. No one bothered to explain why the Maoris would be happier in South Africa in the future than they would have been in 1960—but perhaps no one asked.

THE SOUTH AFRICAN CRICKET TOUR OF ENGLAND

In England, another controversy was raging over the upcoming South African cricket tour of England. The campaign had begun quietly and had not gathered much steam before Sharpeville. In fact, the only publicized voice until then was that of the Reverend Nicholas Stacey of Birmingham, who refused to preach at the "Sportsmen's Service" prior to the England-South Africa test match. He also called for a tour boycott.[55]

In South Africa, most observers felt that Basil D'Oliveira was a good enough athlete to be on the South African team. However, this was against tradition and D'Oliveira had to be satisfied with an offer to play professional cricket in England. D'Oliveira's exclusion from the South African side increased the depth of protest in England.

Unable to finance his own way, a series of benefit games were held, a final one being between a nonwhite team and a white team—an absolute violation of government policy. D'Oliveira later recalled: "I don't know exactly how this match came to be staged or who turned blind eyes, but we knew then . . . that the dogma of Mr. Vorster's cabinet is not by any means a true reflection of the wishes of many South African cricketers."[56]

As in the case of New Zealand, the effect of Sharpeville was dramatic in English sports circles. An organization called Campaign Against Race Discrimination in Sport came out in opposition to the cricket tour. Its secretary, Anthony Steel, maintained that it was the South African cricket body that brought politics into sport.[57] The English cricket star, the Reverend David Sheppard, said he would not play against the South Africans.[58] The pro-tour faction was able to counter Sheppard with the Reverend T. M. H. Richards, who said of Sheppard's decision: "What

Mr. Sheppard is doing is to judge the citizens of a country by the policies of their Government."[59] The Marleybone Cricket Council (MCC), the sports body responsible for cricket in England, deemed it "wholly unjustifiable to identify members of the South African cricket team with political issues."[60] In the meantime, the Anti-Apartheid Movement in England planned to have five hundred demonstrators meet the South Africans when they landed at the airport.[61]

The cricket tour, however, was never seriously threatened. When the team arrived, *The Times* [London] had an editorial welcoming the South Africans, warning Englishmen that they must understand the conditions the South Africans live in. The English were told to be kind to them, as they were England's "old friends."[62] In 1960, this seemed to ring true with the English public.

SASA ACTIVITIES AND THE GOVERNMENT

SASA increased its activity in 1960. It spent a great deal of its energies in the campaign against the New Zealand rugby tour, especially in collecting signatures on the petition opposing the tour. It was doing this in conjunction with the African National Congress and intended to send the petitions to Prime Minister Nash of New Zealand. The petitioning became more difficult to do after Sharpeville, and SASA activists had to drive around late at night so the police would not catch them. One of the leaders, Omar Cassem, later said that he sometimes felt like a "secret agent."[63]

That Cassem's caution was justified was borne out when the police raided the homes of SASA leaders Dennis Brutus and S. K. Rangasamy. They seized all of SASA's documents, including the petitions to Nash and letters from Nash, David Sheppard, Otto Mayer (the IOC chancellor), and Anthony Steel of the Campaign Against Race Discrimination in Sport.[64] According to Dennis Brutus, some petitions with more than 7,500 signatures did reach Prime Minister Nash, however, this was only a fraction of the number of signatures collected.[65]

The police action did not deter SASA; perhaps it even increased its resolve. SASA wrote to the IOC, asking it to put the matter of South Africa's sports policy on the agenda for the Rome session. SASA made the following charges:

1. There was no sport in South Africa in which there was an open, nonracial trial.
2. There was not a single body affiliated to SAOC that admitted all South Africans as members.
3. All offers of affiliation made to nonwhites were made on the condition that the nonwhites accept apartheid in the administration of sport in South Africa.[66]

When Dennis Brutus attempted to go to Rome himself, he was denied a passport. Nelson Mahono, a former member of the Pan-African Congress, then living in Ghana, went to Rome in his stead to represent SASA. The Reverend M. Scott went to Rome from England as a representative of the Campaign Against Race Discrimination in Sport and SASA. The IOC dismissed both men and maintained that the South African Olympic Committee (SAOC) had made "every reasonable effort" to choose its team on the basis of merit.[67] Although it was not disclosed until 1968, South Africa's IOC member, Reg Honey, contradicted his 1959 claim that there was no discrimination in South African sport. At the IOC Rome session, he promised that South Africa would make progress in eliminating discrimination in sport.[68]

SASA also wrote to the Imperial Cricket Conference (ICC), the international body supervising cricket in Commonwealth nations, charging discrimination in cricket in South Africa. The ICC, in turn, wrote to the white South African body, SACA, to inquire about racism, and it, in turn, wrote to Minister of the Interior Naude for clarification. Naude's reply, dated June 16, 1960, was indeed clear:

> The Government does not favour inter-racial team competitions within the borders of the Union and will discourage such competitions taking place as being contrary to the traditional policy of the Union—as accepted by all races in the Union.
>
> The policy of separate development is in accordance with the traditional South African custom that whites and non-whites should organize their sporting activities separately. The inclusion of different races in the same team would therefore be contrary to established and accepted custom.[69]

INTERRACIAL SPORT IN SOUTH AFRICA

There was one last cricket story in 1960: In December, a South African Indian team beat a highly regarded white team led by Peter Walker.[70] That the match took place was significant: it showed there were whites who wanted interracial competition in South Africa. That the whites lost to the supposedly less talented Indian team added to the embarrassment of the whites who opposed such competition. It also did little for those who said that South Africa's national cricket team was all-white because there were no qualified nonwhites.

The same can be said of the interracial boxing tournament staged in Basutoland. Out of three matches, nonwhite Africans won two.[71]

South Africa's sports policy was also making its international friends uncomfortable in two other sports. In February, the English Table Tennis Association refused an invitation from the white South African Table Tennis Union (SATTU) for a three-month tour of South Africa. The English body's reason was that the South African government would not allow it to play against nonwhite table tennis teams.[72] This was the first time that an English sports body had shunned the South Africans.

Of much greater significance, the International Football Federation (FIFA), voted fifty-two to ten at its August congress that FASA must achieve nondiscrimination in football within a year or it would be suspended from FIFA. FASA had managed to get the Bantu Soccer Federation to affiliate to it, but FIFA was unwilling to accept this as proof of significant progress toward nondiscrimination. Meanwhile, the British body lobbied to have FIFA recognize both FASA and the nonwhite South African Soccer Federation (SASF).[73]

1961

Nineteen sixty-one was marked by the increased consideration given to the South African controversy in international sports bodies. SASA continued its lobbying against apartheid sports, and the government kept the pressure on SASA and other potential protestors. Two relatively unimportant (when compared to the 1960 New Zealand rugby tour of South Africa and the South African cricket tour of England) tours took place with relatively mild protest. Interracial South African matches were planned and several did come off. The controversy over Papwa Sewgolum built up. Finally, the controversy over Japanese status in South Africa began.

THE GROWING CONTROVERSY

South Africa's status was changed in three international sports bodies during 1961. The most significant of these was FASA's suspension by FIFA because of alleged discrimination in South African football. FIFA's executive also decided to put the matter before the full FIFA congress in Chile in 1962.[74]

In the hope of a more favorable decision in Chile, FASA helped the Africans form a professional soccer league in November. It also helped to raise R2,000 to start the operation, and the new league became affiliated to FASA.[75]

In September, SASA appealed to the Commonwealth Games Federation to exclude South Africa because of its policy of racial discrimination in sport. When the Commonwealth Games Federation's advisory committee met in October, it decided that South Africa could not compete in the Perth games in 1962 since it was no longer a member of the Commonwealth.[76]

The third international body to change the status of South Africa was the Imperial Cricket Conference. The potential for change in the ICC was far greater than the actual change; the ICC was also a Commonwealth body, and South Africa could easily have been excluded on the basis that it was no longer a Commonwealth member (as happened several months later in the Commonwealth games).

When the ICC met in July, South Africa, represented by Foster Bowley, asked for a rules change so that "test" status could continue. (When a cricket team tours abroad, it usually plays a relatively large number of matches and a few "test" matches. These test matches are the important ones when deciding the country's international standing.)[77] SASA had been in touch with ICC members, asking them to exclude South Africa from the ICC.

The ICC finally decided to put off a decision; in the meanwhile, however, it declared that all test matches with South Africa would be "unofficial." They could retroactively become official if it was later decided to retain South Africa as a member. The deadlock resulted when the three predominantly white member nations voted for a change in the rules to accommodate South Africa, while the three predominantly nonwhite nations vetoed such change. The deputy defense minister of India, Sardar Majithia, protested the deadlock and said that South Africa should have been thrown out of the ICC forever.[78]

This was the first time that an international sports body was split along racial lines and set a pattern for the future, both in the ICC and in other bodies. South Africa's position was questioned but not acted upon in two other bodies: the International Amateur Boxing Association (IABA) and the International Rugby Union Board.

In February, the chairman of the South African Amateur Boxing Association (SAABA) announced that the IABA would exclude the SAABA, which was all white, unless it accepted affiliation from nonwhite boxers. The South Africa Non-European Amateur Boxing Association (SANEABA) was then accepted as an affiliate with the following provisions:

1. A liaison committee was established, with three white and three nonwhite members; the chairman of the white body was the head.
2. The policy would be one of parallel development.
3. There would be no mixed tournaments in South Africa.
4. Mixed teams might tour overseas.
5. Selection would be based on separate trials. If necessary, final mixed private trials might be held.[79]

In April, the International Rugby Union Board refused to interfere with the South African Rugby Board because it did not want to bring politics into sport. At the same meeting, the South African Rugby Union announced that the Welsh Rugby Union had agreed to tour South Africa in 1964.[80] This seemed bound to stir up past grievances because the Welsh National Union of Mineworkers had been in the forefront of the protest against the 1960 rugby and cricket tours of England.[81]

At its first biennial conference SASA had a major breakthrough. It was, in effect, recognized by the fact of Reg Honey's presence. Honey spoke at the meeting and made the following points:

1. Candidates for the Olympic games must belong to the national body in their code of sport.

2. Merit was the only basis for selection.
3. Selections would be made by the national bodies affiliated to SAOC. Nonwhites must affiliate to the national bodies to be chosen.[82]

Honey gave SASA a great deal of ammunition for its struggle when he admitted that he understood its complaints in two main areas: that if nonwhites did affiliate to the white national bodies, they would have to be represented by whites and that separate trials were not a fair basis for selection.[83]

Dennis Brutus countered Honey. First, he pointed out that if nonwhites did affiliate, their total vote would equal that of one white provincial body. Second, even with separate trials, no white beat the record lift of Precious McKenzie; but a white man went to the Olympics in McKenzie's event while McKenzie remained in South Africa. And finally, Brutus himself was not allowed to go to the IOC Rome session because the government denied him a passport.[84] Honey assured SASA that he would present its views at the next IOC meeting (although there is no record that he did this in the IOC minutes) and, in the interim, he hoped SASA would accept the compromises offered by the white bodies.[85]

SASA later announced the launching of Operation SONREIS (Support Only Non-Racial Events in Sport), which was designed to halt participation in or attendance at events organized along racial lines.[86] This program never really got off the ground, perhaps because it was simply too wide in scope. Since all sporting events in South Africa were organized on racial lines, whether by choice or tradition, this would have meant an end to nonwhite sport in South Africa if it was followed absolutely.

GOVERNMENT SPORTS POLICY

On two separate occasions, Minister of the Interior Naude addressed Parliament on the sports issue. On both occasions, he assured members of Parliament that the policy set forth in 1956 still stood and that he would continue to withhold passports and visas to maintain the policy.[87]

According to FASA, the government was responsible for cancelling a planned interracial soccer match in March (SASF maintained that it was FASA that cancelled the match).[88]

To see better the extent to which the government and/or South African sportsmen were willing to go to maintain segregation, one can examine the cases of Theunis Theart and Sidney Trimmer. Theart was suspended for three months from the white cycling body because he rode behind a group of Colored cyclists to show them his form. In September, three Colored gymnasts were barred from observing the white Western Province gymnastic championships. When he discovered what had happened, Trimmer, a judge at the event, left in protest in order to "get people concerned to come out from the façade of 'Government legislation' behind which they have been hiding."[89]

SOUTH AFRICA'S RUGBY AND CRICKET TOURS

Two South African tours did take place in 1961. While both sports in which they took place were very important to South Africans, they were of only secondary importance to the countries which they were playing. In New Zealand, the rugby matches with South Africa are the most important exchange; in England, the cricket exchanges count most. Therefore, when the South African rugby team toured England and its cricket team toured New Zealand, they did not attract the attention they did in 1960 when the exchanges were reversed.

The only notable protest of the rugby tour of Britain occurred when the Edinburgh town council boycotted the civic luncheon held for the South Africans.[90]

In New Zealand, only minor representations were made to Prime Minister Holyoake over the New Zealand cricket tour of South Africa as Maoris, for the most part, did not play cricket and thus were not qualified to be chosen for the tour.[91]

RACIAL CLASSIFICATIONS

An important controversy in 1961 concerned a nonwhite golfer of international repute, Papwa Sewgolum, who had won the Dutch Open twice. As an Indian, his status in South Africa was questionable in terms of participating in white events. The more successful he became, the more questionable his status, following the tradition of all other successful nonwhite sportsmen (such as N'Tuli).

In January, Papwa had applied to play in the Natal Open; the South African Golf Union (SAGU) delayed its decision long enough to keep

Papwa out of the tournament. In March, he applied to play in the South African Open. SAGU sought the advice of two lawyers as to whether Sewgolum needed a permit to play under the Group Areas Act. Although told to do so, he did not apply for the necessary permit in time, and SAGU had to get an MP to intervene with Minister of the Interior Naude. Naude issued the permit but refused to allow Sewgolum to practice on the course or to use the clubhouse facilities.[92]

Seeing how the winds were blowing for nonwhite golfers, Edward Johnson-Sedibe left South Africa to become a professional in England.[93] But Sewgolum stayed to meet the winds head on.

THE JAPANESE-CHINESE CONTROVERSY

The stage was set in 1961 for the controversy over the racial classification of the Japanese and Chinese in South Africa, although it did not affect sport until 1962.

In November, the *Rand Daily Mail* [Johannesburg] reported that a group of Japanese businessmen had come to South Africa to conclude major trade agreements with South Africa. The South Africans were reportedly afraid that they would lose some European markets as the bitterness over their race policies intensified, so the Japanese were given the status of honorary whites in South Africa.[94] This created a thorny problem: the Chinese people living in South Africa were classified as non-whites.

The absurdity of all this was pointed out by what has become known as the Song case. In April, Minister of the Interior Naude had said in Parliament that the decisive test of race was community acceptance. David Song, a Chinese and therefore a nonwhite, was reported by the *Rand Daily Mail* [Johannesburg] as saying, "It is better to be white in South Africa,"[95] and he appealed to be classified as white. More than three hundred whites signed a petition saying they accepted him as a white man, although he was obviously Chinese in appearance. Song (but not members of his family) was reclassified as white.

Several MP's then asked in Parliament if Song should be charged with violating the Immorality and Mixed Marriages Act since he was a white man living with nonwhites—and miscegenation was, of course, the number one enemy of apartheid. Naude held that Song would not be prosecuted because he was married before the act was passed.[96]

And so went race relations in South Africa. Nineteen sixty-one, like the others, was not a very good year.

1962

Nineteen sixty-two appeared to be a magnified instant replay of 1961 in South African sport; however, two new and very significant elements were added: the IOC as a whole pointed an accusing finger at South Africa; and some white South African sportsmen began to ask publicly for change in apartheid sports policy. Fear of isolation in sports was having an effect.

APARTHEID IN SPORTS

The Japanese-Chinese controversy was dragged into sport early in the year when the Pretoria city council announced that it would not permit a touring Japanese swimming team to use its pool in March despite the fact that the members were honorary whites.[97]

A storm of protest quickly followed. *Die Vaderland* [Johannesburg] and *Die Burger* [Cape Town] both ran front-page editorials condemning the council for not consulting the government before making its decision.[98] Neville Gracie, the head of the South African Amateur Swimming Union (SAASU), apologized to the Japanese consul-general in South Africa and to the Japanese swimming officials.[99] Because of the pressure from the government, the Pretoria city council announced that it would rescind the ban.[100]

Pretoria was not out of the news for long; it banned a women's softball tournament ten days later. The team had six Chinese women.[101]

There were other examples of the inconsistency of the application of apartheid in sports in 1962.

It was announced in February that Papwa Sewgolum could not compete in the Natal Open. A government statement said simply that "the policy of the Government is against mixed participation in sport."[102]

The Coastals, a multiracial soccer team in Durban, continued playing after members of the Special Branch, a police agency, warned the white members that they would be in trouble if they did not quit the team.[103]

An interracial soccer match took place in Maseru, Basutoland, in February. Nine thousand watched the white Germiston Callies defeat the (African) Black Pirates.[104]

The government finally decided that enough was enough. In May, it charged two whites, two Indians, and five Coloreds with contravening the Group Areas Act—the act that clearly allots certain portions of the land for separate races—by participating in a multiracial football match in October 1961. The match took place in an Indian area.[105] This was the test case of the application of the Group Areas Act to sports and was, of course, closely followed by the government and sportsmen.

On appeal, the nine were acquitted by the Natal Supreme Court in October on the reasoning that the players had not sat down together as customers in a club; and the Durban Sports Grounds Association, which controlled the grounds the men had played on, was a group of sports clubs and not a group of individuals. The judge maintained that the legislation was aimed at clubs having individual members.[106]

FASA's SUSPENSION

FASA was in the news in January as it attempted to have its suspension from FIFA lifted. The manager of the South African National Football League, a white professional league affiliated to FASA, met with Sir Stanley Rous, the FIFA president, in January. Rous warned him that FASA must make genuine progress in order to have the suspension lifted.

FASA moved to form a high-level committee with an equal representation of whites and nonwhites. The nonwhites would attend FASA's meetings and have a vote. Finally, if FIFA lifted the suspension, South Africa's team for the World cup would be chosen strictly on merit.[107]

When the time for the FIFA congress came in May, FASA brought with it B. P. Morola, the president of their affiliated Bantu Football Association. This was the first time that a nonwhite South African had attended an international sports conference to speak in favor of a white South African body. Morola told the congress:

> Our problem in South Africa will be solved only with time, goodwill and man's natural evolution of thinking and tolerance. It cannot be

imposed from outside, and the world, in trying to help us, should not put too much pressure on us.[108]

There were no representatives from SASF at the congress; the government had refused to issue passports to them. Robert Resha, who had left South Africa earlier in the year, represented SASF at the Congress.

Although it praised FASA for its progress since being suspended, FIFA decided to uphold the suspension.[109]

THE IOC, SASA, AND GOVERNMENT POLICY

The government, SASA, and the IOC continued to spin their strangling web around the IOC charter. SASA was recognized for the first time in the United States when the *New York Times* had a feature story about it on January 29. The story centered around Dennis Brutus, emphasizing the fact that he had been a "banned person" under the Suppression of Communism Act since 1961 for his activities for nonracialism. Brutus was thus unable to attend meetings, which apparently left SASA without its leader. But Brutus was undeterred; he said, "We have a strong case that the Olympic Charter itself outlaws discrimination."[110] Brutus was probably the biggest part of the case himself.

But the government seemed willing to provide more evidence. In February, the new minister of the interior, Mr. Jan de Klerk, announced that "the government policy is that no mixed teams should take part in sports inside or outside this country."[111] The meaning was clear enough: there could be no mixed team at the Olympic games. Reg Honey, in fact, felt that this was so severe a statement that there would be little point in his attending the next IOC meeting; South Africa was certain to be suspended immediately. Honey, however, underestimated the power of South Africa's friends on the IOC.

When the IOC executive board met in March, Avery Brundage noted only that there had been no progress in South Africa regarding the problem of discimination in sports. Brundage said he would seek an explanation and assurances that the promise Honey had made at the last conference in Rome still held. Without these, Brundage said some action would have to be taken.[112] Brundage was apparently not convinced by de Klerk's statement that there was no chance for progress.

Since there were only two months before the full IOC session in June, the government provided the IOC with all the evidence it ever needed to show that not only was there no progress but that apartheid in sports was expanding.

On March 29, de Klerk announced that the government could not approve of mixed sports teams competing in world events; that mixed teams from other nations were not welcome in South Africa; and that *separate* white and nonwhite teams from South Africa could compete abroad in international competitions. Referring to the multiracial events that had taken place in Basutoland, de Klerk said:

> It must be understood that all attempts to evade or undermine the South African custom in neighboring territories by inviting or inducing white and non-white teams to play one another across the border (or by inviting mixed teams from South Africa) in what are clearly not international competitions, but only competitions organized specifically to do there, with South African sportsmen as participants, what is not permissible in South Africa itself, will be viewed in an unfavorable light.
>
> As regards the administration and control of sports activities, it would be in accord with the Government's policy if non-white associations were to exist and develop alongside the corresponding white associations. The latter associations could then act as coordinating bodies between the association at top level, and serve as representatives in the corresponding white bodies.[113]

Olive van Ryneveld, the Progressive party spokesman, immediately warned that South Africa's approach to overseas sports would lead to South Africa's exclusion from them. General Klopper, the president of the South African Olympic Committee, agreed that this was probably true and that SAOC's plan for a mixed team without mixed trials would have been far more acceptable to international bodies. Reg Honey repeated that he saw no point in attending the next IOC session; South Africa would surely be suspended.[114] Even after the March indecision, he still seemed to doubt his international sports friends.

Still the government was not willing to let things rest. The minister of community development stepped to the front of the stage on April 16. There was not a single golf course for nonwhites in South Africa, that is, not a single course of championship calibre. The minister said that until such a course was made available, he would consider applications from Coloreds and Indians (but not Africans) to use white facilities, provided that no "undesirable" effects would result.[115] He did not make clear what he would consider to be undesirable effects.

On the same day, Minister of Bantu Administration and Development, de Wet Nel, said:

> I am against mixed sport meetings in principle. . . . There is sufficient evidence to prove that such a policy would lead to the most distasteful racial tensions. It is senseless injudiciousness to encourage such a thing.[116]

The minister of community development, who had been prepared to allow Indians and Coloreds to use white facilities for the Transvaal nonwhite championship, reversed his stand because of de Wet Nel's position, claiming that unless he did so, the development of nonwhite championship courses would be hindered![117] He failed to mention that it would take eight to ten years to build such a course once development began—which it had not in 1962.

The South African Amateur Athletic Union (SAAAU) had been invited to send *one* team to Mozambique for an international contest. SAAAU boldly announced that it would choose its team on merit and would send one team of whites and nonwhites, all of whom would wear the Springbok colors. Separate trials were to decide who would go. This appeared to be the breakthrough South Africa's critics were waiting for.

But it seemed that SAAAU had a rather unique selection process. Two nonwhites, on the basis of their performances in the trials, qualified for the team; however, they were replaced by two white athletes. These white athletes had achieved better times than the nonwhites but not in the trials! If this was to be the criterion—that is, any time counted during the recent past—two other nonwhites had better times than either the whites selected or the nonwhites excluded. When Matt Mare, the head of SAAAU, was asked why Henry Khosi, whose time was 0.1 of a second faster than the white man selected, was not chosen, he replied, "0.1 second does not really count."[118]

General Klopper was one of the first to oppose the government's policy when he said that he would stand by the Olympic principles. He said that sport must be for all, regardless of race.[119] This was truly a significant stand.

The government made one more regulation before the IOC met: all invitations to overseas teams must be approved by the government before they were sent to the team to be invited.[120] After all that had happened in the previous two months in South Africa, it seemed inevitable that South Africa would be suspended from the IOC.

When the IOC met in Moscow, Avery Brundage confirmed that Honey's promises had not been carried out. Nevertheless, only five members voted for immediate suspension. (It should be noted that there was not a single black African member of the IOC in 1962. The two delegates from Africa, Reg Honey from South Africa and Reg Alexander from Kenya, were both white.) The IOC decided to give the South Africans until October 1963 (the date of the next IOC meeting) to eliminate racism in sports.[121]

Although this decision appeared to be very generous on the part of the IOC, it was viewed as anything but that in South Africa. *Die Transvaler* [Johannesburg] said the decision "confirms what has been happening on South African sports fields for the past five years–that international sport has lost its value. It has now become a battlefield where political differences must be settled."[122] Matt Mare of the SAAAU called the decision "a political trick against the South African Government."[123]

One week after the IOC meeting, Albert Luthuli, former president of the banned African National Congress, recipient of the Nobel peace prize, and ex-chief, and G. M. Naicker, president of the Indian National Congress, took a strong position on sports apartheid. In a joint statement, they appealed for a boycott of all-white events that were sponsored by segregated organizations. They said that those who attend "are in fact–morally and financially supporting the perpetuation of apartheid."[124]

THE DEADLOCK IN THE ICC

The deadlock in the Imperial Cricket Conference remained unresolved after its July meeting. Once again, the nations lined up as they had in 1961: Pakistan, India, and the West Indies opposing South Africa, and England, Australia, and New Zealand supporting South Africa.[125]

Two weeks later, Owen Wynne, a former Springbok cricket star, suggested that a national convention be held to form one Olympic association that would represent all South Africans.[126] It appeared that the fear of isolation in sport was causing white South Africans to reconsider their sports policy.

THE UNITED STATES AAU BAN

In August, the United States AAU banned an American swimming team from visiting South Africa because of the racial choice of the South African team and spectators. This was a major victory for SASA, which announced the decision of the USAAU at a press conference on August 24.[127] This was the first time that an American sports body declined to go to South Africa because of its racial policy in sports. It is possible that the AAU recalled the humiliation of having an earlier swimming team compete against the Germans before an all-Aryan audience when a sign appeared on the entrance gate saying, "Jews are not wanted."[128]

THE FORMATION OF SAN-ROC

Perhaps the most important event of the year, in terms of long-run effects, was the formation of the South African Non-Racial Olympic Committee. SAN-ROC, an outgrowth of SASA, was organized so that it could apply to the IOC as the truly representative Olympic committee in South Africa.[129] It was destined not only to lead but also to become the very symbol of the struggle for nonracial sport in South Africa.

1963

In 1963, Dennis Brutus became the international symbol of the struggle for nonracial sport in South Africa, and Papwa Sewgolum became the symbol of what the struggle was about. The government, for the first time, threatened to introduce legislation to solidify its position on apartheid in sport. The IOC took a stand that was to become the guiding principle with regard to South Africa at its Baden-Baden session. And, finally, the white national sports bodies in South Africa increasingly sought compromises with the nonwhite bodies in order to placate the international federations.

THE STRUGGLE FOR NONRACIAL SPORT

It was apparent in 1962 that the government was becoming more and more concerned with the seemingly inconsistent allowance of letting Sewgolum play in white events. Everything came to a head when Papwa beat 113 whites to win the Natal Open Golf Championship in January 1963.

For Papwa, the sweet taste of victory (he was the first nonwhite golfer to win a major title) was quickly blunted by the humiliation of apartheid. Under the provisions of the Group Areas Act, Papwa could not enter the clubhouse to join his fellow professionals in the awards ceremony. Instead, he was forced to accept his prize outdoors in the pouring rain. Adding to the humiliation was the fact that members of Sewgolum's race were inside the clubhouse–serving the white golfers.[130] Furthermore, the South African Broadcasting Corporation refused to report the results of the tournament. A spokesman for the station said, "We do not broadcast multi-racial sport."[131]

Minister of Community Development, Jan Botha, announced that Sewgolum did not have a permit to play in the tournament and that "the question of what steps will be taken is under consideration."[132]

The result was that the victory that should have propelled his career to new heights actually put Sewgolum's career in jeopardy. He was allowed to compete in the South African Open in March, finishing second. His accomplishments in these two tournaments should have assured him a place on South Africa's Canada cup team. However, he was ruled ineligible for the team since he was not a member of the white Professional Golfers' Association.[133] While Sewgolum may have been traveling on the road to professional obscurity in South Africa, the international publicity surrounding his case made him a symbol of what apartheid sport meant for nonwhite South Africans. Papwa Sewgolum became the first real martyr for those opposing South Africa's sports policy. It was not long before there were others.

What happened to Sewgolum in 1963 does not even compare with what happened to Dennis Brutus, the leader of SAN-ROC. Brutus was still under banning orders, which meant, among other things, that he could not attend meetings. In May, he was arrested for failing to comply with the banning orders.

When Brutus had attempted to meet a Swiss journalist, Robert Basliger, who was in Johannesburg doing a story on racism in sport, he was arrested.[134] Other SAN-ROC leaders were convinced that Frank Braun, the new head of SAOC, had called the police. It is possible that this theory is correct since the police came from the office next to Braun's.[135] Frank Braun explained the incident in this way:

> The meeting was set for the Olympic office. The head of the SAN-ROC delegation at that time was a man named John Harris, who had succeeded Brutus. When I arrived I found Brutus was there. It was illegal for him to speak to a meeting this large, and I told him so. I said, "Dennis, you know that you cannot speak to this meeting. Will you please leave?" Harris said that Brutus was there only to introduce us all, since he knew everyone. But I could have done the same thing. I knew everyone there. But before anything else could take place, the special forces came in and arrested Brutus and took him away for breaking the law. I have been accused of having tipped them off, but that would have served no purpose. I think myself that Harris tipped off the special forces simply to create a disturbance and a martyr.[136]

This episode in Brutus' career as an anti-apartheid leader was dwarfed by the events of September. Brutus had decided to go to Baden-Baden for the IOC meeting in October to present SAN-ROC's case against SAOC. Traveling on a valid Rhodesian passport, he left South Africa and was working his way north when he was stopped by the Mozambique police, who took him to the South African police.[137] The question of the legality of this action subsequently brought protests from Britain and the United Nations, since Brutus was a British subject traveling on a valid Rhodesian passport.[138]

In any case, Brutus was brought back to Johannesburg. He was admittedly afraid because all his friends believed that he was safely on his way to Baden-Baden; therefore, he tried to escape when the police car stopped. He jumped on a bus, but the driver pushed him off, and a police officer shot him in the stomach.

Brutus was lying in the street, bleeding profusely, when the ambulance came. It had been called by someone who had seen the light-skinned

Brutus from some distance away. When the ambulance driver realized that Brutus was Colored, he drove off because it was a whites-only ambulance. It was an hour before a Colored ambulance took him to the hospital.[139]

The publicity over this incident, occurring a mere three weeks before the IOC meeting, undoubtedly had a marked effect on the decision the IOC reached in Baden-Baden.

To complete the round-up of SAN-ROC leaders, the South African police arrested John Harris on his way to Baden after Dennis Brutus was arrested.[140] Harris, however, did manage to get a tape recording of SAN-ROC's position to the IOC.

In that tape, Harris gave three basic reasons why SAOC should be suspended. First, it had violated the Olympic charter through discrimination. Second, the situation was worsening, not improving, as the Moscow declaration had said it must. Finally, the South African government was clearly interfering in sport with no objections from SAOC. Harris ended the tape by urging

> that the SAOC . . . be suspended. And we ask for this strong medicine because this committee has shown that it will not listen to advice, that it will not accept warnings, that threats have very little—if any—effect. Action is needed. . . . And when racialism has been eliminated in this way, we will welcome the lifting of the suspension of the SAOC.[141]

THE IOC's RESOLUTION

The IOC meeting was originally scheduled to be held in Nairobi; however, when Oginga Odinga, the Kenyan minister for home affairs, insisted that the representatives from South Africa and Portugal be multiracial, the IOC rescheduled the meeting for Baden-Baden.[142]

At the Baden-Baden meeting, the South Africans brought along J. R. Rathebe, a Bantu boxing official, to advise Frank Braun.[143] Before the meeting, Braun publicly stated that "every application to join the Olympic team for Tokyo will be treated on its merits in the light of Government policy."[144]

As for Rathebe, the *Post* [Natal], a nonwhite South African newspaper, reported that nonwhites had been surprised by his selection; he was felt to be unrepresentative of South African nonwhite opinion. John Harris called him a "smoke-screen."[145]

The South African delegation told the IOC that apartheid was an internal matter and one that should not concern the IOC. It said that it would hold trials outside South Africa if it found them impossible to hold them within South Africa (this seemed to be a particularly curious pledge; it was absolutely clear the government would never have allowed this). The South Africans said the government would grant passports for worthy nonwhites to participate in the Olympics and claimed that all opposition to this policy came from political agitators, not sportsmen.[146]

Members of the IOC expressed grave concern that no mixed trials would be held to select the team. Although it still refused to suspend South Africa outright, it took an important step in that direction when it passed the following resolution by a vote of thirty to twenty:

> That the SAOC be told that it must make a firm declaration of its acceptance of the spirit of the Olympic Code and in particular of Principle 1 and Rule 24 read together, and must get from its Government by December 31st 1963 a change in policy regarding racial discrimination in sports and competitions in its country, failing which the South African National Olympic Committee will be debarred from entering its teams in the Olympic Games.[147]

According to Otto Mayer, the IOC chancellor, the resolution put the "responsibility squarely on the South African Government."[148]

The *Evening Post* [Port Elizabeth] reported Prime Minister Verwoerd's reaction: "Verwoerd, in a speech at Swellendam at the weekend . . . specifically mentioned that the principle of segregation must be maintained in sport."[149] Matt Mare, president of the AAU, described the IOC decision as

> . . . short-sighted and marking the start of the break-up of the Olympic Games. I am very personally perturbed and disappointed to think that the IOC could have reached such a decision. We have devoted a considerable time to the building up of machinery to help the non-white athlete attain his present standard.[150]

Mare seemed to be indicating that he felt the "machinery" was worthless and that it was built up merely to keep South Africa in the Olympic games.

A *Die Burger* [Cape Town] editorial held that if South Africa's membership in the IOC was related to foreign demands on the republic, "then our attitude in this matter cannot be different from what it is in other international spheres."[151]

Jan de Klerk, the minister of the interior, announced that South Africa would not change its position merely to pacify the IOC. And General Klopper, the former head of the SAOC and the first South African sports administrator who openly said South Africa would stand by the Olympic principles (in 1962), stated, "We have got a way of life in this country and we cannot change it because some people want us to."[152]

As early as February, the government had made it clear that it was not going to change its policy. In fact, it threatened to introduce legislation on its sports policy if there were future violations of it. The legislation, according to Minister of the Interior de Klerk, "will clearly determine this positive policy in regard to the participation or non-participation in mixed sport within and outside the country."[153] On February 4, de Klerk made the following (and now familiar) policy statement:

> South African custom is that within the boundaries of the Republic, whites and non-whites exercise their sports separately and this custom must be adhered to, that is; that within our boundaries, whites and non-whites must not compete with each other, either in individual items or in teams or as members of teams.
>
> Participation of mixed teams as representatives of South Africa as a whole in world sporting tournaments or competitions cannot be approved. Where, for example, whites take part in such tournaments individually, they must do so as the representatives of the whites of our country and, in the same way, non-whites will represent non-white South Africans.[154]

However, he continued, South Africans could compete outside South Africa with men of other races who were not South Africans.[155] Taken together, de Klerk's statements should have made it clear to the IOC that it would have been impossible for the SAOC to comply with the Baden resolution. But, as has been seen, the IOC has not been hasty in its actions regarding South Africa.

COMPROMISES BY THE WHITE BODIES

In 1963, for the first time since 1958 when a nonwhite cricket team toured Kenya, nonwhites traveled abroad to compete.

The first was an amateur boxing tour of the United States in March. When the tour was announced, several nonwhite groups affiliated to the white SAABA. A total of five whites and three nonwhites were chosen for the team. The government issued the passports for all without any difficulty. This was a momentous occasion, but apartheid won out at the departure: the whites left on one plane and the nonwhites left on another; the South African press was not allowed to photograph whites and nonwhites together; and none of the boxers was awarded the Springbok colors, although they all wore the same blazers (without the Springbok emblem). After leaving South Africa, however, both groups lived and traveled together.[156] The South African Broadcasting Corporation broadcast this event because it was within government policy to have multiracial sport overseas.[157]

The second tour was not even partially multiracial. During the summer, ten African athletes toured Great Britain for six weeks. The tour was approved by the government and passports were issued, but the athletes were not allowed to wear the Springbok emblem. One member of the team, Bennett Makgamathe, set a new South African record in his event and clearly would have had to have been a top candidate for any South African Olympic team.[158]

Chris de Broglio maintains that these tours were initiated to soften South Africa's image abroad, that is, to show that white sports administrators were interested in the welfare of nonwhites.[159] In addition to the tours and the affiliations that resulted in boxing, the white South African Cycling Federation (SACF) announced in February—just before the IOC meeting—that it would seek closer ties with nonwhite cyclists and that it would send qualified nonwhites overseas, possibly even to the Olympic games. The nonwhite South African Amateur Athletic and Cycling Board of Control remained affiliated to SAN-ROC, however.[160]

One case that not only backfired, but also caused white sports administrators considerable embarrassment, was that of Precious McKenzie. McKenzie, the top weightlifter in his category, belonged to the weightlifting body affiliated to the nonracial national federation. In August, the white body offered McKenzie the opportunity to become the first nonwhite to wear the coveted Springbok colors as a representative of South Africa in the world championships in Stockholm. (In light of all previous cases, as well as all those to follow in the period covered in this study, it is doubtful that the government would have allowed McKenzie to wear these colors, although it probably would have allowed him to go to Stockholm.) All McKenzie had to do was to join the nonwhite body affiliated to the white national body, thus disavowing his loyalty to the nonracial body. In one of those rare moments in which an athlete shuns the chance for glory to stand on a principle, McKenzie refused the offer.[161] In explaining his decision, he said:

> The National Weightlifting Association wants me to join them now so that they can gain official recognition with the world body and say they have no apartheid. But I don't swing so easily.
>
> Why do they want me in such a hurry now? Is it because pressure is being applied because of their racial policy?[162]

Not only was this a defeat for the white body, but also, as John Harris explained, it had great meaning for SAN-ROC:

> We in SAN-ROC extend to you our sincere personal and official congratulations on your magnificent stand for the highest principles of non-racialism in sport. The sacrifice you have made will have meaning in sporting circles all over the world. Aside from your past and future weightlifting achievements, your outstanding action will be an example which will place the name of Precious McKenzie in a very special and unchallenged position in South African sport for all time. You may be sure that what you have done will become a famous part of our country's sporting history.[163]

And so, McKenzie's name was added to those of Sewgolum and Brutus as martyrs in the fight for nonracial sport in South Africa. There can be little doubt that the cases of all three affected the IOC's decision in October. Before that, however, there were two tours involving South Africa that stirred up some controversy.

The first was an Australian rugby tour of South Africa in August and September. The Secretary for Colored affairs had asked the Bloemfontein city council to allow a limited number of Colored (but not nonwhites in general) spectators to watch the match with Australia at the local stadium. The city council refused, arousing the wrath of the South African Rugby Board. (As it turned out, the all-white audience at the event was involved in several bad incidents, even without nonwhites in attendance.)[164]

During the last match of the tour (in Port Elizabeth), there was a serious disturbance. The nonwhite spectators had booed the South African team throughout the match. When South Africa took the lead at the end of the match, groups of nonwhites began to "riot"—at least according to white sports officials.[165] The next week, the Eastern Province Rugby Union decided to raise the price of nonwhite (but not white) tickets and to ban booing.[166]

While the idea of attempting to ban booing at a sports event might take on a humorous connotation, what followed in Parliament was utterly humorless. It was reported in December that legislation had been proposed to ban all nonwhite spectators at stadiums in South Africa. Reg Honey called this "monstrous" and predicted that it would mean the end of international sport for South Africa.[167]

The second tour involved the South African cricket team in Australia. The selectors ignored Basil D'Oliveira and picked an all-white team. This fact resulted in several demonstrations against South African sports policy during the Australian tour. The Springbok captain actually met with Prime Minister Verwoerd, who briefed him on how to answer questions while he was in Australia.[168]

COMMONWEALTH SPORTS RELATIONS

South African sports administrators were successful in three international and Commonwealth sports bodies in 1963. Although South Africa was no longer a Commonwealth member, it was permitted to send an all-white team to compete in the 1963 Commonwealth golf championship in Australia.[169]

South African cricket relations also remained on an even par. Although many felt it was a certainty that South Africa would finally be expelled from the Imperial Cricket Conference, plans for future tours were retained at the insistence of the British body, the MCC. After the ICC meeting, it appeared likely that South Africa would be granted the status of an associate member.[170]

Dennis Brutus reflected on the lack of sympathy for the nonwhite situation by the South African Cricket Association:

> We went to see Mr. Arthur Coy, then president of the South African body, in my home town, Port Elizabeth. To our suggestion that the MCC might take action against South Africa if it continued to flout the spirit of cricket and exclude players on the grounds of race, his reply was an arrogant: "Go ahead and try." And Algy Frames, the then secretary of South African cricket, went further; "My boy," he told me loftily, "if we were to include any blacks in our team to England there would be a riot."[171]

THE LIFTING OF FASA's SUSPENSION

The most striking success for South African sports administrators in 1963 was FIFA's lifting of FASA's suspension.

Sir Stanley Rous, the president of FIFA, had led a two-man delegation to investigate South African football. Rous said there was nothing in FIFA's constitution demanding multiracialism, so FIFA's only interest was to see if FASA furthered the cause of football as best it could. He saw nonwhite facilities and said he was satisfied with them.[172] He met with the rival groups–FASA and nonwhite SASF. White FASA thought he was very fair; SASF maintained that Rous was very biased toward the white body.[173] In any case, when the FIFA executive met later in January, it lifted FASA's suspension, which, it claimed, merely impeded football in South Africa. Rous said that FASA did not practice discrimination (a curious claim in light of his view that FIFA was not concerned with multiracial football). Rous announced that an African team would be sent as a test of FASA's sincerity.[174]

George Singh, who was to SASF what Dennis Brutus was to SAN-ROC, said of this decision:

> There is not even a semblance of justice done to the overwhelming majority of non-white footballers who have been clamoring for the past 50 years for full international recognition and the right to play for their country.[175]

In Cairo, where the FIFA executive had met, the African Football Confederation announced that it would not send a team to South Africa as FIFA prescribed. The AFC spokesman, General Mustapha, said the AFC would now treat South Africa "as if she belonged to another continent."[176]

The AFC meeting was attended by Rous and J. J. McGuire of the United States (McGuire went with Rous to investigate conditions in South Africa). Rous told the members of the AFC, "You should not let your Government policies interfere with your decision."[177]

An interesting side note is that in 1935, amid the controversy over the 1935 German football tour of England, Stanley Rous, then secretary of the British Football Association, chastised those protesting in England for bringing politics into sport and insulting their German friends.[178] Rous was rapidly becoming for FIFA what Avery Brundage had become for the IOC—a "friend" for South Africa in international sports.

But the football story for 1963 was not yet ended. FASA announced that it would send an all-nonwhite team to the World cup in 1966 to keep in line with government policy (as opposed to sending a mixed team). But FASA wanted SASF to affiliate, along with its professional counterpart, the South African Soccer League (SASL). SASF/SASL refused on the grounds that a mixed team should go to the World cup.[179] This refusal led Vivian Granger, manager of the white professional National Football League (NFL), to declare "total war" on SASF/SASL affiliates by attempting to get them banned from using municipal facilities for their matches.[180] This, in turn, led to SASF/SASL's calling for a nonwhite boycott of the NFL game in December.[181] All was not tranquil in South African football as the year came to a close.

SUMMARY

Apartheid was not only extended into South African sport but was also completely accepted by white administrators by the end of 1963.

Only General Klopper's statement that he would abide by the Olympic principles stood as an exception, and even he soon withdrew this statement. At the same time, nonwhites, as represented by SASA and SAN-ROC, clearly did not accept sports apartheid. Nevertheless, with the threat of IOC suspension, white sports authorities were promising some concessions (such as the boxing tour and the offer to Precious McKenzie). The second stage of increased international protest and more concessions by the white authorities was next to come.

3

The Growth of Protest Against Apartheid Sport: 1964-1968

1964

The IOC decision at Baden-Baden was the key to the events of 1964. The question of South African participation was raised in six major international federations in 1964 as these federations were forced to confront the issue. Zambia became the first country officially to break sports relations with South Africa. The controversy over South African participation spread so fast that it even affected a bowling tour of Britain, not to mention the usual problems in Australia and New Zealand. Inside South Africa, SAN-ROC achieved new success throughout the first half of the year, only to have its very existence endangered in July.

THE IOC's SUSPENSION OF SOUTH AFRICA

According to the Baden-Baden resolution, the SAOC had until December 31, 1963, to persuade the South African government to change its sports policy. When the SAOC did not meet this deadline, IOC Chancellor Otto Mayer announced that the IOC would grant an extension until January 15 so that the SAOC could draft its reply.[1] On January 15, Mayer announced that the SAOC had rejected the IOC's demand to integrate sports in South Africa, but it still hoped to go to Tokyo. Accordingly, Mayer said that the IOC would make a final decision at its Innsbruck meeting at the end of the month.[2] South Africa had been given a one-month reprieve, but it seemed certain that it would be suspended when the IOC met.

At the IOC meeting, Frank Braun confirmed that the South African government was not willing to change its policy. Nevertheless, he said, the SAOC (now called the South African Olympic and National Games Association–SAONGA) affirmed its loyalty to the Olympic principles and would conduct trials, either inside South Africa or abroad, to meet IOC standards. Any nonwhites selected would be granted passports by the government.[3] Lord Exeter pointed out that the SAONGA had not publicly and officially declared that it disassociated itself from the sports policy of the government, and Braun said this was true.[4]

The IOC, in light of this, passed the following resolution, which began by noting that SAONGA had made very real progress:

> The South African National Olympic Committee has, however, another duty under Rule 24 "to conduct its activities in accordance with the Olympic Regulations and high ideals of the Olympic movement." . . . To fulfill this obligation it was essential that it should collectively, clearly and publicly disassociate itself from the policy of non-competition in sport and non-integration in the administration of sports in South Africa between whites and non-whites, and would continue to urge this point of view. The IOC considers that the SANOC has not carried out this obligation adequately.
>
> Under these circumstances, the resolution passed at Baden-Baden still stands and the invitation to the South African team to compete in Tokyo is withdrawn.
>
> When the SANOC has carried out its duty under Rule 24, it will then be in a position to return to the IOC for reconsideration of this decision.[5]

The last part of the resolution was the key: if SAONGA would declare its opposition to the government sports policy, it would be allowed to attend the Tokyo games. It had only to do this by the August deadline for entering teams for the games.[6] Persuading the government to change its position was no longer a condition.

According to Braun, "The IOC resolution was a face-saving device for the IOC."[7] South Africa would hold trials outside the country to allow whites and nonwhites to compete together.[8]

Thus, in effect, the IOC had extended its deadline from December 31 to January 15 to the end of January and, finally, to August. Not only had it extended the deadline, but it had drastically changed the conditions that had to be met by the deadline.

John Harris of SAN-ROC immediately petitioned members of the IOC, the national Olympic committees (NOCs), and the international sports federations concerning the pending August decision on South Africa. Harris maintained that Braun's statements since the Innsbruck meeting indicated that a deal must have been struck between the SAONGA and the IOC executive. Harris also pointed out that South African sportsmen were no longer so important when measured against other African athletes. As evidence, he cited that in 1958 South Africa would have won 29 of 32 athletic events in competition with other Africans. In 1964, the South Africans would have won only 7 of 32, while Kenya alone would have won 8.[9] The other nations of Africa were now fast challenging South Africa athletically as well as politically.

Meanwhile, Otto Mayer announced his resignation from the IOC: "It is situations like this [South Africa] that make the job of Chancellor really unbearable."[10]

The first South African games were held in March and April. Separate events were held for whites and nonwhites. (In fact, the nonwhite games were not held until late April and ran into May.) Both series of games were used as pre-Olympic tests, and several nonwhites were tentatively selected. The SAONGA reaffirmed its loyalty to the Olympic principles.[11]

It seemed obvious that these moves were designed to influence the meeting of the IOC executive in late June, but the IOC merely noted the further progress that the SAONGA had made and set the deadline for August 16.[12] From the events that followed this announcement in South Africa, it would appear that both the SAONGA and the South African government fully expected to be invited to Tokyo by the IOC executive. Minister of the Interior de Klerk immediately announced that nonwhites would never represent South Africa in international competition and that apartheid in sport would remain.[13] Furthermore, since the IOC refused to make any concessions, the South African government would follow its lead.[14]

General Klopper, the former head of the SAOC, blamed the IOC for keeping South African nonwhites out of the Olympic games.[15] This charge had been leveled before and would be made again and again in the future.

In July, *Dagbreek* reported that the arrangements made by the SAONGA would have been rejected by the government if they had attempted to go through with them. *Dagbreek* had sought the government's advice and had been told that two teams would have gone to the Olympics: white athletes would have represented white South Africa and nonwhites nonwhite South Africa. The teams would have had to travel and live separately, could not have competed in the same events, and could not have worn the same uniforms.[16] Nevertheless, the government never contradicted the SAONGA statements while it appeared that the team might be invited to Tokyo.

THE ARREST OF JOHN HARRIS AND THE EMERGENCE OF PETER HAIN

In July, SAN-ROC leader John Harris was arrested for the bombing of the Johannesburg railroad station, in which a woman was killed and fifteen people were hospitalized. Harris was charged with murder and two counts of sabotage.[17] Although his actions had nothing to do with SAN-ROC, the bombing left an indelible mark on the nonracial movement for sport in South Africa. With SAN-ROC's former leader in prison and its present leader charged with sabotage, it became very easy to dismiss SAN-ROC as a group of revolutionaries. Brutus maintained that Harris' action virtually ended SAN-ROC's chances for leadership while it tried to function inside South Africa.[18]

Would the South African Government have made its bold statements of June and July if it had known that it was going to be dealt the prizewinning card in Harris' capture? Would the IOC have then readmitted South Africa for the Tokyo Games after a nonracial movement for sports had seemingly been thoroughly discredited by Harris' action? It is purely speculation, but, nonetheless, is interesting.

When the official word came that South Africa was irrevocably out of the Tokyo Games, Dennis Brutus was still on Robben Island serving his 18 months in prison. He recalled the effect of the announcement:

> It gave us great satisfaction. The cheering in the quadrangle at Robben Island, where we were breaking stones, must have deafened the guards.[19]

It came to light during Harris' trial that he had warned the police and two newspapers that the bomb had been planted, but no action was taken to clear the railroad station. An eminent private psychiatrist examined Harris and declared that he was legally insane at the time of the bombing and could not be criminally responsible. However, two government psychiatrists held that he was responsible, and Harris was found guilty and sentenced to death.[20]

Although not attempting to condone what Harris did, Dennis Brutus remembered him as "a very charming, gentle, intelligent young man. There may have been some instability. He may have been frustrated with the kind of effete liberalism of the official Liberal Party."[21]

During the trial and while waiting for the execution, Harris' wife lived with another white family in Johannesburg, the Hains. All had been activists in the Liberal Party and Mr. Hain had been jailed in 1961 and was under banning orders at the time of Harris' execution. The night before the funeral service, the police told Mr. Hain that he could not deliver the eulogy as planned.[22]

Mr. Hain's 15 year old son, Peter, delivered the eulogy in his place and led the group in singing, "We Shall Overcome." Four years later, Peter Hain was to capture the imagination of another nation in one of England's largest and most successful mass movements. But of this time, his only memory is one of bitterness. This, perhaps, eventually led to South Africa's second greatest defeat in international sports. In an interview in his London home during the Stop The Seventy Tour (STST) campaign, Hain said:

> This was the beginning of my life as an activist. Until then, I never really understood; I was never committed. For me, the time had come. I did not know what form it would take or when it could happen. But here we are.[23]

Much more will be said about the 'form' in the next chapter. But the irony is obvious: while the South Africans apparently had rid themselves of their number one sports nemesis in SAN-ROC, it indirectly gave birth to another powerful leader and movement.[24] And SAN-ROC itself was not to play dead for very long.

THE EFFECT OF THE BADEN RESOLUTION

Because of the Baden-Baden resolution, other international federations considered the South African issue.

In late June, Alex Metreveli of the U.S.S.R. and Istvan Gulyas of Hungary refused to play tennis against Abe Segal, a South African tennis player, at Wimbledon.[25] Another South African player broke down and was unable to compete when confronted by anti-apartheid demonstrators at Wimbledon.[26] In early June, the International Lawn Tennis Federation (ILTF) met in Vienna. After a heated debate, it passed two landmark resolutions:

1. In no circumstances shall there be racial discrimination at international tournaments.
2. Teams or players whose entry has been accepted shall not withdraw except for reasons of health or bereavement or unless with the permission of the organizing committee. Any transgressor will be refused entry to future competitions unless a written guarantee is given that such acts will not again occur.[27]

The second resolution was obviously undertaken to avoid any future actions like those of Metreveli and Gulyas. However, the public relations value of this tactic was not easily forgotten by the socialist countries, and future transgressions did, in fact, occur.

In September, the International Table Tennis Federation met in Prague, where it censured South Africa for continued discrimination in sport, especially the withholding of passports from nonwhites.[28] (The South African government had refused to issue passports for a nonwhite team to compete for the All-African championship in Ghana.)

In October, the Russians proposed that South Africa be expelled from three international federations: the International Amateur Boxing Association (IABA), the International Swimming Federation (FINA), and the International Amateur Athletics Federation (IAAF). In the IABA, the motion was dismissed on a technicality: the Russians had not submitted the motion in time for it to be placed on the agenda. In FINA, the Soviet motion was defeated 2 to 1, and in the IAAF by 145 to 82.[29]

The International Rugby Board actually met in South Africa during the SARB's jubilee celebration. Obviously there was no chance of a confrontation in the IRB. The SARB invited two leading Maoris to attend the meeting, and this prompted speculation that Maoris would be allowed in future New Zealand rugby tours of South Africa.[30]

There was, however, one federation that did take action against the South Africans. As has been seen, the racial composition of South African football had been a major controversy since the early 1950s. In January, the National Football League (white) cancelled its invitation to a Portuguese team when it learned that several members of the Portuguese team were nonwhite.[31] In March, the Colored Football Association decided to end its affiliation to the white body, FASA.[32] The playing grounds of the Bantu body in Johannesburg were closed, and the Bantu association was told that it would have to affiliate to FASA if it wanted new grounds to play on.[33] The Colored association in Johannesburg was told in June to affiliate to FASA if it wanted to continue using its sports grounds.[34] Finally, the Bloemfontein city council refused the request of an NFL official to allow six leading nonwhite players and officials to attend matches there to improve their playing standards.[35] When the International Football Federation (FIFA) met in October, the full body overrode the 1963 decision of the FIFA executive to lift the suspension of FASA.

FIFA's president, Sir Stanley Rous, argued at length that there was no discrimination in South African football. He maintained that his investigation of 1963 was definitive and that the executive's decision was completely within its jurisdiction.[36]

O. Djan, the representative from Ghana, maintained that since nonwhites could not join whites on international teams from South Africa and since they could not play together inside South Africa, South Africa was clearly violating the FIFA statutes. Two delegates from FASA (one white and one nonwhite) told the congress that all nonwhites in South Africa were happy with the situation and that to suspend FASA would only hurt the nonwhites.[37]

The FIFA congress voted forty-eight to fifteen for the suspension of the South African body.[38] This was a major blow to the South Africans.

OVERSEAS DEMONSTRATION AGAINST SOUTH AFRICAN TEAMS

Overseas demonstrations against South African sportsmen increased in 1964. The South African cricket tour of Australia and New Zealand aroused several protests. The Australian Trade Unionists passed the following resolution: "The cricket team from South Africa cannot expect the same warm welcome as other visiting teams. We are not against the South African cricketers as individuals. We are against apartheid."[39] In Wellington, the wicket was damaged before a test match with South Africa. The demonstrations also brought about a substantial reduction in the number of people attending the matches.[40] As a result of the violence–such as the damaged wicket–during the tour, the New Zealand National Council of Churches met with sports bodies in December and resolved that all national teams would be chosen without regard to race and that sports contact with countries practicing discrimination had value.[41]

In May, anti-apartheid demonstrators disrupted the Davis cup match between Norway and South Africa in Oslo. There were fifty arrests after a hundred people stormed the court. The match had to be moved to a private court, where police checked everyone attempting to gain entrance to the match.[42]

A bowling tour of Britain was constantly disrupted: the lord provost of Glasgow refused to have the customary civic luncheon for the visitors; the South Africans were confronted by demonstrations in Cardiff, Wales; and a match was cancelled in Dublin.[43]

The South African AAU was forced to cancel a mixed European tour (whites and nonwhites were to go as separate teams without Springbok colors) when de Klerk's statement was made public in June.[44]

Finally, Zambia announced on November 4 that it would terminate all sports contacts with South Africa because of apartheid.[45]

1965

The South African government made two dramatic incursions into sports policy in 1965. One involved spectators inside South Africa; the other radically affected its sports relations with New Zealand and even became an election issue.

In international federations, it was a relatively tranquil year for South Africa. Even the IOC seemed to virtually ignore the South African question save for a brief moment at its Madrid session. The lack of international pressure may have been largely due to the fact that SAN-ROC's hands were completely tied: Harris had been executed early in the year and Brutus, although released from prison, was still under crippling banning orders.

GOVERNMENT INCURSION

The first government incursion in 1965 came in February with the issuance of Proclamation Number R26. This was an extension of the Group Areas Act and included individuals. In particular, it required permits for mixed spectators at events. It applied to "any place of public entertainment," which made it far broader in scope than Proclamation 255 of 1960 (which it replaced), which was limited to "any public cinema."[46]

At first, it was difficult to determine how easy it would be to obtain permits. Beginning in March, there were clarifications as to how Proclamation R26 would affect sports events. The minister of community development announced that a sports facility in a white area should generally be used only by whites. However, if separate facilities (seating, entrances, and toilets) existed, nonwhites could attend provincial and international events if it would not disturb the whites; Bantus could never attend events below the provincial level, while Indians and Colored people could–if it did not disturb the whites. The minister of Bantu administration confirmed this policy. Still, the policy was ambiguous, since the definition of what would disturb the whites was not made clear. Nonwhites were granted a permit to attend the stadium in Newlands; however, the government ordered that a six-foot-high wire fence be erected to separate them from whites.[47]

The second, and much more threatening, government incursion into sports policy occurred in September at the end of the South African rugby tour of New Zealand. The tour had gone well with no disruptions, a result of assurances that Maoris would be welcome in South Africa in future New Zealand rugby tours. These assurances were confirmed during the first days of September by a member of the South African Rugby Board (SARB) and by Kobus Louw, a senior civil servant in the Department of Coloured Affairs and rugby tour manager. Statements by the latter two men were interpreted in the South African press as indicating that the government itself had agreed to allow the Maoris to tour South Africa in 1967.[48]

All illusions were quickly dispelled. On September 4, Prime Minister Verwoerd himself spoke out:

> When we are the guests of another country we have to behave according to their tradition. We will play there in the exact way it has been arranged by New Zealand. Like we subject ourselves to their customs, we expect that, when other countries visit us, they will respect ours of no mixed teams.[49]

An editorial in the September 7 *Die Transvaler* attempted to give the speech (called the Loskop Dam speech) a philosophical base:

> It must be ascribed to one particular factor that the white race has hitherto maintained itself in the southern part of Africa. That is that there has been no miscegenation. The absence of miscegenation was because there was no social mixing between whites and non-whites. Social mixing leads inexorably to miscegenation. . . . It is today the social aim of the Communist. . . . In South Africa the races do not mix on the sports field. If they mix first on the sports field, then the road to other forms of social mixing is wide open. . . . With an eye to upholding the white race and its civilization not one single compromise can be entered into–not even when it comes to a visiting Rugby team.[50]

Minister of the Interior de Klerk tried to explain the Loskop speech with the same philosophical base but with other implications:

> I also want to emphasize that it is wrong to assert that this is political interference in a purely sporting matter. The Government was elected to oppose the various forms of integration, including social integration. It had to see the national policy was respected in the field of sport as in all other spheres. . . .
>
> In conclusion, I want to say that it is a pity but typical of United Party leadership that they are seeking political advantage out of this, with a view to the elections, and are also trying to create the false impression that the National Party will become divided and will split on the issue.
>
> The continued existence of peace and order within white South Africa is of the utmost first importance. It does not tolerate any concession to the United Party's policy of integration of black and white for which, in this case, it is seeking a breakthrough in a subtle way with help from the outside world.[51]

While it might be difficult to understand how two or three Maoris on a New Zealand team would lead to the dreaded miscegenation, it seemed to be a real fear for the white South Africans. That the National party leadership was able to discern a conspiracy of the Communists, the United party, and the New Zealand government that would lead to miscegenation through social mixing is illustrative of the paranoia under which they make decisions. Verwoerd's statement renewed old grievances with New Zealand dating back to the 1959-1960 controversy. On September 30, Verwoerd attempted to put the blame on New Zealand: "It is not South Africa but New Zealand which draws a distinction between the Maoris and the white Zealanders. If they are one nation, why refer to Maoris at all?"[52]

Up to this point, official New Zealand reaction to the Loskop Dam speech was negligible. In fact, Pat Walsh, one of the Maoris who had gone to South Africa in 1964 for the meeting of the International Rugby Board, showed how well South Africa's propaganda machinery had worked when he said of the Loskop speech, "I only hope the New Zealand public doesn't make a political issue out of this."[53] But Verwoerd's speech was more than other New Zealanders could take and prompted Prime Minister Holyoake to respond:

> I have certainly not tried to dictate otherwise or suggest that South Africa should suspend its racial policy as I believe that the composition of the South African team is a matter for South Africa. Rather it appears that the South African Prime Minister is trying to dictate the composition of the New Zealand team and is asking New Zealand to suspend its racial policy for South Africa's sake.[54]

In spite of the unequivocal statements by the South African government, Dr. Dannie Craven, head of the South African Rugby Board, curiously enough asked the government in December to allow Maoris to take part in the 1967 tour. The government refused.[55]

Why did Craven even ask? It was not the first time that a sports administrator had made statements for mixed sports in South Africa in the full knowledge that the government would not permit such hopes to become reality. Why, then, did they make these statements? Probably because sports administrators in South Africa wanted the international federations to believe that it was the government and not they who were responsible for apartheid in sports.

THE IOC

It was not only South Africa that proposed to keep out foreign athletes on political and/or racial grounds. To keep things in some global perspective, it should be noted that, in April, the French government announced it would not guarantee visas for East German athletes scheduled to compete in the Grenoble winter Olympics in 1968.[56] This decision sent a shock wave through the IOC, and it was this issue—not that of South Africa—that dominated the IOC meeting in Madrid in October. At that meeting, the French NOC assured the IOC that the East Germans would be allowed to compete in Grenoble.[57]

The South African question was discussed from the point of view of excluding South African administrators (who refused to disassociate themselves from the government's policy) from the IOC meeting.[58] This discussion was led by the African delegates who had previously threatened to walk out of an NOC meeting if Reg Honey of South Africa was admitted.[59] In August, the South Africans had invited Avery Brundage to come to South Africa to inspect their sports administration, but he did not go.[60]

The only international action taken against South Africa in 1965 was that its team was excluded from the University World Games in Budapest. The South Africans had already selected an all-white team at the time of the withdrawal of the invitation.[61]

SAN-ROC's IMPORTANCE

The importance of SAN-ROC can, perhaps, best be seen in this year of 1965 when it was virtually inoperative. In 1963, the Baden-Baden resolution had been passed amid a great deal of publicity surrounding the arrests of John Harris and Dennis Brutus as they attempted to attend the IOC session. In 1964, South Africa was officially excluded from the Tokyo games, and the South African issue was raised before more than a half-dozen international federations. But in 1965, SAN-ROC was out of the picture and the South African issue seemed to be a dead one internationally. The South African government made certain that things would remain this way when Dennis Brutus' prison sentence ended. Brutus described what happened:

> I was banned the day before I was released from prison in Caledon Square in Cape Town. I was given a series of orders lifting all the bans which had been imposed on me in '61 and which were to run until '66; and then given a fresh set of bans starting in '65 and running to 1970. They included all those previously on me with many more, one of them being social intercourse; another confining me to house arrest for 12 hours every day and all the weekends; and another which not only forbade me to publish as had been the case in the past but also forbade me to write anything that might be published. There were no reasons given.[62]

1966

For white South Africans, 1965 proved to be the lull before the storm, which gathered force in 1966 and eventually ripped South Africa from the heart of the global sports map.

SAN-ROC's ability to function within South Africa had been reduced to zero. Its leaders had been hounded, banned, arrested, exiled, or executed. There was no future for the group in South Africa. Two leading SAN-ROC figures, Chris de Broglio and Reg Hlongwane, prominent South African weightlifters, had moved to London in self-exile, and the process of rebirth was completed for SAN-ROC in 1966.[63]

The rebirth of SAN-ROC meant trouble for South African sports. After the tranquility of 1965, the South African issue was raised in four international federations, as well as in the IOC, in 1966. Sports relations with six countries were challenged. This unrest brought the promise of more compromises from the South African sports bodies for nonwhite South Africans. Of equal importance to the reemergence of SAN-ROC in London–and to a large extent precipitated by that reemergence–was the founding of another sports organization in Bamako in December, the Supreme Council for Sport in Africa (SCSA).[64]

THE GOVERNMENT AND PAPWA SEWGOLUM

By 1966, Papwa Sewgolum was a three-time winner of the Dutch Open, and his international standing was secure; but in South Africa, his opportunity to play continually seemed to be at the whim of the government. He had been refused several permits to play in South Africa in early January. The South African Golf Union intervened on Sewgolum's behalf, and the government agreed that he could enter any tournament that he had competed in prior to 1966.[65] However, five days later, Jan Haak, the South African minister of planning, refused to allow Sewgolum to compete in the Western Province Open, even though he had played in it before.[66] The ruling was applied inconsistently throughout the year.

SAAAU's SUPPORT OF APARTHEID SPORT

In February, the South African AAU made the strongest statement by a sports body up to that time concerning apartheid in sport. Colonel Vissier, a SAAAU leader, said: "We are one of the strongest bodies in the country and the time has come for us to say how we feel on this point. We must make it clear that there can be no deviating from Government policy."[67] In response to the SAAAU's policy statement, Britain's international athletes voted sixty-one to nine in a referendum to stop competition with South Africa until there was no discrimination in South African sports.[68]

IOC ACTIONS ON SOUTH AFRICA

As the Rome meeting of the IOC was about to get underway, the Kenya National Sports Council announced that it had withdrawn an invitation to two nonwhite South Africans to compete in Nairobi in July. The invitation had been made by Reg Alexander, the white IOC delegate from Kenya, who had visited South Africa. The Kenya National Sports Council called the invitation "a move to undermine the stand taken by the African Olympic Association on the question of segregation in sport practiced in South Africa."[69] The Kenyans feared that the invitation might show the South Africans in a favorable light before the IOC. Alexander further embarrassed the Kenyans at the IOC meeting; he said that when he visited South Africa, he had been impressed by what was being done for nonwhite sport and that whatever failures did exist were not the fault of the South African sports administrators.[70]

Before the meeting began, there was a great deal of speculation in the South African press that SAONGA would be excluded from the Mexico Olympics at the Rome session.[71]

When the session began, Braun told IOC members that SAONGA was ready to create a committee composed of half white and half nonwhite members. SAONGA had, according to Braun, received the government's permission to do this. In addition, Braun reaffirmed SAONGA's faith in the Olympic regulations.[72]

Avery Brundage advised the IOC that to suspend South Africa at that time would seriously jeopardize the negotiations in progress between the South African government and the SAONGA, and he suggested that the IOC allow time to see if the new proposals would work. The IOC accepted this suggestion and decided to send an investigative committee to South Africa before the next session at Tehran. The committee was to consist of Brundage (or his representative) and two African delegates.[73]

The minutes of the IOC session make no mention of the fact that South Africa would have to send two teams to the Olympics: one representing whites and another representing nonwhites. Minister of the Interior Pieter LeRoux had made this quite clear when he warned that South Africa would never allow a mixed team to represent all of South Africa.[74]

It should be noted that since there were only two black African nations represented on the IOC, one of the members of the IOC investigative team would have to be Reg Alexander of Kenya, who had already delivered his own favorable report on South Africa as a result of his visit there. At this point, it seemed that the white South Africans would be assured of a favorable report as the second proposed member, Avery Brundage, said after the IOC meeting: "We would like to see South Africa back in the Olympic Games. We all regard this new proposal as a considerable step forward—we have made progress. We have not had time to consider all its implications, but it seems to be a favorable move."[75] Later in the year, Brundage was quoted as having said that "the IOC was now prepared to lift the suspension of South Africa as great progress had been made."[76] This statement brought a quick SAN-ROC appeal to the Afro-Asian members of the IOC to protest Brundage's statement.[77]

Brundage's remarks bring to mind those he made to United States athletes *before* he left to investigate conditions in Germany in 1934. He told the athletes to prepare for the games, strongly implying what the result of his investigation would be.[78] The implication proved correct in 1935, as they did in 1968 when the commission report was released.

THE INTERNATIONAL FEDERATIONS

In May, the controversy over the New Zealand All-Blacks team was raised again when the New Zealand Federation of Labor voted to refuse service to sports teams chosen on a racial basis. This was no small matter, as the federation's services included all travel facilities.[79]

The U.S.S.R. again raised the issue of South Africa before the International Lawn Tennis Federation (ILTF) meeting in July. In a system known as "weighted voting," the Russian proposal to exclude South Africa was defeated, 80 percent to 20 percent, according to ILTF Secretary Basil Reay. Under this weighted voting system, the major tennis-playing nations (all are predominantly white nations) control the vast majority of the votes.

Reay said that the ILTF did not expect the SALTU to be responsible for changing South Africa's laws. J. L. Barrie and B. S. L. Franklin, SALTU's representatives at the ILTF meeting, announced that SALTU had given nonwhite tennis players monetary as well as technical help and that nonwhite bodies would henceforth take part in the administration of tennis at the national level.[80]

Barrie went still further and said that he anticipated the day when nonwhite South Africans would compete in international tournaments. He hoped that the nonwhite bodies would immediately become affiliated to SALTU so that it could begin with its assistance.[81] SAN-ROC leader Chris de Broglio nevertheless sought South Africa's expulsion from the ILTF in 1968.[82]

In August, Franklin attempted to dispel rumors that South Africa's tennis allies were deserting it:

> The Americans especially were both surprised and annoyed that their name had been linked in reports with the expulsion move. They said that the reports were 102% wrong. . . . It was apparent that the vast majority of the delegates of the 50 to 60 nations represented were firmly opposed to attempts to introduce politics into the administration of the game, or to interfere with the domestic politics of any particular country.[83]

Franklin warned the nonwhite bodies that they must affiliate to SALTU if they had any hope of gaining international standing.[84] Barrie later announced that Frank Waring, the minister of the newly created Department of Sport, had told him that SALTU's new policy regarding nonwhites was within the government's guidelines for sports policy.[85]

DENNIS BRUTUS AND SAN-ROC IN EXILE

Although SAN-ROC was trying to regain the momentum it had built up before the John Harris affair in 1964, it seemed that without Dennis Brutus' leadership, it was a lost organization. So was Brutus a lost man in South Africa. He recalled:

> After a year under house arrest and very difficult conditions, part of which I had spent unemployed, I gave up and began to make seri-

ous efforts to get out of South Africa, roughly between May and June of 1966. By July the permission had come through and I got away.[86]

Chris de Broglio helped Brutus get his British passport back (it had been taken away by the South African police) by having MP Jeremy Thorpe intervene in London,[87]

Brutus arrived in London in August and, after only four days, he flew to Jamaica for the Commonwealth games. He announced that he was going after the international federations, especially the IAAF and the FIHC (weightlifting). Of white South Africans, he maintained: "They are sports mad. When they were deprived of their rugby test matches against the New Zealand All-Blacks, there was a sense of all-pervading gloom over the country."[88]

South Africa's membership in the IAAF was a particular target of SAN-ROC for two primary reasons: Vissier's statement on apartheid in February and one made by IAAF leader Harold Abrahams in April. Referring to the possibility of the SAAAU being expelled from the IAAF if the IOC decided to expel the South African body, Abrahams had said: "I do not believe South Africa is in danger of being expelled [from the IAAF]. What would such a move achieve? The Olympic body forbids the practice of segregation. The IAAF does not."[89]

SAN-ROC began its campaign by sending a memorandum detailing the SAAAU's actions of discrimination to all the African and Asian delegates on the IAAF. It asked that an investigative committee go to South Africa.[90] This memorandum prompted the Sierra Leone National Sports Council, among others, to petition the IAAF to exclude the SAAAU.[91]

SAN-ROC's efforts with the IAAF were subverted when, at its annual meeting in Budapest, the IAAF adopted a weighted voting system that gave 37 predominantly white nations 244 votes and 99 predominantly nonwhite nations only 195 votes.[92] The motion to exclude South Africa, although discussed, was thoroughly defeated as a result of the new voting system.[93]

There were also several compelling reasons for SAN-ROC to single out the struggle in weightlifting. First, this was where the struggle had begun in 1946. Second, Chris de Broglio, Brutus' top aid, had been a white South African weightlifting champion from 1953 through 1962. Finally, it was in weightlifting that the nonracial movement had its best case since three nonwhites, Ron Eland, Precious McKenzie and Reg Hlongwane, all had to leave South Africa in order to gain recognition in international weightlifting circles.

The campaign began before Brutus arrived in London. Chris de Broglio sent letters to all the national weightlifting federations affiliated to the international body, the International Weightlifting Federation (FIHC), in which he called for the expulsion of the white South African Amateur Weightlifting Union and the recognition of the nonracial South African Amateur Weightlifting Federation (SAAWF).[94] He also wrote to the South African provincial weightlifting associations asking them not to affiliate to the white body. He assured them of SAN-ROC's support at the Berlin meeting of the FIHC.[95]

In August, de Broglio drew up the document for the FIHC, charging the SAAWU with violating the FIHC constitution. When the FIHC met, twenty-two of the thirty nations present had signed SAN-ROC's expulsion declaration. In spite of this petition, the FIHC executive refused even to discuss the possibility of expulsion; instead, it decided to send a three-man investigative team to South Africa.[96]

The SAAWU had brought a Colored official, Billy Francis, with it to the FIHC meeting. The nonwhite *Golden City Post* immediately protested on the grounds that Francis did not represent nonwhite opinion. In fact, he had been expelled from the SAAWF, and the association that he represented had fewer members than the smallest unit affiliated to the SAAWF.[97] Nevertheless, the white national bodies of South Africa usually brought a nonwhite administrator to the meetings of the international federations. At best, their ability to speak for nonwhite South African opinion was questionable. Dennis Brutus referred to them as "stooges."[98] While this may be a harsh generalization, in 1966 Brutus was beyond question far more representative of nonwhite South African opinion than a Billy Francis or a B. P. Morola.

Although SAN-ROC members were distressed that the question of expulsion was not even discussed, they were pleased to know that a top-level investigative team would be going to South Africa.

SOUTH AFRICAN INTERNAL POLICIES

By August 1966, professional football in South Africa had all but consumed itself. The white NFL had succeeded in keeping the nonwhite

SASL out of most of South Africa's sports grounds, while the nonwhite boycott had all but ruined the NFL. In August, both groups attempted to start again, although it was not certain what the regrouped SASL would do.[99] *The World* [Johannesburg], in an editorial, pleaded with the nonwhite groups to affiliate to the NFL so that football could again become a major sport in South Africa.[100]

In November, FIFA decided that it could not temporarily lift its suspension of FASA so it could invite a team to play it during FASA's seventy-fifth anniversary.[101] Dave Marais, FASA's president, said of FASA's suspension:

> The tragedy is that most of the important countries are sympathetic. But there is such a large bloc of African countries that when it comes to one man, one vote, we don't have a chance of reversing the decision. I think there should be a qualified vote. It is absurd for each little country to have the same voting power as countries like England or Italy.[102]

The importance of a weighted voting system in international federations became obvious: in the ILTF and the IAAF, both with voting systems weighted in favor of European nations, South Africa's membership was upheld; in FIFA, where one country, one vote was the rule, the South Africans had been suspended.

Frank Braun, who was also the head of the South African white boxing body, announced that there would be a nonwhite tour of Italy if all the nonwhite groups became affiliated to his white SAABA. Without affiliation, there would be no tour.[103] Although this type of pressure could hardly be called subtle, it was not an untypical tactic of white South African sports administrators.

Later in August, Minister of the Interior LeRoux refused to allow a university rugby team to tour Japan at the expense of the Japanese. LeRoux said that he did not want to do anything that might disturb the existing friendly relations between Japan and South Africa.[104] He did not elaborate on how such a tour might affect those relations in a negative manner.

THE FORMATION OF THE SUPREME COUNCIL OF SPORT

The role of South African sport in South Africa's overall international relations was clearly stated in an editorial in the *Star* [Johannesburg]:

> However absurd it might be, in the mass mind today national images are created on fields of sport, and since South Africa is at the bottom of any popularity poll for political reasons, we are particularly fortunate to have young people overseas winning acclaim not only for their brilliant performances but for their sportsmanship. South Africa's successes are remarkable since this is a small country and its representatives are drawn from only a minority of the people. Take politics out of sport and Springboks overseas would do more for the image of South Africa than all our propaganda offices put together.[105]

But if there was ever a chance that politics could be taken out of sport in regard to the case of South Africa, that chance was forever extinguished when the Supreme Council for Sport in Africa was formed by thirty-two African nations in Bamako in December 1966. Although its general purpose was to coordinate and promote sport throughout Africa, Dennis Brutus, who attended the original conference in Bamako, maintained that a primary motivating force in the formation of the SCSA was an attack on South Africa's apartheid sport.[106]

The SCSA's major resolution was:

> It is the firm decision of the Supreme Council to use every means to obtain the expulsion of South African sports organizations from the Olympic Movement and from International Federations should South Africa fail to comply fully with the IOC rules.
>
> Finally, the Supreme Council invites all its members to subject their decision to participate in the 1968 Olympic Games to the reservation that no racialist team from South Africa takes part, and to ask all national Olympic committees to support the attitude of the Supreme Council for Sport in Africa.[107]

The wording left no doubt that there was a clear boycott threat for the 1968 Olympics. When the African nations actually carried out this threat, fourteen months later after the IOC Grenoble decision to allow South Africa to compete in Mexico, the IOC charged that the decision was totally unexpected. In spite of this claim, the warning was unequivocal. After this resolution was passed at Bamako, South Africa's international sports relations were never the same again. The African nations had seized the opportunity; they have still to let go.

1967

The attitude of the South African government was more rigid at the beginning of 1967 than at any other time since the Nationalists came to power. It was, in fact, so rigid in its attitude toward Basil D'Oliveira that it brought upon itself a tumult of criticism from abroad and, more significantly, at home. Concessions made later in the year by the new prime minister, Mr. Vorster, can be directly attributed to this criticism.

The South African issue dominated the IOC at its Tehran meeting in April, and the IOC commission went to South Africa to investigate charges of discrimination in November. SAN-ROC and the SCSA continued their uncompromising stands and were joined by the American Committee on Africa (ACOA) and the United Nations. In addition, fourteen nations became involved in the South African sports controversy. Finally, black American athletes began to talk of an Olympic boycott, primarily because of racism in sports in the United States; however, the expulsion of South Africa from the Olympics was one of their six demands.

THE POSITION OF THE SOUTH AFRICAN GOVERNMENT

Basil D'Oliveira, the Cape Colored cricket star who had gone to England to play professional cricket in 1960 because he could not play in South Africa for the all-white Springboks, had become an international star for England. He was such a good player that it had become expected that whenever an English team went overseas, he would be on that team. Nevertheless, when the MCC, the body responsible for English cricket, had scheduled a tour of South Africa for late 1968, there was considerable speculation as to whether the South African government would allow D'Oliveira to come with the English team. All doubts should have been ended when Minister of the Interior LeRoux said in January 1967: "Our policy is clear. We will not allow mixed teams to play against our white teams here. If this player [D'Oliveira] were chosen, he would not be allowed to come here. That is our policy. It is well known here and overseas."[108] Indeed, the fate of the Maoris and the now-cancelled 1967 All-Blacks tour of South Africa had made the government's attitude well known in South Africa and overseas. There was, however, a slight twist in this case; the player in question was a native South African.

The reaction of the MCC in London was an indication of the new rules of the game of cricket. MCC spokesman S. C. Griffith said of the impending confrontation, "We will cross that bridge when we come to it."[109] *The Guardian* [Manchester] interpreted his statement as meaning that two cricket seasons would have to pass before the MCC made its selections for the team and it might be possible that D'Oliveira would not be quite as proficient at the time of selection. This would avoid the confrontation with the South African government and the tour could go on as planned.[110]

In case LeRoux's statement was not clear enough, Minister of Sport Frank Waring told Parliamant: "At this stage the question is hypothetical. However, the Government has on many occasions made it quite clear that it opposes mixed sport in South Africa."[111]

The South African press promptly condemned the government's decision and, at the same time, praised D'Oliveira as a man who was apolitical.[112] And, indeed he was—so much so that he, frankly, annoyed many leaders of the nonracial movement for his failure to publicly criticize apartheid in sports. D'Oliveira was in South Africa coaching Colored cricketers when the controversy began. When he got back to London, he refused to become involved in the controversy: "I think responsible people like the MCC can make fair and just decisions. . . . I am going to sit tight."[113]

The MCC had, in fact, assured the British government that its team would be chosen solely on merit; if South Africa would not accept a team with D'Oliveira as a member, the tour would be cancelled. British Minister of Sport Dennis Howell praised the MCC for its decision.[114]

By the end of January, everything seemed quite clear-cut: the South Africans would refuse permission for D'Oliveira to play and the MCC would then cancel the tour. But it was not so simple.

South African sportsmen were convinced that if the MCC cancelled the tour, the sports associations of New Zealand and Australia would follow directly.[115] Barbados had already withdrawn invitations to three South African cricket stars in retaliation for the government's stand on D'Oliveira,[116] and three British athletic champions announced that they would not tour South Africa because of apartheid in sports.[117]

With the pressure mounting on the South African government, LeRoux denied that he said D'Oliveira could not come. However, he hastened to add: "The Government under its new Prime Minister would be just as inflexible and immovable on principles. . . . There should be no mixed sport in South Africa."[118] By the end of February, *Dagbreek* ran a front-page editorial predicting that Vorster would ease the application of apartheid in sport because of the controversies over the cancellation of the New Zealand tour and the D'Oliveira affair.[119] This was the first sign of a breakthrough, and South African sportsmen knew all too well that they needed a major breakthrough soon if they were to remain in the Olympic movement. While the D'Oliveira affair was temporarily laid to rest, the approach of the Tehran IOC meeting was what concerned South Africans. While it was true that a new policy was being formulated, events that the South African government had not foreseen caused more embarrassment and made its diplomatic task more difficult.

A leading South African tobacco company offered to sponsor a cricket series between South Africa and the West Indies to be played in Britain.[120] Minister of Sport Waring quickly responded to this proposed series: "If whites and nonwhites start competing against each other, there will be such viciousness as has never been seen before."[121] Vorster, in a March 4 speech at Oudshoorn, emphasized that the National party had only one policy: that each group's sport be practiced and administered separately. South Africa, he said, should not open sports relations with the West Indies, Pakistan, and India because it did not have traditional sports relations with those countries.[122] He also criticized the tobacco company for interfering with the functions of the National party.[123]

In mid-March, Tunisia and Morocco withdrew from the International Cross Country Championships in Cardiff because of South Africa's presence. Ted Skipper, and Anti-Apartheid Movement (AAM) leader, announced that the AAM was ready to give "one of the greatest demonstrations against South Africa's colour policy this country has seen."[124]

Seeing the need to move quickly, Frank Braun announced the so-called Tehran concessions before the prime minister had the opportunity to explain them in Parliament. There were several points:

1. South Africa would send a mixed team to the Olympics.
2. All members would march under the same flag and wear the same colors.
3. South Africans of different racial groups could compete against each other at the games.
4. A nonwhite Olympic committee would be formed, and each racial group would designate its candidates for selection.
5. A liaison committee of whites and nonwhites, under Braun's chairmanship, would make the final selection of team members.[125]

Lord Exeter, a British member of the IOC, commented: "It is definitely a very great step forward and I am very pleased to hear it."[126]

The next day, Chris de Broglio hastily put together a SAN-ROC press statement condemning the concessions, which he said showed how much the government interfered in sport. He pointed out that the idea of mixed teams from South Africa was not new.[127] While it was true that South Africa had sent whites and nonwhites abroad before, it had never sent a unified team overseas.

The South African sports administrators had clearly seized the momentum before Tehran. Braun was particularly pleased with the reaction of the influential nonwhite sports writer, Leslie Sehume. In his column in the March 29 issue of *The World* [Johannesburg], Sehume urged all nonwhites to get together so that nonwhite sport could develop more rapidly to the point that nonwhites would be able to compete with whites in all sports and not just the few they had parity in at that time.[128]

SOUTH AFRICAN SPORTS RELATIONS WITH UGANDA

The South Africans even managed to obtain an invitation to the Ugandian International Tennis Tournament. The acting director of the tournament, John McKenzie, invited South Africa because "a suitable basis for cooperation which will benefit all concerned can be worked out."[129] *The People* [Kampala], which was the government newspaper in Uganda, condemned McKenzie's one-man decision as a breach of the Organization of African Unity (OAU) decision of imposing a total sports ban on South Africa until it stopped racial discrimination. The editorial succintly stated the political value of the sports issue to Africa:

> Here is a field in which Africa does not need to plead, cajole or threaten other powers to take action against apartheid; we can act decisively ourselves . . . the South Africans do not consider it minor. As Jim Barrie, President of the South African Lawn Tennis Union said, "this will be a major step in overcoming the threat of international sports isolation."
>
> What is our policy toward this infiltration? . . . If we wish to accept their offers—baited hooks, they have been called—let us say so openly. . . .
>
> Unless we face these complex problems, they are going to be a serious threat to the OAU. Once South Africa gets a hold INSIDE the OAU, that is the beginning of the end of our anti-colonialism stand.[130]

The Ugandans used an approach similar to that used by the South Africans. While the South Africans maintained that they could not allow Maoris to come to South Africa because it would be the beginning of the end of apartheid, the Ugandans maintained that they could not allow the South Africans to come to Uganda because it would be the beginning of the end of the OAU's anticolonialism. Just as the Maoris did not go to South Africa in 1967, neither did the South Africans go to Uganda.

OTHER CONCESSIONS AND OTHER BANS

In South Africa, it had barely been noticed that a group of Colored spectators had been ejected from an international tennis match because there were no separate toilet facilities. A "whites only" sign then had to be posted on the door of the stadium.[131] But the mood in South African sports circles was still positive. The Ugandan tour had not yet been cancelled, and a group of nonwhite boxers left for a tour of Italy (they were not awarded Springbok colors but wore the badge of the Kudu head) on the same day that it was announced that the newly formed South African Rugby Union (nonwhite) would be sending a twenty-five-man team on an overseas tour in 1968 or 1969 (players from the nonracial South African Rugby Federation would not be allowed to tour unless they affiliated to the SARU).[132]

In Yaounde, the Supreme Council for Sport in Africa, in an attempt to regain the momentum as the Tehran meeting approached, announced on April 10 that the African nations might boycott the Mexico games if a "racist team" from South Africa was there.[133]

However, it was Prime Minister Vorster who gained the headlines the next day in a speech in Parliament that clearly set out South Africa's sports policy—new and old. He began the speech on an idealistic note:

> This matter should not be dragged into politics, because in my humble opinion it is a matter which does not belong there. . . . The policy of South Africa, and not only of the National Party, is separate development . . . a policy which has never been based on hate or prejudice or fear . . . it does not mean the denial of a person's human dignity . . . South Africa has never demanded of any state that it also accept this policy, and similarly South Africa will never allow the policy of another state to be forced onto her in this regard. . . . Differences in domestic policy are not an obstacle to peaceful cooperation between countries. As far as that is concerned, separate development also applies to the field of sport.
>
> I therefore want to make it quite clear that from South Africa's point of view no mixed sport between whites and non-whites will be practiced locally, irrespective of the standard of proficiency of the participants. . . . We do not apply that as a criterion because our policy has nothing to do with proficiency or lack of proficiency. If any person, locally or abroad, adopts the attitude that he will enter into relations with us only if we are prepared to jettison the separate practicing of sport prevailing among our own people in South Africa, then I want to make it quite clear that, no matter how important those sports relations are in my view, I am not prepared to pay that price. On that score, I want no misunderstanding whatsoever . . . in respect of this principle we are not prepared to compromise, we are not prepared to negotiate and we are not prepared to make any concessions.

> In the second place our attitude in respect of sport is that attendance of members of one group at such recreational events of the other group takes place by way of permit, if at all . . . provided that separate facilities are available and as long as it does not result in situations which are conducive to friction and disturbance, and, I want to add, provided that it will not hamper the development of their own facilities.[134]

This last clause was characteristic of South African government officials who were justifying denying the use of white facilities to nonwhites. What they were saying was that by using the white facilities constantly, nonwhites would see no need to develop their own facilities; furthermore, nonwhites who attended white events would not develop an appreciation of their own nonwhite sportsmen. It is a curious form of logic.

Vorster was laying the framework of what seemed to be a dogmatic policy with no hint of change. Still, he did advocate the policy of sending one team to the Olympics:

> I want to make it quite clear that a decision was already taken in this regard by my predecessor. It is not a decision taken in my time. . . . The Olympic Games is a unique event in which all countries of the world take part, and our attitude in respect of that event was that if there were any of our Coloured or Bantu who were good enough to compete there, or whose standard of proficiency was such that they could take part in it, we would make it possible for them to take part. . . . Only one team from each country is allowed to take part in the Olympic Games.[135]

This seemed to be a curious statement for Vorster; his predecessor's policy toward the Olympic games was clearly that if nonwhites were to compete, they would compete as a separate team representing nonwhite South Africans. A white team would represent white South Africans. Vorster was obviously trying to create the impression in the right-wing Parliament that he was not making any new policies. He continued:

> Because the Olympic Games lay it down as an absolute condition, the people who are then selected will take part as one contingent under the South African flag. . . .
>
> Then we come to other sporting matters. . . . I have no objection to the Canada Cup tournament taking place here in South Africa.

> In fact, I have issued an invitation to that effect. . . . The same applies in respect of the Davis Cup competition. . . . If it were to happen that we had to play against a Coloured country in the finals, we would do so, whether in that country or in South Africa, because here one has to do with an inter-state relationship. . . . We must draw a very clear distinction between personal relations on the one hand and inter-state relations on the other.
>
> To illustrate it even further . . . it is not our policy that there should be social mingling of whites and non-whites in South Africa, but because I was dealing with an inter-state relationship in that instance, I could receive the Prime Minister of Lesotho as I did, because it was not a personal relationship but an inter-state relationship. I received him as the Prime Minister of his country, just as my forefathers received people of that rank many years ago. . . . I therefore say that this is my attitude in respect of the Olympic Games and in respect of the Canada Cup tournament and in respect of the Davis Cup competition.[136]

Vorster seemed to need to show that his policies were continuations and not innovations. Yet, in respect to international events, they clearly were innovations.

According to *The Times* [London], Vorster's speech also implied that Maoris and Basil D'Oliveira would be able to compete in South Africa.[137] Vorster confirmed this in Parliament the next day when he said that Maoris had been on New Zealand teams that had come to South Africa in 1929, 1949, and 1960: "We received those people and we treated them as we would treat any member of the New Zealand team—there were no difficulties."[138] Vorster was again attempting to demonstrate that his policy was merely business as usual. However, according to the records, no Maoris had come to South Africa in those or any other years as members of the All-Blacks. (While it might have been possible that people would have already forgotten the composition of the 1929 and 1949 All-Blacks tours, the 1960 tour was all too fresh in their minds.) In any case, the *New York Times* reported Vorster's policy as a major breakthrough—and that was undoubtedly what Vorster hoped the outside world would believe.[139] However, his hopes that South Africans would not interpret it in this way fell through as both right-wing MP's and members of the opposition responded that the policy was a radical change. Most South African newspapers agreed with them. In answer, Vorster attempted to cover his policy: "If there are people who in any way believe or think that it can be inferred from my speech that all barriers will now be removed, then they are making a very big mistake."[140] In an obvious reference to the D'Oliveira affair, he said: "One thing I do not believe in is what people have tried in the past—namely, long before a tour takes place, to name an individual and ask whether we will accept him or not. That sort of thing is only asked to cause trouble where trouble does not exist."[141]

Thus, the fact of the MCC tour was once again uncertain. Some of the inconsistencies in the "new" (or old, if one believed Vorster) policy began to surface. After a close reading of the speech, it became obvious that, while South Africa's international sports policy was liberalized, it was largely at the expense of a hardening of the internal sports policy: the ban on mixed spectators was strengthened; the inequality of opportunity in training of and competition for nonwhites was solidified; and the interference of the government in sports policy was made absolute, with no pretense of the possibility of an independent policy by sports administrators. A prime casualty of the new policy was Papwa Sewgolum; Vorster ruled that he could never again compete with white golfers in South Africa.[142]

Most sportsmen (at least, most white sportsmen), both at home and abroad, were willing to overlook the new inconsistencies. Frank Braun immediately announced that a conference, composed of an equal number of whites and nonwhites, would be held to establish the nonwhite Olympic committee.[143]

SAN-ROC, perhaps fearing the loss of its own influence in South Africa, announced it might support the new committee. Chris de Broglio commented:

> There was a time when we thought the granite wall of sport apartheid would never crack. If Mr. Braun can now convince the IOC that this is the start of a new deal for non-white sportsmen in South Africa, we might even ask to join the new Olympic committee.[144]

SAN-ROC even went so far as to suggest how to establish such a committee. It proposed two alternative plans:

1. Hold a national convention to elect a caretaker executive to supervise the merger of all existing bodies into one national body for each code of sport. If it was impossible for the merger to take place rapidly enough, the caretaker executive could supervise nonracial trials for the Olympic team.
2. Open membership of all organizations affiliated to SAONGA to all South Africans. The provincial bodies in each code of sport would be represented on the executive of the national organization by one white and one nonwhite delegate for a transitional period of two to four years. During such a period, SAONGA would also be composed of one white and one nonwhite delegate from each code of sport.[145]

Just as Vorster's policy seemed to be a major departure internationally, so did this position by SAN-ROC. Based on its previous stands, it seemed completely incongruous that SAN-ROC would consider separate representation, even if only for a transitional period. Chris de Broglio, who signed the new position paper, later agreed that there was some inconsistency, but he maintained that things were happening so fast at the time leading up to the IOC Tehran meeting that SAN-ROC wanted to appear reasonable and remain in the forefront of the nonracial movement.[146]

IOC officials also praised Vorster's new policy. IOC Chancellor Westerhoff said: "This seems a giant step forward. In Tehran, Mr. Braun will have every opportunity of convincing South Africa's enemies and friends that this is the start of a new era for non-white sportsmen in South Africa."[147] Lord Exeter, a member of the IOC executive, commented:

> South Africa has kept its promise . . . and, now Mr. Braun will have to clarify things for us in Tehran. With this fine opportunity, I am sure everybody will vote him all the time he needs to put his case.
>
> We want assurance that these concessions are a sincere intention of bigger things to come.[148]

Westerhoff and Exeter seem not to have read Vorster's follow-up speech: there were no "bigger things to come."

The Sunday Times [Johannesburg] had high praise for Vorster, especially in light of Verwoerd's policy. It called the "extremists" in the National party an "irritant minority":

> What is important at this stage is that Mr. Vorster has enunciated a new and enlightened principle, which represents a magnificent reversal of earlier trends.[149]

The *Sunday Tribune* [Durban] carried an article by its parliamentary correspondant calling Vorster "the sportsman of the year." It warned, however, that Vorster had not changed apartheid itself.[150] *The Sunday Express* [Johannesburg], although praising the new policy, warned sports administrators not to interpret the policy freely since "his concessions are specific—not general. They apply to individual sports and events; they do not confer carte-blanche on all sports to engage in mixed competitions."[151] But the sternest warning came from Alan Paton, the Liberal party leader:

> It would be wrong of the MCC and the All-Blacks for instance, to consider that the immoral practice of apartheid has been relaxed merely because South Africa will now allow Maoris and Basil D'Oliveira to play here.
>
> They must not forget that in many centers here Africans are not allowed in the stadiums in which test matches are played—not even as spectators.
>
> In no cases are they allowed as spectators on the golf courses on which whites play.
>
> And Mr. Vorster has made it clear that South African non-whites will never be allowed to play against whites on the sports fields of this country.[152]

While most white South African sports administrators welcomed the new sports policy, the SAAAU and the South African Amateur Swimming Union (SAASU) had mixed reactions. While Frank Braun told the SAAAU that it could send a mixed team to international matches in Belgium, Germany, and France, Matt Mare of the SAAAU said that he was not enthusiastic about sending a team to the "little Olympics" in Mexico in 1967 (this was a pre-Olympic event, run by the IOC).[153] Neville Gracie, president of the SAASU, said he was not prepared to allow his swimmers to be "used as instruments to get South Africa back in the Olympic Games."[154] But South African officials had always placed swimming in a separate category from other sports. Frank Braun had once "scientifically" explained why there were no qualified nonwhite swimmers in South Africa, "Some sports the African is not suited for. In swimming, the water closes their pores so they cannot get rid of carbon dioxide and they tire quickly."[155] He hastened to add, lest the interviewer think him biased, "But they are great boxers and cyclers and runners."[156]

As the opening of the Tehran IOC session neared, officials from the black African nations began to react to the possible readmission of South Africa to the Olympic games. Ato Tessema, head of the Ethiopian Sports Confederation, threatened that if South Africa was readmitted, Ethiopia would boycott the Mexico games. Tessema predicted all African nations would join the boycott.[157] Isaac Luganzo, head of the Kenya National Sports Council, announced: "We must resist any pressure brought to bear to have South Africa readmitted to the Olympic Games until apartheid in sport in the Republic is broken 100 per cent."[158] Dennis Brutus wrote to Brundage, describing how South Africa was still violating Olympic principles.[159] The African national Olympic committees met in Tehran on May 2 before the IOC session opened and passed an important motion, which read:

> The African NOC's are firmly resolved to use every means to obtain the expulsion of South African sports organizations from the Olympic Movement and from the International Federations, should the NOC of this country fail to comply with the IOC rules.
>
> The African NOC's reserve their decision to participate in the 1968 Olympic Games in case the South African team would be allowed to participate in such Games without complying fully with the Olympic Charter, of which the IOC is the supreme guardian.[160]

In a meeting with the NOCs, President Brundage said that it could not be expected that the Olympic movement "can be used as a stick to achieve political aims."[161] Due to reports to be made in Tehran, as well as the upcoming IOC commission visit to South Africa, he said, "No decision can and will be taken before the next IOC session in Grenoble."[162] (The IOC commission to South Africa was supposed to make its report at the Tehran meeting; however, it had not even been able to go to South Africa before the meeting because the NOC of South Africa had failed to supply the commission with the preliminary information that it had requested.)[163]

THE IOC's TEHRAN SESSION

On May 4, Frank Braun met with the IOC executive and read a lengthy statement, which contained all of the Tehran concessions. He said:

> South Africa has been in the doldrums of exclusion. . . . The stigma of being looked upon as an outcast has not been an easy cross to bear. . . . This is a plea not based on compassionate grounds only. . . . For the Olympic Games in Tokyo . . . seven non-whites had been nominated for the South African team. . . . Last year in Rome we were able to indicate that non-white sports administrators nominated by their own national committees would be given a meaningful share and say in the selection of participants. . . . We did not hesitate to reaffirm our adherence to the principles and requirements of the Olympic Committee.[164]

Braun then announced the five new concessions to the executive:

1. One team would represent all South Africans.
2. The team would travel together.
3. The team would live together, wear the same uniform, and march together as an integrated team under one flag.
4. Whites and nonwhites could compete against each other at the games.
5. An equal number of whites and nonwhites, under Braun's chairmanship, would select the participants.[165]

Braun admitted that he could not foresee integrated sport or mixed trials in South Africa. He asked the IOC to act immediately because, if he went home empty-handed, those who opposed the concessions in the first place would want them rescinded. He maintained that, with each new concession, South Africa's opponents raised a new issue. Braun concluded, "We have no alternative than to request of you to accept, or otherwise, to reject us on the position as it now stands."[166] Dennis Brutus gave his reaction to Braun's speech:

> My first reaction in reading the concessions was that they were really quite spectacular. Compared to South Africa's previous position they represented a real advance.
>
> But equally important were the admissions to the kinds of charges that we had been making about racism in sport which Braun was factually stating as being part of the previous structure and promising that they would change.
>
> I had the uneasy feeling that Braun was, in fact, in desperation promising the IOC more than he could deliver in the hope of getting in and forcing a decision at that time . . . and, of course, my suspicions were confirmed when, getting the South African papers, I read that Vorster was warning the sportsmen not to make promises which they could not deliver.
>
> There was a very considerable satisfaction to me in seeing how far we had pushed Braun and the white sports into making concessions, but I knew that we were by no means where we wanted them to be and, in fact, I anticipated it was going to make things very difficult for us in heading them off from Mexico.[167]

In an attempt to get around that difficulty, Brutus and de Broglio had met with Señor Vasquez, president of the organizing committee for the the 1968 games. They persuaded Vasquez to agree not to invite South Africa to the Little Olympics because it was still officially under IOC suspension, SAN-ROC released this information on May 5.[168]

When the IOC opened its full session the next day, Reg Alexander of Kenya presented a resolution that the IOC not communicate with SAN-ROC as long as it used "Olympic" in its name. The resolution was passed unanimously, and SAN-ROC's hand was officially slapped, but it was a small price to pay for what it considered a very significant victory.[169]

By the ninth, the IOC had decided, after noting tremendous progress, that it would put off a decision on South Africa until Grenoble.[170] Prime Minister Vorster's reaction to this decision was fast and furious.

The Eastern Province Herald [Port Elizabeth] reported that there was a full-scale revolt by National party MP's over SAONGA's statements. (It had been reported in South Africa that Dennis McIldowie, Braun's associate in Tehran, had offered mixed trials outside South Africa. Braun had clearly made no such promise in his official text.) Vorster said: "I feel compelled to warn sports administrators to read my policy statement on sport very carefully and not to raise expectations that cannot be fulfilled."[171] Braun denied that he was seeking to ease the application of apartheid in sport in South Africa.[172]

The *Cape Argus* [Cape Town] ran a front-page banner headline, "NO CONCESSIONS BY SOUTH AFRICA TO GET INTO THE OLYMPICS."[173] There was considerable confusion in South Africa after Braun's statement of "no concessions." The full text of his speech was never reported in the South African press. In it, he had clearly stated that there would be no more concessions other than those he outlined and that there could be no mixed trials. Therefore, much of the confusion in South Africa can be attributed to poor reporting. However, considering the previous history of the IOC's delays of final decisions on South Africa and subsequent reactions in South Africa, this overreaction may have merely been part of the pattern. South African officials obviously hoped to be readmitted to the Olympics immediately on the basis of the concessions already granted (as Braun had also stated in his speech).

In any case, Braun said of the commission:

> We are happy to go back from here and prepare for the Commission to meet African officials of the bodies controlling Olympic-type sports.
>
> We are happy provided that the Commission goes to report on the willingness of the non-white controlling bodies to administer Olympic-type sports—to ascertain that the position is as we have stated here.[174]

Braun gave the impression that he was setting down ground rules for the IOC commission.

It had been announced in New York City on May 8 that the South African sports issue had finally reached the United States. The American Committee on Africa (ACOA) issued a letter to Douglas F. Roby, president of the USOC, asking it to commit itself to keeping South Africa out of the Olympic games. The letter contained a list of charges and had been signed by thirty prominent Americans, including Jackie Robinson, Arthur Ashe, Roy Campanella, Oscar Robertson, Buddy Young, I. W. Abel, Floyd McKissick, Bayard Rustin, Stokely Carmichael, Langston Hughes, Percy Sutton, Ruby Dee, Ed Sullivan, Pete Seeger, and Reinhold Niebuhr.[175] ACOA's lead was to have a significant impact later in the year when the Olympic boycott movement in the United States started.

Dennis Brutus wrote to Brundage expressing approval of the decision not to readmit South Africa but also expressing dismay at the fact that the IOC would listen only to one side of the story (a reference to the IOC resolution on SAN-ROC).[171] In June, Chris de Broglio announced that SAN-ROC would henceforth be called the South African Non-Racial Open Committee in deference to the IOC.[177]

EVENTS OF JULY

In July, the SAAAU sponsored two groups of athletes to tour Britain: a white group and a Bantu group. The Bantu group was not allowed to wear the colors of South Africa; instead, it wore the colors and badge of its own Bantu association. The teams had separate itineraries, but they were scheduled to compete together in White City stadium.[178] At the urging of SAN-ROC, teams from Kenya, Nigeria, Pakistan, and India withdrew from the White City event.[179]

The Department of Sport in South Africa wrote to the two groups requesting that they not appear in the same meet and, especially, in the same event. The athletes ignored this. A *Star* [Johannesburg] editorial condemned the Department of Sport action and praised the athletes for leaving the anti-apartheid demonstrators outside the stadium with nothing to protest since they were running together.[180]

Also in July, the mayor of Johannesburg gave a civic buffet dinner for officials and players in a Colored interprovincial rugby tournament. Seventeen city councilors were refused government permits to attend; permits for the mayor and deputy mayor were granted on the condition that they sit apart from the Colored guests.[181]

Dennis Brutus was a speaker at the U.N. international seminar on apartheid, racial discrimination, and colonialism in Southern Africa, held in Lusaka, beginning on July 24. Brutus emphasized that all nations should follow the 1966 recommendation of the Brasilia seminar of the U.N. that "all states should refrain from cultural and sports relationships with South Africa as long as apartheid and white supremacy prevail in that country."[182] Brutus recognized the actions taken by Kenya, India, Nigeria, and Pakistan with regard to the White City athletic events, as a welcome sign that nations were beginning to follow the Brasilia recommendation.[183]

Newark, N.J., proved to be the setting of what turned out to be July's most important event. It was in Newark at the first National Conference on Black Power that a boycott of the Olympics by black American athletes was proposed. A boycott of professional boxing was another proposal (due to the fact that Muhammad Ali had been stripped of his crown by the World Boxing Association).[184] Although the boycott of the Olympics had no form in July, the important thing was that the idea had been planted.

THE IOC COMMISSION TO SOUTH AFRICA

In South Africa, August was a month for preparing for the September visit of the IOC commission. Lord Killanin had been named to replace Avery Brundage on the commission. Brundage instructed Killanin that the commission was to make a report and not to make recommendations. It was not to judge apartheid per se:

> Our concern is with the NOC and what it is doing to comply with Olympic regulations, especially articles 24 and 25. . . . We must not become involved in political issues, nor permit the Olympic Games to be used as a tool or as a weapon for extraneous causes.[185]

In a statement that was curious only because of its timing, Minister of Sport Frank Waring told the Natal Congress of the National party that South Africa would not allow any country to interfere with its internal sports policy; mixed sport could only lead to racial friction.[186] Coming only three weeks before the arrival of the IOC commission, this speech was obviously not designed for diplomatic impact but to allay the fears of the right wing of the National party.

Kenya, perhaps to attract attention to the nonracial movement for the IOC commission, banned a group of tennis pros who had been playing in South Africa. That this did not exactly drive the pros into retirement was indicated by Rod Laver, a well-known tennis star: "We will never give up the tour in South Africa for three days in Kenya."[187]

There had been considerable speculation as to the reception of the only black member of the commission, Sir Ade Ademola. Shortly before the group arrived, Braun announced that apartheid would be suspended for Ademola. He could live and travel with Killanin and Reg Alexander.[188] However, it was reported that once the commission actually arrived, social functions, including most meals, were held in private. Photographers were not allowed to photograph Ademola and Frank Waring together at lunch in Pretoria. That Ademola was not interested in testing apartheid was shown in an incident that occurred shortly after his arrival. The *Daily News* [Durban] reported that Ademola

> is proving an undemanding guest. There was a flutter among the press cars in Pretoria when the bus taking the IOC delegation to Atteridgeville township pulled up in front of a suburban cafe and Sir Ade marched purposefully toward the pavement—but entered the Chemist shop next door.[189]

When a group of Indian sports administrators told the commission that the reason for their poor facilities was lack of aid from the government and the Durban city council, Ademola apparently shocked them with the following comment:

> But why are you so dependent on the Government and City Council for finance? Why don't you go ahead and do something yourselves? When we want stadiums and other facilities in Nigeria, we charge an entrance fee. . . . Surely there are enough Indians in Natal to provide finance."[190]

One of the Indians explained that under their lease (which they were about to lose), they were not permitted to improve the land.[191] Ademola made no further comments.

In a private meeting with Lord Killanin in Pretoria, Prime Minister Vorster said that he stood by the Tehran proposals. The only change he wished to make in Braun's speech was the substitution of "one team" for what Braun called an "integrated team." Vorster reaffirmed at the meeting that South Africa would rather withdraw from the Olympics than hold mixed trials. South Africa would not crawl if the IOC would not trust its selection committee.[192]

The commission met with many nonwhite sportsmen and administrators. Killanin said that they were wary of "government stooges" among those interviewed.[193] One nonwhite they met was Wilfred Brutus, a former SAN-ROC leader and brother of Dennis Brutus. Wilfred had been under banning orders (he had been banned under the Suppression of Communism Act in 1964) and was then out on bail for contravening the orders.[194] Shortly after meeting Ademola, Brutus escaped from South Africa and joined his brother in London. According to Dennis Brutus, his brother felt that Ademola had given him an "unfavorable hearing."[195]

Toward the end of the commission's stay, Frank Waring made a speech similar to the one he made just before they had arrived. He addressed a National party meeting in Caledon:

> Our policy is a separate sport and if the demand is made on us–a political demand–that we must change our pattern of sport and mix it, we are not prepared to pay the price.
>
> We are quite prepared that our non-whites should take part in the Olympic Games. We will pick a white and a black team.[196]

His statement seemed to once again raise the possibility of South Africa attempting to send two teams to Mexico and rekindled doubts in many minds as to the sincerity of the South African government.

An early reading of the commission's impressions came from Killanin and Alexander. Killanin said, "I never imagined that the problem would be so complex. I suppose before I came out I had imagined it to be simply a problem of black and white."[197] Alexander added:

> I had imagined that most countries in Africa were in very close touch with South African non-whites. They certainly give the impression that they know what non-whites here are thinking.

> Since arriving here I have found that nothing could be further from the truth. These countries are obviously not in touch at all with the situation here.[198]

Furthermore, *The Times* [London] reported that Killanin had been quite impressed with what he saw of South African sports.[199]

Before leaving, Killanin made an agreement to meet with SAN-ROC representatives in Lausanne. It is a good indication of how highly South Africans held Dennis Brutus' power of persuasion when the *Sunday Tribune* [Durban] said that South Africa's chances of being readmitted to the games would be finished when Brutus met the commision.[200] When asked if SAN-ROC intended to wreck the IOC's work in South Africa, Chris de Broglio responded:

> Decidedly not. We have even watered down some of our demands to be fair to everybody. We will settle for a mixed national athletic championship and mixed national trials for the Olympic Games in 1968.
>
> We realize that the problems are great and cannot expect them to be solved completely in nine months. Just the above concessions will be enough to satisfy us for the moment. Of course, things must escalate from there until the end principle of complete sporting integration is reached. . . . We want to help.[201]

Representing SAN-ROC at the Lausanne meeting were Reg Hlongwane, Precious McKenzie, Chris de Broglio, and Dennis Brutus.

Hlongwane told how he was the top weightlifter in South Africa for his division but was recognized only as the nonwhite champion because only whites could be national champions. He had not been selected for the 1964 Olympics because the South African NOC demanded that national, not Olympic, rules be followed.[202]

Precious McKenzie testified that in 1958 his total lift was higher than Reg Gaffley, the white weightlifter who represented South Africa in the Commonwealth games and won the gold medal. In 1960, McKenzie had set the South African record but was not invited to the national championships or the Olympic trials. In a separate nonracial trial, he outlifted the white man who was selected. In 1963 he was offered a position on the South African Olympic team provided he resigned from the nonracial federation and joined the nonwhite federation affiliated to the white body. He refused and later emigrated to Great Britain, where he won a gold medal in the 1966 Commonwealth games representing Britain. He told the IOC commission, "I wear a British blazer, but my true ambition was to represent my own country."[203]

Chris de Broglio told the commission that when he joined SAN-ROC in 1963, he was forced to stop competing despite the fact that he had been a South African weightlifting champion from 1953 through 1962. He had also been the head of the white weightlifting body and, as such, allowed nonracial competition to take place before the security police forced him to leave the country.[204]

Dennis Brutus merely had to retell his already well-known story. He later recounted the mood of the commission in Lausanne: "We certainly threw everything we had at them. The feeling I got was that they were listening but they weren't impressed and that possibly they had already made up their own minds."[205] That this was, in fact, the case can hardly be doubted after reading the IOC commission's report, which came out in February 1968. In the summary, it describes SAN-ROC in terms that it would not have gathered from the testimony in Lausanne:

> The evidence before the Commission tends to show that the SAN-ROC, now operating from London, is supported only in spirit by the majority of non-whites in South Africa; but its methods are a cause of embarrassment to the majority in South Africa for whom it claims to speak. The Commission must assume that those who gave evidence voluntarily before it, with courage and conviction, were men of good faith. One witness, previously a leading member of SAN-ROC, summarized this opinion in South Africa when he said, "I do feel that these who are outside the country are self-exiled and I feel that wherever they are they should not dictate to us here because we have to face the situation, not them."[206]

THE BLACK AMERICAN BOYCOTT MOVEMENT

By late November, the black American Olympic boycott movement was about to get underway officially. A few days before the expected announcement, Dennis Brutus cabled a fellow South African at UCLA, Dan Kunene. Brutus asked him to get in touch with Harry Edwards, a professor at San Jose State College and a former first-class athlete at San Jose, and to ask the Americans to tie South African expulsion into their demands.[207]

Before the opening of the Western Regional Black Youth Conference, Edwards said to the press:

> Is it not time for black people to stand up as men and women and refuse to be utilized as performing animals for a little extra dog food? Would not an excellent beginning point be the 1968 Olympic Games?[208]

A resolution calling for the boycott of the games by black Americans was made at the conference. After the conference, Edwards again spoke to the press:

> This is a significant stand because I know of no other group of people who can make our feelings known. I hope the country can see what these black athletes have done. This is the last chance to avoid a racial catastrophe in this country.
>
> This is our way of pointing out that the United States has no right to set itself up as a leader of the free world. It is a simple fact that America has to be exposed for what it is. America is just as guilty as South Africa ever was.[209]

Edwards claimed that about fifty to sixty athletes would join. The group already included Lew Alcindor (now Kareem Abdul Jabbar), Lucius Allen, Mike Warren, Lee Evans, and Tommy Smith.[210]

In December, Edwards' movement picked up considerable strength when Martin Luther King, Floyd McKissick, and Louis Lomax joined. The group drew up six demands:

1. Avery Brundage must resign as head of the IOC because he was anti-Semitic and antiblack (as evidence, they pointed out that Brundage owned the Montecido Country Club in Santa Barbara, which did not allow Jewish or black members).

2. The New York Athletic Club must end its policy of discrimination against Jews and blacks (it did not allow them as members).
3. Muhammad Ali must be reinstated as heavyweight champion.
4. The USOC must appoint one more black as an Olympic track coach.
5. A black must be appointed to the USOC itself.
6. The United States must stop competing with South Africa and Rhodesia.[211]

King said, "No one looking at the six demands can ignore the truth in them,"[212] and Lomax added, "Clay's loss of the heavyweight title was a total castration of the black people in this country."[213]

Avery Brundage responded immediately to the charges that he was a racist and an anti-Semite:

> I have opposed racial and religious discrimination all my life.
>
> In 1936, as Chairman of the USOC, I supported the Jews against Hitler. It was our threat to take the Olympic Games away from Berlin that forced Hitler to include two Jews . . . on the German national team, to demonstrate that Nazi Germany observed Olympic principles.
>
> As far as the Olympic Games are concerned, it is a matter of record that the Games are open to athletes of all races, colors and creeds.[214]

Brundage twisted the facts quite a bit in regard to the 1936 games. Virtually he alone had been responsible for keeping the games in Berlin against the wishes of nearly every Jewish group in the United States; it was Brundage himself who said that he thought Germany was on the "right path" *after* seeing firsthand what was happening there in 1935 and 1936; as to whether Nazi Germany observed the Olympic principles, Brundage's point is certainly debatable. Referring to the country club, he said: "The club is entirely run by its members and I have nothing to do whatever with its operation. I go there only two or three times a year and haven't played golf in 40 years."[215] On the antiblack charge, Brundage said, "If the American Negro athletes boycott the Olympic Games, they won't be missed."[216] The next day, he boasted to his colleagues in

Lausanne, "It made them furious when I told them we would not miss them."[217]

THE SUPREME COUNCIL'S LAGOS MEETING

The Supreme Council for Sport in Africa met in Lagos in December. Dennis Brutus and Ade Ademola had a difficult time over South Africa. Brutus recalled the scene:

> I must say that I never felt happy with him and I never felt worse than when I addressed the meeting of the Supreme Council in Lagos where I had warned them that the South Africans were going to get in at Mexico; that the IOC Report would not keep them out. Ademola, as a member of that Commission, told me that I was exaggerating the dangers, and I was quite wrong. But it turned out that he signed the report that got them back in.[218]

At Lagos, Jean-Claude Ganga, the secretary-general of the SCSA, said, "If, in spite of the country's segregationist tendencies in sports, the Committee [IOC] decides to admit it, we will withdraw from the world body."[219] The SCSA decided to put off a final decision until after the IOC's Grenoble meeting, but it gave the executive committee full power to make a binding decision if South Africa was readmitted at that time.[220] Ganga was reported as having said that the IOC "was convinced that the country was discriminatory in all spheres of sport."[221] But an IOC spokesman in Lausanne said of Ganga, "He has no right to say such a thing. . . . He must have imagined all this since the report has never been issued."[222] In any case, the SCSA was poised and waiting for the Grenoble decision.

Hoping to avoid a political cloud which was already about to burst, French NOC president, Count Jean de Beaumont, suggested that South Africans be allowed to compete as individuals rather than as a team from South Africa.[223]

NONWHITE SOUTH AFRICAN OPINION

In South Africa, the *Post* [Natal] ran an end-of-the-year editorial that began by spelling out all aspects of nonwhite sport in South Africa. It continued:

> In spite of this, *Post* still believes that we should go to the Olympics next year.
>
> If we are barred from the Olympics, officials at all levels will not have the same incentive to improve our facilities and our sport—and it will be another triumph for apartheid, even if whites have to suffer.
>
> South Africa's chances . . . are not helped by the deafening silence of white sportsmen. White sportsmen should say clearly that, while they have to keep the laws of the land, they are against these laws.
>
> South Africa is condemned by its own mouth—a tightlipped mouth that, it seems only opens to condemn other nations for bringing politics into sports and never raises a voice against the cause of all the trouble—apartheid.[224]

It was an eloquent description of the feelings of a large section of the nonwhite community in South Africa.

SOUTH AFRICAN FOOTBALL

The final episode of 1967 concerned football, which appeared to be on its deathbed at the end of the year.

In November, the African Football Confederation, at the urging of SAN-ROC, submitted a list of charges against FASA to the International Football Federation (FIFA). It held that:

1. FASA had convinced the municipalities to refuse sports grounds to SASF/SASL affiliates.
2. FASA was responsible for the banning orders on George Singh, SASF's secretary.
3. FASA gave "blood money" to affiliated nonwhite organizations.
4. Braun's offer to send a nonwhite team to the 1968 Olympics was merely an attempt to woo FIFA and the IOC.[225]

These charges, however, were merely like kicking a dead animal. The two men most responsible for the death of SASL, Marais and Granger, had spent the year putting together a new nonwhite league to replace it—the South African National Soccer Association. However, even it was stillborn after the Johannesburg Non-European Affairs Department announced that only African clubs could play.[226]

Nineteen sixty-seven was a turbulent year for all those interested in South African sport. But it was a cakewalk compared to 1968.

1968

By February 1968, it seemed as though all of South Africa's problems were over and the potential nightmare of international sports isolation was ended. However, the very event that caused South Africa to feel secure led to a genuine nightmare for the international sports community.

As a result of the IOC's Grenoble decision to allow South Africa to compete in the Mexico games, more than fifty countries joined the controversy over South Africa. In addition to the Olympic question, South Africa tangled with six other nations over other sports issues. The most important of these was the culmination of the D'Oliveira affair, which had begun in 1967.

The South African sports question was once again focused on at both the Organization of African Unity and at the United Nations; almost every major international sports federation at least discussed the issues involved.

With their dream of Olympic competition deferred, the South Africans organized their own sports festival for 1969—the South African games, which were to become the center of yet another controversy for South Africa.

Finally, although only tangentially related to the South African question, the black American protest in sports had both high points and low points in 1968. Whatever one's attitude may have been in relation to what the black athletes did, there can be no doubt that it ended the era of the apolitical black athlete as well as introduced the issue of racism in American sports to a dramatic new level.

Of all these developments in 1968, it was unquestionably the IOC's decision to allow South Africa to compete in Mexico that became the most controversial.

THE REPORT OF THE IOC COMMISSION ON SOUTH AFRICA

Rumor about the IOC report and what would take place at the Grenoble IOC meeting was the order of the day in January. SAN-ROC had learned that the report would treat South Africa favorably and that the IOC would conduct a postal vote on lifting South Africa's suspension.[227] On January 16, SAN-ROC contacted the Afro-Asian Solidarity Committee and asked all its members to raise objections to South Africa's readmission with their respective NOCs.[228] In addition, it also contacted Harry Edwards and asked him to join SAN-ROC in Grenoble.[229] A private SAN-ROC document revealed how little faith it actually had in its allies, especially if the ballot was a postal one. The document said:

> And the real danger of this is that the Socialist countries will have a fairly free hand because they will not have a) control over their members' votes and b) there will be no real way of accounting for how the vote went. . . . All we have on our side are uncertain votes of some friends.[230]

On the other side of the fight, Frank Braun seemed to envision himself as the James Bond of sports. Asked how he felt facing the "plotting of the Afro-Asian and Communist nations," Braun said, "One has got to go over there and fight. The job has to be done by someone."[231] Braun admitted that South Africa's chances had improved tremendously.

Not knowing what the outcome of Grenoble would be, the international sports federations requested that the IOC allow South African federations that did not practice discrimination to compete in Mexico,[232] to which SAN-ROC replied that all sports bodies in South Africa that were recognized by the IOC practiced apartheid.[233]

On the eve of the release of the IOC report, the African National Congress (ANC) broadcast an appeal over Radio Tanzania about the Olympics, simultaneously distributing the text to the press. It said, in part:

> It is in the sphere of sports, the arts and culture that South Africa can be made to feel the full weight of international moral

> indignation against apartheid. . . . It is a cynical act of hypocrisy even to suggest that they will march under the same flag and sing the same National Anthem when they are prohibited from doing so inside South Africa. The test of whether there is race discrimination or not against the black people in South African sport can only be demonstrated by what happens inside South Africa. . . . We are paying a very heavy price for apartheid; our only crime is that we were born black. We now appeal to all men of good will, fair play and justice to exclude the white South African sports from the Olympic Games.[234]

These sentiments gave the world an equally eloquent statement of the other side of nonwhite South African opinion as that quoted in the *Post* editorial of December 24.

When the report of the IOC commission on South Africa was released on the afternoon of January 30, it appeared to be favorable to South Africa.[235] It concluded with the following six points:

1. The government policy was one of separate and parallel development and was imposed on sport through indirect laws.
2. Up to 1963, the SANOC did nothing to change this policy.
3. Between 1963 and 1967, the SANOC made serious representations to the government, resulting in the Tehran proposals; SANOC also declared its acceptance of IOC principle One in 1966. Principle One states that no discrimination is allowed against any country or person on the grounds of race, religion or political affiliation.
4. The overwhelming evidence from all sports administrators and competitors in South Africa was that the Tehran proposals were "an acceptable basis for a multi-racial team to the Mexico Olympic Games. . . . Sportsmen of all communities in South Africa were prepared to accept the selection by the joint body as provided for in the Tehran statement."[236]
5. SAN-ROC was not representative of South African nonwhite opinion.
6. A great deal had been done to develop facilities and grounds and to provide coaches and trainers for nonwhites to give them the same opportunities available to whites.[237]

Sensing what was apparently about to happen in Grenoble, those opposing South Africa got to work. Dennis Brutus wrote to Avery Brundage and attempted to take advantage of the considerable material in the report that outlined where discrimination did exist in South African sport; he warned that the Olympic movement would be split wide open if South Africa was readmitted. He was also highly critical of the quote by the unnamed former SAN-ROC member whose statement supposedly represented South African nonwhite opinion of SAN-ROC. Brutus said, "We cannot treat the quote seriously."[238]

In a statement for the American Committee on Africa, Harry Edwards said:

> I am deeply opposed to the presence of South Africans or Southern Rhodesians as team members or as individuals at international sporting events or events in the United States if there is any form of racism and on that there can be no compromise. Black athletes will refuse to participate in the Olympic Games if South Africa or Southern Rhodesia are permitted into the Games while racism still exists at any level.[239]

Again under the ACOA's auspices, a group of professional athletes, including the man who broke the color barrier in American professional sports, Jackie Robinson, came out against South Africa's readmission to the Olympics. He urged the USOC to fight South Africa's readmission and called the Tehran proposals a fraud. Of the black boycott, he said, "Basically, I'm supporting these kids. I think it takes a great deal of courage for them to give up a chance at a gold medal to help the Negro cause."[240] The support of Robinson, who was generally viewed as a moderate in the black community, added immeasurably to Edwards' movement. In addition, Edwards' and Robinson's support tied the black American boycott movement, once only tangentially connected with the anti-South African campaign, to that campaign for the duration of their now-joint struggle.

As the Grenoble meeting neared, Frank Braun was constantly asking that the people of South Africa accept and support the prevailing political and social order in South Africa. This brought the wrath of the normally agreeable *Post* [Natal], which criticized Braun's statements:

> It is an arrogant, incorrect and political assumption to say that the POPULATION of South Africa supports the prevailing political and social order.
>
> Mr. Braun might be speaking for the majority of the WHITE population of this country. But he cannot—and should not—pretend to speak for the majority of ALL people here.
>
> Non-whites are just as anxious to see the South African flag flying at the Mexico Games—but not at the price of having to say we support apartheid and all the agony it has brought.[241]

THE GRENOBLE IOC DECISION

When the IOC did meet, it passed the following resolution on the South African issue:

> Having studied the report of the commission on South Africa, the IOC notes with grave concern that racially discriminatory internal policies of the South African Government prevent the NOC of the country from achieving fully the aims of the IOC under Fundamental Principle 1 of the Olympic Code.
>
> It is, however, encouraged that positive efforts by the South African NOC have resulted in a firm undertaking to implement the proposals announced at the IOC session at Tehran in May 1967 whereby a multiracial team will be selected on merit.
>
> It now resolves that the South African NOC may enter a team which conforms with Fundamental Principle 1 in the Olympic Games in 1968 in Mexico and on the understanding that it continues vigorously its efforts to have all forms of racial discrimination in amateur sport removed and the IOC will reconsider the question by the end of 1970.[242]

The resolution was curious, for several reasons. For one, the first sentence says that SANOC cannot achieve the aims of principle 1, but the third sentence notes that SANOC may enter a "team which conforms with Fundamental Principle 1." Furthermore, the first sentence states that the South African government's internal policies affect the SANOC. This itself violates IOC rule 25, which states that the "NOC must be completely independent and autonomous and in a position to resist all political, religious and commercial pressure."[243] Finally, the third sentence said that the resolution was being approved on the "understanding" that SANOC would continue its efforts to have "all forms of racial discrimination in amateur sport removed." That there was no such understanding is attested to by Frank Braun's Tehran statement:

> It would amount to nothing less than dishonesty to envision anything at this stage beyond that which we have informed you of. . . . We have no alternative than to request of you to accept or, otherwise, to reject us on the position as it now stands.[244]

Even though the resolution was riddled with contradictions and inconsistencies, it was passed by the IOC.

On the next day in his press conference, Avery Brundage claimed that the IOC had won a major victory:

> I think, in the circumstances, it was only the power of the Olympic Movement that could have secured this change, and this is the first time by any organization that anything has been accomplished for the non-whites in South Africa.[245]

The reaction in South Africa was one of joy. Braun praised the IOC commission for its fair report and particularly thanked Ademola, who, he said, "fought for us like a hero. He must rate as one of the people who have most helped South Africa to get back into the Olympics."[246] Reg Honey also praised South Africa's friends for backing them to the hilt.[247] Prime Minister Vorster, whose policy had now been vindicated, said, "I am glad for the sake of our young sportsmen and athletes that they can again take part in the Olympic Games, which it is their right and privilege to do."[248]

A Nationalist MP analyzed what the IOC's decision meant to Vorster and the party:

> Nothing succeeds like success. Nationalists are supporting Mr. Vorster enthusiastically now for the simple reason that his policies work. The preliminary reports we have received from the constitu-

encies show that the tide of popular opinion is suddenly swinging in strongly behind the outward-looking policies. Our people now know what it all means.[249]

Humphrey Khosi, South Africa's top nonwhite athlete, called himself "the happiest man in the country" as a result of the IOC's decision.[250]

Editorial comments in Britain and the United States generally praised the IOC. *The Times* [London] emphasized how important sport had become as a lever for diplomacy; that sport was the primary weapon of those who wished to end apartheid. It called for those contemplating a boycott to reconsider their stand and "to occupy the ground gained in the Olympic decision, hold the Games successfully, and go on from there."[251] The *Daily Telegraph* [London] believed that the decision was sound and that the best way to cope with South Africa was to establish as many points of contact as possible.[252] According to the *New York Times,* South Africa had made revolutionary concessions and, therefore, the boycott should be called off.[253] On the other hand, the *Observer* [London] called for support of the position of SAN-ROC and the boycotters.[254]

IOC Chancellor Westerhoff warned those who might boycott that "the IOC does not like threats and boycotts will not change our decision."[255]

The British Anti-Apartheid Movement called for multiracial trials for the selection of South Africa's team.[256] However, it was obvious that, as Braun himself had said, there was absolutely no chance of that happening.

Dennis Brutus, in a letter to Brundage, asked how South Africa could be readmitted by a resolution in which it was stated that racial discrimination in South African sport was a fact of life. Brutus neither expected nor received a reply; he merely wanted the IOC to know that the fight was far from over.[257]

Algeria and Ethiopia became the first nations to announce their withdrawal from the games. In announcing Ethiopia's decision, Y. Tessema, secretary-general of the Ethiopian Sports Confederation, said:

> This is a victory for the policy of apartheid and not for SANOC. . . . What happens after the Games? Each athlete will return to South Africa and join his segregated club. What has the IOC achieved if the status quo is maintained in South Africa after the Mexico Games?[258]

The U.S.S.R. called the IOC decision a "flagrant violation of the Charter of the IOC."[259] The next day, it withdrew from the NYAC track meet after black Americans put pressure on the Soviet embassy in Washington.[260]

The *Sunday Times* [London] reported that Mexico had asked the South Africans to withdraw and that they had agreed.[261] However, the next day Frank Braun denied that strongly: "There is not a chance of our withdrawing."[262] This was in spite of the fact that Guinea, Gambia, Uganda, Tanzania, Ghana, and the U.A.R. had joined the boycott.[263]

Count Jean de Beaumont, an IOC delegate from France, called the IOC decision "the most retrograde step the IOC has made in 18 years."[264]

Frank Braun, in a statement not designed to win South Africa friends in the Third World, called the African boycott a giant bluff "by a lot of spoiled kids. They may form their own Afro-Asian Games instead of competing at the Olympics. That should restore the old prestige of the Games."[265] Dennis Brutus labeled this statement "racist" and continued:

> What we have seen so far of boycott intentions is the tip of the iceberg. After the African states have met in Brazzaville we should get creditable reactions, not only from Africa and Asia, but also from the Eastern European countries and at least one Western European country.[266]

Brutus proved prophet again. The Prime Minister of Malaysia, Tunku Abdul Rahman, said that Malaysia should join the boycott, and Somalia became the ninth nation to join.[267]

When Kenya became the tenth nation, the Olympics lost several world-class athletes, including Kip Keino, the world record holder for three thousand meters. When the Kenyan government announced the decision, a somewhat despondant Keino said:

> We as sportsmen have to obey the decisions made by the Kenya Government. It is the policy of the Government to have nothing to do with South Africa and we can do nothing but accept this policy. I do not mind running against anybody. But if I am told I cannot run against certain people, I will not.[268]

The statement has an oddly familiar ring to it: if you substitute "South African government" for "Kenya government," it could be a statement by a white South African athlete saying he would compete against non-whites but the government would not allow it. Frank Braun then made an offer Keino could resist: "If Keino and others can compete individually South Africa would then be delighted to invite them to accompany our mixed team and train with us."[269] He also asked the boycotting nations to come to Mexico for this "historic event."[270]

However, by the time Braun had made his remark, Syria, the Sudan, and Zambia had joined the boycott. Only Denmark and South Korea had publicly supported the IOC decision.[271] This, however, was hardly a true indication of the support South Africa was receiving from European and American nations.

The Organization of African Unity's (OAU) ministerial council passed the following resolution:

> In the event of the IOC refusing to exclude South Africa from the Olympic Games, so long as that country persistently pursues the inhuman policy of apartheid, all member states of the OAU, and other states and sports organizations that are inspired by the same racial equality, should refrain from participating in the Games.[272]

Although this was a clear message to the Supreme Council for Sport in Africa, scheduled to meet two days later in Brazzaville, Avery Brundage held a press conference in the hope of stopping a greater erosion of the games. He must have chosen his words carefully:

> South Africa has not been invited to the Games of the XIXth Olymiad in Mexico. . . . The Olympic Games are between individuals and not between nations. . . . South African non-whites have long sought this opportunity and it is unfortunate that some who pretend to be their friends would deprive them of it. They are not responsible for the policies of their Government. . . . There was the same flurry in 1936 about fascism when the Games were held in Berlin although the German Government had nothing to do with them.[273]

His attempt to show that it was not South Africa but a group of fine sportsmen who only happened to be from South Africa who would go to Mexico had little effect on the boycott movement. The Supreme Council of the OAU committed its thirty-two member nations to the boycott:[274] Dahomey, Gabon, Sierra Leone, Togo, Burundi, Nigeria, Uganda, Ghana, Upper Volta, the C.A.R., Congo-Brazzaville, Congo-Kinshasa, Algeria, Sudan, Gambia, Zambia, Kenya, Tanzania, Morocco, Mali, Mauritania, Senegal, Chad, Ivory Coast, Madagascar, Cameroon, Guinea, Tunisia, the U.A.R., Liberia, Ethiopia, and Niger.[275]

Soviet diplomatic sources were quoted as saying that the Soviet Union would probably join the boycott. All of this prompted Italian IOC member Giulio Onesti to call for an extraordinary meeting of the IOC to reconsider the decision to readmit South Africa.[276] Although it appeared that the Olympic movement itself was crumbling, Avery Brundage merely said, "The Games will go on. There is no doubt they'll proceed and will be a tremendous success."[277]

In the United States, the NCAA announced that Lew Alcindor, Lucius Allen, Mike Warren, and Bill Hewitt, all All-Americans in 1968, had boycotted the Olympic basketball trials.[278] As Brundage and Lord Exeter announced that there would not be a special IOC meeting, Guyana, Barbados, and Trinidad joined the boycott.[279]

Apparently still convinced that they would be going to Mexico, the South Africans established their first mixed selection committee for boxing. It was composed of four whites and four nonwhites under Braun's chairmanship.[280] On the same day, Saudi Arabia became the thirty-seventh nation to officially join the boycott.[281]

The *New York Times* reported on March 2 that Mexico had asked the IOC to reconsider its decision on South Africa. Although Brundage refused to say that it was for that purpose, he announced that the IOC would meet within sixty days.[282]

Meanwhile, in South Africa, Fred Thabede, a nonwhite boxing official, condemned the boycotters:

> The African states know as well as any of us that for the past seven years South Africa's OC has been struggling to have an integrated team at the Olympics. Now they slap us in the face in the most bla-

> tant showing of discrimination against our whites—and non-whites—that I have ever seen.[283]

Thabede's appeal fell on deaf ears as Pakistan and Kuwait joined the boycotters.[284] But the key still seemed to be the Soviet Union. If it pulled out of the games, as had been rumored from the start, either the IOC would have to change its mind or the games would be dead. With thirty-nine nations from the Third World having announced their intention of boycotting the games, the Russians appeared to have to make a move. *The Times* [London] reported that Peking was ready to take full advantage of a Soviet decision to participate.[285] On March 7, the NOC of the U.S.S.R. announced:

> If the IOC refuses to convene an emergency session and insists on its decision about South Africa, the USSR OC will be impelled to reconsider the question of the participation of Soviet sportsmen in the Summer Olympics of 1968.[286]

Dennis Brutus was the man who had been pushing Soviet sports officials for a commitment since the Grenoble decision. He later admitted that he believed the lure of potential gold medals in Mexico would have ultimately kept the Russians in the Olympics. While he was convinced of this, he knew that keeping the threat of a Soviet boycott alive was almost as important to the outcome on South Africa.[287]

In any case, the *New York Times* reported on March 10 that the following countries would go to Mexico under any circumstances: Britain, West Germany, Italy, Greece, Denmark, Australia, Israel, Turkey, Brazil, Uruguay and, in all likelihood, Japan.[288] Two days later, it reported that a majority of the IOC executive wanted a full meeting of the IOC before the scheduled April 20 session of the executive; Brundage refused.[289]

In the meantime, Frank Braun told reporters in South Africa that there were not many nonwhites who could qualify for the Olympic team but he was "certain that there will be a lot more candidates when we pick up our side four years from now."[290] It sounded as if Braun was attempting to gradually inform the public that the number of nonwhites on the South African team might not be as high as had been originally expected.

A week later, SAN-ROC announced that Poland, Hungary, Rumania, Bulgaria, Czechoslovakia, and the German Democratic Republic were ready to join the boycott, which had also recently claimed North Korea;[291] however, it was not likely that those countries would have joined if the Russians did not do so first.

In spite of all the boycotting nations, the IOC gave South Africa its accreditation on April 2, which, according to the *Eastern Province Herald* [Port Elizabeth], virtually made South Africa's participation a certainty.[292] This is a fair indication that the IOC still had no intention of reversing its decision when the executive met three weeks later.

In the United States, the ACOA held a major press conference on April 10 and announced that sixty-three important amateur and professional athletes (thirteen of whom had competed in previous Olympic games) endorsed the Olympic boycott because of South African participation.[293] At the same press conference, Steve Mokone, a former South African nonwhite soccer star, then going to school in the United States, read from letters that he had received from nonwhite South Africans. Mokone maintained that these letters were truly the sentiments of the majority of nonwhite South Africans. He quoted one of the letters:

> The grapevine says everybody is against the idea [South African participation]. The trouble is that no one has the nerve—Robben Island is very near. Conditions are really bad here and they are getting worse. . . . We don't need the Olympics as much as they do because we have never been there. It hurts them more being thrown out than it does us.
>
> None of us want to see them take South Africa back. But what can we do. . . . How do people outside feel about this? . . . We saw many of the countries are boycotting. We all hope Russia will join too. We have kind of lost hope the African states will stick together for the sake of their brothers here who can't do or say much.[294]

These were strikingly different than the "official nonwhite opinions" being released in South Africa.

Mokone told of his being arrested five times in South Africa. He was particularly critical of Gary Player, who had been telling the press that nonwhites in South Africa were very happy. Mokone said, "I don't know which black people he talked to. Probably his maid. He never talked to any people I ever heard of."[295]

The situation in the United States had changed a great deal in the past weeks, mostly because of Martin Luther King's assassination early in April. This caused conservative blacks to sound moderate, and moderate blacks to sound radical. Ralph Boston, the great black athlete who had refused to join the boycott, said that King's death had forced him to reconsider his stand. Harry Edwards, looking beyond the sports field, predicted, "That is the end of nonviolence. Now it will be life for life."[296]

In a last effort to drum up more support in the IOC, the SCSA sent a letter with a collection of opinions from around the world that opposed South Africa's readmission to the Olympics. SCSA also said that the boycott would take place, for better or for worse, if the IOC failed to reverse its stand.[297]

It was announced in South Africa that a nonwhite would carry the flag in the opening ceremony of the games.[298] This news, coming so close to the IOC meeting, was, perhaps, meant to balance the distressing news that right-wing pressure in South Africa resulted in the design of a new badge for the Olympic team.[299] Thus, even in the Olympic games, nonwhite South Africans were still to be denied the use of the Springbok emblem. If the South Africans had been allowed to remain in the games, it is not unlikely that such pressure would have forced further erosion of the Tehran concessions.

Four days before the IOC executive board was to meet, Avery Brundage flew to South Africa, ostensibly to visit a game park: "In view of the climate existing in some parts of the civilized world, I thought it might be refreshing to spend a few days with the animals in their natural habitat."[300] Asked if he had come to request that South Africa withdraw, Brundage replied, "All I can say is that you people have very vivid imaginations. . . . I would like to see South Africa in the Games."[301]

Frank Braun said that Brundage told him he would rather resign than approve an unfair judgment. Brundage showed Braun a legal opinion to the effect that the invitation to South Africa could not be legally withdrawn:

> Still, Mr. Brundage hinted to me when he was here that it might be the diplomatic thing to withdraw. . . . You know what I told

> him? I said, "Mr. Brundage, I would rather be shot in Mexico City than lynched in Johannesburg."[302]

The IOC delegate from the Soviet Union charged that Brundage was "defending racism" by going to South Africa. It is not insignificant that two days before the IOC was to meet, Malawi became the first African nation to announce that it would not join the boycott.[303] This introduced a new factor into the equation for the diplomacy of international sports: economics and geography joined politics and race as variables.

THE REVERSAL OF THE GRENOBLE DECISION

When the IOC executive met on April 20 and 21, it engaged in two days of what it called harsh discussion. Finally, it came up with the following proposal, which it immediately cabled to all IOC members:

> In view of all the information on the international climate received by the Executive Board at this meeting, it is unanimously of the opinion that it would be most unwise for a South African team to participate in the Games of the XIXth Olympiad. Therefore, the Executive Board strongly recommends that you endorse this unanimous proposal to withdraw the invitation to these Games.[304]

Brundage explained the decision:

> We are very sad because the fundamental basic Olympic Principle is to welcome the youth of the world and it is very unfortunate that some of the youth of the world will be excluded in Mexico. . . . We seem to live in an age when violence and turbulence are the order of the day. We are of course concerned with the safety of the participants and the dignity of the Games.[305]

The Times [London] reported that factors in the decision included King's death, a speech by Enoch Powell on explosive color conflicts in England, the fact that Brundage's Chicago hotel was sacked by blacks while he was in it, and the potential for racial violence in Mexico.[306] In an editorial, the paper said that the IOC had bowed to the political realities of the day and the Olympics might just as well be governed by the United Nations as by the IOC.[307]

Reg Honey called the IOC proposal "illegal and immoral" and called for the IOC to resign. Braun said: "This is virtually an instruction to members to vote against South Africa. It is quite unconstitutional. If the Mexicans cannot guarantee the safety of competitors, they should not be holding the Games."[308] He claimed that "the strong-arm boys have turned the others around" and that the IOC would lose a tremendous amount of face.[309]

In an attempt to ward off criticism of political interference in the IOC, Brundage held another press conference on April 24. He noted:

> It should be emphasized that in adopting this recommendation the IOC is not bowing to threats or pressures of any kind from those who did not understand the true Olympic philosophy. Boycott is not a word used in sports circles.[310]

Brundage had certainly changed his opinion about the African nations; only a few short years before, he had praised them as the hope of ridding the Olympic Movement of its imperfections.[311] He had also predicted that sports would be a primary source of African unity.[312] He was certainly correct on the latter point. About the proposal, Brundage continued:

> You will find in a carefully worded cablegram . . . that there is no criticism of Mexico, no criticism of South Africa and no criticism of the IOC. There were no suspensions, no expulsions nor were there any legal technicalities mentioned. Such procedures are foreign to the sport world, which is based on fair play and good sportsmanship.[313]

It appeared from this statement that Brundage's memory had temporarily escaped him. In May 1959, the IOC had expelled Nationalist China.[314] In addition to the suspension of South Africa in 1964, it had suspended Indonesia in February 1963.[315] As for not mentioning any legal technicalities, this was true because Brundage had himself secured legal opinions that said the IOC had not a leg to stand on in withdrawing the invitation to South Africa.[316]

The final vote on the executive's proposal was forty-seven for, sixteen opposed, and eight abstentions.[317] The reaction in South Africa was to be expected. Prime Minister Vorster predicted:

> If what has happened is to be the pattern of how world events are going to be arranged in the future, we are back in the jungle. Then it will be no longer necessary to arrange Olympic Games, but rather to have tree-climbing events.[318]

An editorial in the *Sunday Express* [Johannesburg] maintained that

> politics, not the Olympic ideal, mob law and not the Olympic Movement's legal procedures had won the pre-Olympic test. . . . It has been shown that validly taken decisions . . . can be reversed because of the vile threats of a venemous and vociferous pressure group.[319]

The pressure group it referred to was SAN-ROC. The newspaper warned that sports administrators should continue to press for recognition and not revert to sports isolation, as members of the Nationalist party were demanding. The *Sunday Times* [Johannesburg] reported that the right-wing Verkramptes were very pleased with the IOC decision because it would force Vorster to tone down his outward policy. In an editorial, the same paper said that the reasons given by the IOC for their withdrawal were absurd and were obviously the result of pressure politics.[320]

Nonwhite South African sportsmen and administrators (at least those quoted in the South African press) were disappointed with the IOC decision. Humphrey Khosi, the outstanding runner, described himself as the "unhappiest man in the world. . . . It is really terrible when you try so hard to represent your own country and then find people do something like this to you."[321] Fred Thabede, the nonwhite boxing official, said: "It breaks my heart to think that all the work we have put into having an integrated team should have gone to waste; and I can't understand why the African states have been the ones behind this."[322] Edward Sono, vice-president of the South African Non-European Athletic Association, agreed: "I'm sure all non-whites are sad about our exclusion from the Games, and not just the athletes."[323]

THE SOUTH AFRICAN GAMES

With the possibility of competing in the Mexico games behind them, the South Africans embarked on a new venture to assuage the pain of the loss of the Olympics. They decided to revive the South African games, last held in 1964, the year of their initial suspension from the Olympics.

In May, the Shell Oil Company announced a grant to promote national sports festivals in South Africa,[324] which provided the initial financing for the South African games.[325] The scale of these games was to be far greater than those of 1964. The organizers planned to invite international stars who had competed in the Mexico games to South Africa in 1969. There would be separate games for whites in Bloemfontein and for nonwhites in Umlazi.[325]

An editorial in the *Star* warned that the games would seriously damage the international sympathy that was created for South Africa by the IOC decision. It said that the segregated games would merely serve to confirm the allegations that South Africa was using its nonwhites as a passport to the Olympic games. Fred Waring of the Department of Sport had decided to make the games segregated.[326] Waring also did nothing to improve South Africa's international image when he ordered all sports bodies to consult the Department of Sport before they invited overseas teams. The chief aim of this, he explained, was to avoid embarrassment "to both parties which might arise in the case where a member of the invited team turned out to be non-white."[327]

An indication of the unimportance of the nonwhite version of the South African games was given when Frank Braun announced in August that the nonwhite games would be postponed until October 1969.[328] The first to accept invitations to the white games were the Australian and Swedish teams.[329] Pressure groups opposing international competition for South Africa, still savoring the taste of victory over the Olympic decision, barely seemed to take notice of the South African games in 1968.

There were still other international federations that had to meet in 1968, and many South African sportsmen feared that the Olympic decision was only the beginning in terms of international sports isolation. While SAN-ROC began to sense that its moment had finally come, federations inside South Africa began to move to a position to block it.

SAN-EABA's PROPOSAL

At the end of May, the South African Non-European Amateur Boxing Association (SAN-EABA) proposed a meeting of all athletic national nonwhite organizations to form South Africa's first nonwhite Olympic games council. (The one that Braun had proposed earlier in the year never had time to get off the ground.) SAN-EABA suggested that this organization and a similar white organization merge to form a new South African NOC, which would then become affiliated to the IOC.[330] This would solve the problem the IOC would seemingly have because of past grievances with the present SANOC. Because SAN-ROC had been trying for years to hold a national sports convention to establish a unified national Olympic committee, Dennis Brutus felt that SAN-EABA's plan was designed to undercut SAN-ROC.[331] That SAN-EABA was a body affiliated not only to a white organization but to the white SAABA headed by Braun himself made their plan perhaps more suspect than it otherwise might have been.

SAN-ROC AND THE UNITED NATIONS

In June, SAN-ROC made a special presentation to the United Nations. It set out the question of apartheid in sports and described its own activities to change this. The result was a five-page report published by the United Nations Special Committee on the policies of apartheid, covering the issues raised by SAN-ROC.

THE POSITION OF SOUTH AFRICA IN TENNIS

Tennis was the next target of SAN-ROC, which by now had expanded its horizons and included Rhodesia as a nation to be expelled from world sports bodies because of its racial policies. Although its case against Rhodesia could hardly be compared to that against South Africa, some progress was made in 1968. In May, more than a thousand demonstrators had stormed the stadium in Baastad, Sweden, to protest a Davis cup match between Sweden and Rhodesia. The demonstrators had a violent confrontation with the police, who told the Davis cup organizers to call off the match.[332] But the biggest victory against Rhodesia came when the United Nations Security Council resolved on May 29 that all U.N.

members were to deny admission to anyone carrying a Rhodesian passport.[333] This decision meant that the Rhodesians could not compete in the Olympics.

The tennis issue was still alive in South Africa. The Russians confirmed that they would move that the South Africans be expelled from the ILTF when it met in Monte Carlo in July.[334] In June, Brutus wrote to the ILTF, spelling out how South Africa violated the ILTF constitution.[335] On June 6, SAN-ROC announced that Rumania had decided to withdraw from the Davis cup rather than compete against South Africa.[336] However, when the ILTF meeting was finally held in July, the South Africans had rallied enough support to defeat the Soviet expulsion motion by a three-to-one majority.[337]

THE SOUTH AFRICAN ATHLETIC TOUR OF BRITAIN

In July, SAN-ROC was involved in a protest of a tour of nonwhite South African athletes to Britain. Dennis Brutus wrote to Queen Elizabeth, a Royal Patron of the British Amateur Athletic Association, asking her not to attend the AAA championship and to withdraw her royal patronage because of the presence of the South Africans.[338] In explaining what he termed a difficult decision, Brutus said: "After much discussion, we feel we must protest against the presence of non-white athletes from South Africa who represent sports bodies affiliated to the racist South African sports organizations."[339] Although these activities failed to keep the South African team out of the meet, SAN-ROC did have some success at the IAAF meeting in Mexico, where Matt Mare of South Africa was removed as the representative for all of Africa and replaced by H. Agabani of the Sudan,[340] the first black man to represent Africa on this organization.

THE POSITION OF SOUTH AFRICA IN OTHER INTERNATIONAL SPORTS

In other international federations, the biggest blow to the South Africans was their expulsion from the International Amateur Boxing Association (IABA) in October. This was done by an executive decision and resulted in an immediate protest from Frank Braun, the head of the South African body. Braun has not even bothered to attend the meeting, which was supposed to have been an informal one.[341] This brought to five the number of sports in which South Africa could not compete internationally. The others were table tennis, judo, fencing and football.

In an attempt to get back into the football federation (FIFA), South Africa announced in October that it would attempt to form a Southern African Confederation of Football Associations. FASA felt that by doing this it would gain an additional nine votes at the next FIFA meeting.[342] (FASA was a member of the All-African Confederation of Football Associations but was not allowed to attend their meetings).

A Soviet move to have South Africa expelled from FINA, the international swimming federation, was ruled out of order because nations could not be expelled unless they did not pay their membership fee or contravened the rules (there was no FINA rule against racial discrimination).[343]

Finally, the international weightlifting federation (FIHC) gave the South African federation nine months to prove that it opposed racial discrimination. If it did not do this, it would be suspended.[344]

In addition to the episodes in the international federations, South Africa's traditional sports ties with several countries became increasingly controversial in 1968.

France

France was approached to cancel its competitions with the South African rugby and gymnastic teams. In the first instance, SAN-ROC cabled Charles de Gaulle; in the second case, it made its request for cancellation to the French minister of sport.[345]

New Zealand

The upcoming 1970 All-Blacks tour of South Africa was raising sports tensions in New Zealand. The Citizens Association for Racial Equality (CARE) sponsored a public meeting on South African sports on August 5, and the Maori community began to show more concern over this tour than it had over all previous ones.[346] The stage was set for a prolonged battle in 1969 and in early 1970.

Ireland

In Ireland, the Anti-Apartheid Movement focused increasing attention on the sports issue. It was unsuccessful in its attempt to persuade the Irish Rugby Football Union to refuse to send its players on the Lions tour of South Africa; it was also unsuccessful in its attempts to persuade the IRFU to cancel its invitation to the South Africans to come to Ireland in late 1969. On the positive side, the Irish AAM did manage to get an invitation withdrawn that would have brought the South African nonwhite track team to Ireland. And, although it must have felt a bit self-conscious in listing it as a sports success for nonracialism, the Irish AAM convinced the Irish National Ploughing Association to withdraw from the world ploughing championships in Rhodesia.[347]

Great Britain

No relationship was more seriously questioned in 1968 than the South African relationship with Britain. The MCC was to send a cricket team from Britain to tour South Africa in fall 1968. When it was announced in South Africa that if Basil D'Oliveira, the former Cape Colored cricket star, was selected, he would not be allowed to come, the MCC announced that if this was, in fact, the case, the tour would be cancelled; the British government approved this decision. The picture was muddled slightly when the South African minister of the interior denied that he had ever said that D'Oliveira could not come; however, his speech had been widely reported, and there was little doubt that the policy of no mixed sport still stood. The South Africans clearly hoped that all problems could be avoided by the MCC not selecting D'Oliveira for the tour.

With the day of selection only forty-eight hours away, Prime Minister Vorster, apparently unaware of what the MCC would decide, launched an attack on the anti-apartheid activists in England. He warned the British government that relations between the two countries were seriously endangered by Britain's housing these "Communist controlled and Communist-inspired" people. He said: "We kicked these people out because they were rotten and now Britain allows them to continue with their devilish activities–activities which are not only aimed at South Africa, but at civilization itself."[348]

On August 28, it was announced in London that Basil D'Oliveira had not been selected for the tour. According to MCC Secretary, S. C. Griffith:

> No preconditions as to the selection of the touring party have ever been laid down by the South African Cricket Association (SACA). The team has been picked solely on the basis of providing the best players in a cricketing sense to beat the South Africans.[349]

Basil D'Oliveira refused to comment in the midst of a swell of protest, both in England and in the nonwhite community in South Africa.[350]

There was no protest in white South Africa. When Minister of the Interior Lourens Muller interrupted a speech he was giving on student unrest to relay the news, members of the National party broke out in loud applause.[351]

As protests in England became widespread, the MCC had the tour captain, Colin Cowdrey, explain why he supported the tour: "Sport is still one of the most effective bridges in linking people." He added, however, that he "disliked the whole principle of apartheid."[352]

But the issue was not dead yet: the *News of the World* [London] announced that it had hired D'Oliveira to cover the tour. South Africa accused the *News of the World* of deliberately attempting to embarrass South Africa,[353] and South African sports writers said that it would be harder to cope with D'Oliveira as a reporter than as a player because he could not obtain a blanket exemption from the Group Areas Act. They pointed out that he would not be able to eat or drink with the players for the purpose of interviewing them and would probably have to sit in the nonwhite stands during the matches.[354] D'Oliveira's response was: "I undertook that commission in the sincere belief that I could complete the assignment without infringing any of the rules which I know so well in a country in which I grew up."[355]

This assurance was apparently insufficient for Prime Minister Vorster who announced, "Guests who have ulterior motives or who have been sponsored by people who have ulterior motives usually find that they are not invited."[356] Colin Cowdrey then said that if Vorster did not allow D'Oliveira to go to South Africa as a reporter, he would have to reconsider his captaincy.[357]

There was a dramatic turn of events on September 16 when the MCC announced that D'Oliveira had been selected to replace an injured member of the team. *The Times* [London] reported that D'Oliveira would be allowed to go on the basis of Vorster's speech of April 11, 1967.[358] This was a short-lived fantasy as Vorster announced his decision to cheering Nationalist MPs on the same day that the story appeared:[359]

> We are not prepared to accept a team thrust upon us by people whose interests are not the game, but to gain certain political objectives which they do not even attempt to hide.
>
> The team as constituted now is not the team of the MCC but the team of the Anti-Apartheid Movement, the team of SAN-ROC, and the team of Bishop Reeves. . . . The matter passed from the realm of sport to the realm of politics. . . . Leftist and liberal politicians had entered the field of sport and wanted to use it to suit their own purposes and pink ideals.[360]

In England, the British minister of sport, Dennis Howell, called Vorster's speech "one of the most ludicrous statements I have heard. This amounts to a monstrous libel on the MCC."[362]

In South Africa, most newspapers reported that Vorster's decision meant cricket isolation for South Africa.[362] *The Sunday Express* [Johannesburg], in an editorial, blamed Dennis Brutus for politicizing the case.[363] *Die Transvaaler* [Johannesburg] and *Die Burger* [Cape Town] supported Vorster's decision.[364] Ben Schoeman, Vorster's close aide and minister for transportation, told the MCC not to waste their time trying to make the government change its mind.[365]

When representatives from SACA and the MCC met on September 24, D'Oliveira said "If this is, even at the eleventh hour, the chance that we hope for to save the tour, then I am delighted."[366] But it was not to be. The MCC statement read:

> The Committee was informed that the side selected to represent the MCC in South Africa is not acceptable for reasons beyond the control of SACA. The MCC Committee, therefore, decided unanimously that the tour will not take place.[367]

D'Oliveira said that he hoped this would not affect future tours between Britain and South Africa.[368] The MCC agreed and confirmed this position at a special meeting of the MCC in December.

The meeting was called by the Reverend David Sheppard, himself an MCC member, to protest the MCC's conduct in handling the tour. He proposed three resolutions, including a censure of the MCC's handling of the tour and a suspension of future cricket relations with South Africa until there was proof that cricket in South Africa was becoming non-racial. All three resolutions were soundly voted down by almost 75 percent of the MCC (more than 5,900 members voted).[369] Thus, the MCC decided to go ahead with plans for the 1970 South African cricket tour of Britain.

The *Guardian* [Manchester] then quoted Lord Monckton, who had once said, half-facetiously, "I have been a member of the committee of the MCC and of the Conservative Cabinet and, by comparison with the cricketers, the Tories seemed like a bunch of Commies."[370]

THE MEXICAN OLYMPIC GAMES

The final story of 1968 is that of the Olympic games themselves and, in particular, the black American protest at the games.

At the end of July, Avery Brundage called Mexico "the most stable and fastest growing country in Latin America" and claimed that "the Olympic Movement had had no little part in making it so."[371] Within days of this statement, a student strike began in Mexico City that provoked the worst government crisis in thirty years, according to *The Times* [London]. As the opening of the games neared, thirteen were killed and hundreds injured in a three-day riot. It was an ironic scene: Olympic posters saying, "With peace, everything is possible," were plastered everywhere in the city.[372] Brundage, it seems, was slightly premature in his evaluation of the stability of Mexico, but he was not premature in saying that the Olympic movement had helped to make Mexico what it was. Of the several reasons given by the students for the riots, one was that the incredibly high cost of staging the games was a national disgrace.

But all the political news was not bad for the Olympics; black Americans had called off their boycott of the games.[373] This left only the basketball team without some of the great black stars, especially Alcindor, since the trials had been held while the boycott was still on. However, it was announced that some appropriate action would be taken at the games themselves.

Harry Edwards explained why the boycott was called off by the Olympic Committee for Human Rights (OCHR), as Edwards' group came to be known. OCHR had previously decided that the boycott would be off if only two-thirds of the athletes wanted it; during the trials, only 50 percent voted to boycott. OCHR felt that there was no point in staging a partial boycott because nonboycotters could easily replace those who did, thus making their sacrifice meaningless. The establishment could then point to the nonboycotters as the real black representatives, undermining everything OCHR had worked for. But, perhaps most important, was that OCHR feared a partial boycott would destroy the growing black unity among athletes.[374] Edwards announced that "the plan was to run at Mexico City; but no black athlete was to participate in any victory celebrations."[375] Athletes were to wear black armbands to protest injustice to blacks. Edwards continued:

> The Star Spangled Banner, the national anthem of the United States of America, was to be the focal point of the victory stand protest. . . . For the black man in America, the national anthem has not progressed far beyond what it was before Francis Scott Key put his words to it—an old English drinking song. For in America, a black man would have to be either drunk, insane, or both, not to recognize the hollowness in the anthem's phrases.[376]

In late September, Avery Brundage warned that any protest in Mexico would result in a quick trip home, and twenty-one black athletes immediately called for him to resign because of racial remarks. Brundage denied he had made any such remarks.[377]

The fireworks began on October 15 when sprinter Tommy Smith said, "I don't want Brundage presenting me any medals."[378] A hint of what was to come came in the heats when Smith and John Carlos wore knee-length black socks. But this was nothing compared to the victory ceremony. After the ceremony, Smith explained to Howard Cosell the symbolism of his and Carlos' actions:

> I wore a black right-hand glove and Carlos wore the left-hand glove of the same pair. My raised right hand stood for the power in Black America. Carlos' left hand stood for the unity of Black America. Together, they formed an arc of unity and power. The black scarf around my neck stood for black pride. The black socks with no shoes stood for black poverty in racist America. The totality of our effort was the regaining of black dignity.[379]

The photograph of their gestures became the very symbol of the Mexico games, much to the chagrin of the IOC. Smith and Carlos were given forty-eight hours to leave the Olympic village. USOC president Roby apologized to the IOC and warned other blacks not to protest.[381] The *New York Times* made a survey of United States athletes and found that thirteen supported Carlos and Smith, five opposed them, and one was undecided.[381] It went unreported in the press that the man who had finished in second place in the race with Smith and Carlos—an Australian, Peter Norman—wore the official badge of the OCHR in the victory ceremony.[382]

On October 18, three black Americans—Lee Evans, Larry James, and Ron Freeman—swept the four-hundred-meter race. In the victory ceremony, all wore black berets and raised their closed fists as their names were called. Evans said, "I won this medal for the black people in the United States and all over the world."[383]

The hypocrisy and/or craving for gold medals of the USOC became clear when it did not ask these three athletes to leave the Olympic village. They were three-fourths of the sixteen-hundred-meter relay team that had yet to compete. Carlos and Smith had had no more races to run when they were evicted.

When Harry Edwards said that OCHR had assumed that the USOC would throw Smith and Carlos out, the more moderate blacks, especially Ralph Boston and Bob Beamon, joined the protest.[384]

October 20 became a big day for the OCHR when the sixteen-hundred-meter relay team composed of Evans, James, Freeman, and Vince Matthews (who became better known after his protest in the 1972

Munich Olympics) won the race. All four wore black berets and held up clenched fists in the ceremony.[385] An all-black women's relay team won its event and dedicated its gold medals to Smith and Carlos.[386] The Cuban men's four-hundred-meter relay team gave its silver medals to Stokeley Carmichael, while the Cuban women's four-hundred-meter relay team gave its silver medals to Harry Edwards.[387]

For the USOC and the IOC, Smith, Carlos, Evans, James, Freeman, Matthews, Boston, and Beamon became antiheroes. But there was at least one black American who did not fit into this category, although he, too, engaged in a political display. George Foreman, the former heavyweight champion, won the gold medal in the heavyweight division in Mexico. After he won, he walked around the ring, carrying a United States flag and calling out, "United States power." He was cheered wildly by the crowd and became and instant television celebrity on his return to the United States.

Edwards used the contrast in the treatment of the protesting blacks to that given to Foreman, despite his "blatant political performance," to sum up what the OCHR was all about:

> Foreman's act and the manner in which it was received and the behavior of Smith and Carlos and the way it was received, proves that white racism dominates the United States athletic establishment. It once again pointed out that what is in the interest of whites is de facto acceptable, and what is in the interest of blacks is de facto condemned in white America. "Foreman is a good nigger," was the remark by a Southern graduate student. . . . But then, too, so were many of us at one time or another.[388]

In a survey taken four years later, the gestures of the black athletes in Mexico were still controversial in America. Fifty-seven percent of the blacks surveyed thought the athletes were justified in their actions (9 percent were undecided), while only 32 percent of the whites questioned (8 percent were undecided) felt the same way.[389]

In any case, politics aside, black athletes dominated the track and field events. At his press conference at the close of the games, Avery Brundage was asked why he felt this was so. He answered:

> This is nothing new. Even as far back as 1936, one could see, particularly with Jesse Owens, how the Negroes could excel in athletics. Their muscle structure lends itself to this sort of competition about which we are all delighted, moreover. However, there are still sports where the Negro is in the minority and in which they have to make a great deal of progress.[390]

Brundage's statement about "their muscle structure" is similar to the South African attitude: when Humphrey Khosi, the great South African nonwhite sprinter, had a slow time in a meet, the white athletic official explained:

> You must understand that Africans cannot perform well on a chilly day, because of their black skin. They are black because their skin must absorb heat so that they do their best in warm weather. . . . So, Khosi, under the circumstances, has done quite well.[391]

As for the sports in which "they have to make a great deal of progress," we may recall Frank Braun's less-than-scientific description of why blacks are not good swimmers (see page 92).

In the same press conference, Brundage was asked what progress the Olympics had made in human relations. He replied:

> Right here in Mexico, thanks to the "Juegos Deportivos," the Mexicans have proved that boys and girls are able to become better citizens, as they are stronger and healthier and have acquired a sense of discipline and national morale.[392]

Perhaps Mr. Brundage had missed the riots a few days before the opening of the games, which took strong police action to stop in time for the games.

Brundage's most curious statement came in response to a question asking him how the Olympics could survive as long as politics continued to become more and more involved in the games. His response was: "Who said that politics are becoming more and more involved in the Olympics?

In my opinion this is not so. . . . You know very well that politics are not allowed in the Olympic Games."[393]

Finally, the IOC held a session during the Mexico games. The African NOCs presented a motion to the IOC with the following points:

1. It requested the IOC to reaffirm explicitly that South Africa would not be readmitted until it complied with the Olympic charter.
2. It requested the IOC to suspend South Africa according to article 25.
3. It recommended that all the international federations suspend South Africa.[394]

SAN-ROC had already written to all the international federations meeting in Mexico, spelling out South Africa's violations of their respective charters and asking for South Africa to be suspended.[395] It also combined forces with the ACOA in Mexico and held numerous joint press conferences on the South African issue. SAN-ROC was represented by Chris de Broglio and Dennis Brutus, while the ACOA was represented by Steve Mokone and Jim Bouton, the controversial baseball star and author of *Ball Four.*

In spite of their efforts, South Africa retained its membership in the IOC, at least until the IOC's Warsaw meeting in June 1969. Those who fought for South Africa to be excluded were led by Jean-Claude Ganga of the Supreme Council, who said that opposition to South Africa would be dropped if mixed trials for international events were held in South Africa, even if they resulted in an entirely white team. Ganga maintained that if South Africa agreed to do this, it would be welcomed with open arms at the next All-Africa games.[396] It was not likely that the South Africans would be there.

SUMMARY

So ended the second stage of the historical study. Despite the compromises offered by the white sports authorities in South Africa and the resulting split in the nonracial movement in South Africa, the international protest against apartheid sport grew and kept South Africa out of the 1968 Olympic games. The key to this protest was the rebirth of SAN-ROC in London and the formation of the Supreme Council in Africa. These groups were not willing to accept the compromises offered as anything more than tokenism. All of this prepared the way for the final stage: either South Africa would have to move toward sports integration or it would face complete isolation in international sport.

4

Militant International Opposition to Apartheid Sport and the Resulting Isolation of South Africa: 1969-May 1970

The next stage of the extension of apartheid into South African sports was characterized by the growth of militant international opposition to South African sports policy. By 1969, the demands were for complete sports integration, both inside and outside South Africa. South Africa's refusal to meet these demands resulted in its virtual isolation in international sport by May 1970.

1969

Nineteen sixty-nine was filled with events that had long-term implications for the future of South Africa's international sports relations. The South African games gave an indication of how susceptible South Africa's supposed allies had become to pressure from the black African states. This development was further reflected in the IOC and seven international federations.

Two crucial tours were scheduled for 1970: the All-Blacks from New Zealand were to go to South Africa, presumably with Maoris on the team, and the South African cricket team was to tour Britain and Ireland. Both took on a significance far greater than any previous tours as campaigns were mounted to stop them in New Zealand, Britain, and Ireland, with support from many predominantly nonwhite nations. This was particularly true in England, where the Stop The Seventy Tour (STST) campaign was begun in spectacular fashion. STST used the 1969-1970 Rugby tour as a warm-up for the cricket campaign, resulting in the largest and most successful sports protest movement in history.

All of this had vast repercussions in South Africa, where an early election had to be called for 1970 because of growing opposition to Vorster's outward policy, particularly as it pertained to sports. On the other end of the South African spectrum, sports administrators began to make bold pledges for reform in the face of their crumbling international sports ties.

THE SOUTH AFRICAN GAMES

The South African games were to be comprised of completely separate events, in different cities and at different times, for white and nonwhite sportsmen, with the nonwhite games postponed from spring to fall 1969. In fact, these games did not take place at all in 1969, but rather almost as an afterthought in 1970. There was no way to pretend that the games were to be separate but equal. It was the white games that mattered and, when one talked about the South African games, one really meant the white South African games.

It was not known until March that it was Prime Minister Vorster himself who called for the games without consulting sports officials.[1] This was disclosed in an editorial in the *Sunday Tribune* [Durban] of March 16, which went on to say:

> Everyone is supposed to be satisfied with the cosy assurance that this is not race discrimination—that the non-whites will have their own Games. Let's stop fooling ourselves. The very fact that two sets of Games are being held is discrimination. If ever the likes of SAN-ROC and other anti-South African organizations wanted evidence that there was race discrimination in our sport, they have it in the South African Games. . . . By sending them [South Africa's friends] invitations to Games organized on frankly racial lines, we have only embarrassed our friends. We have forced them to declare themselves—and to make it more difficult for them to support South Africa's case at future IOC meetings.[2]

However, this editorial had been written with the benefit of hindsight—for, at the beginning of 1969, it did appear that many of the so-called friends of South Africa would, in fact, participate in the games. Then the roof started to leak and eventually caved in on the proud head of South African sport and government.

The AAU of the United States refused to allow the four American athletes, who had been invited, to attend. It did not pull any punches as to its reasons:

> After due consideration, it was decided on the basis of a resolution passed two years ago that no American athlete under AAU jurisdiction would be allowed to compete in South Africa because of its racial laws.[3]

The French decided not to send members of its track team, reportedly because "the French track star, dusky sprinter Roger Bambruck . . . was not invited."[4] Australia announced that its athletes would not compete, and two of the six invited British athletes—John Webb and John Boulter—refused to compete in events for whites only.[5]

The West Germans, undeterred by any of this uproar, announced, "No matter what other European countries decide, there is no doubt whatever that we will be sending a team."[6] Belgium and Greece also accepted their invitations in early January, prompting Frank Braun to say, "I am not worried about it. I am sure that the standard at the Games will be world class."[7] The truth of this statement, however, was, at best, doubtful since there would be no black Americans, Asians, African, or athletes from the socialist nations. By the start of the games, the pickings were to be even slimmer.

By that time, SAN-ROC had swung into full action against the games. A press release called them "the greatest racist sports festival ever planned."[8] SAN-ROC appealed to the meeting of Commonwealth prime ministers that the South African games would endanger Commonwealth relations.[9] Dennis Brutus wrote to the manager of the West German athletic team, warning him of the serious implications that West Germany's participation in the games would have on the 1972 Munich Olympics. Brutus' strongly worded letter read, in part:

> It is a regrettable fact that the West German sports bodies have been among the strongest supporters of the racialist organizations

> in South Africa, and one must ask if this has any relation to the past racial influences in German sport.[10]

The South African AAU made what was, perhaps, a major tactical mistake at the end of January when it invited Rhodesia to both the white and nonwhite games.[11] Considering the international position of the Rhodesian government, this invitation could do nothing but harm in regard to the acceptance of invitations by other countries. The invitation to Rhodesia was made on the same day that teams from Austria and Switzerland announced that they would go to South Africa.[12]

In the February 7 edition of *News/Check* [Johannesburg], SAN-ROC's concern about the games was noted: "What about the black sportsmen? They can wait until later in the year—no date has been set, no money allotted by any oil companies, no venue chosen, nobody invited."[13] But in the same article, it was accused of hypocrisy for praising the victories of blacks only in the 1968 Olympics while maintaining a supposedly nonracial stand. Dennis Brutus later revealed how and why this happened:

> This was one of those occasions when Chris issued a statement on behalf of SAN-ROC which I probably would not have, Chris being more forthright (and putting his foot in things occasionally). It's a useful ploy when talking to non-white countries to express their own developing sports prowess and I guess when talking to black South Africans, too, one has to remind them of the achievements of blacks elsewhere.[14]

All in all, though, February 7 did not turn out to be such a bad day for SAN-ROC in its fight against the games. Brutus flew to Lausanne to show Avery Brundage the commemorative stamp for the games being issued in South Africa. The stamp contained the symbol of the Olympic movement—the five Olympic rings. Chris de Broglio maintained that "South Africa's use of the Olympic symbol is illegal because the Republic practices racialism in sport, and because it has no permission from the IOC to print the symbol."[15] To which Minister of Sport Waring replied:

> South Africa is a member of the IOC, and even though we did not participate in the Olympic Games at Mexico City, we have the

> right to use the five-ring symbol in this connection.
> As far as the SAN-ROC people are concerned, this is the type of propaganda they would like to use. They are not interested in sport, only in destroying it.[16]

But the IOC eventually came around to SAN-ROC's position and sent the SANOC the following cable:

> The Executive Board of the IOC, having seen the use of the Olympic symbols on insignia, stamps, etc., in connection with the "all-white South African Games", censures the SANOC for the misuse of these symbols with Games contrary to Olympic principles and ideals.[17]

Lord Killanin added:

> I must warn you that there is now a likelihood that instead of South Africa's participation in Munich, the issue at stake in Warsaw may well become a battle just to insure the SAOC's continued membership in the organization.[18]

The games were in trouble. Even if everyone came to them, the cost was obviously going to be high. With criticism growing in early February, the Bloemfontein ban on nonwhite spectators became another potential source of trouble. Therefore, the government went to the Bloemfontein city council with a request to lift the ban.[19] The council agreed two weeks later, but only under certain conditions—especially that the government bear the cost of constructing the separate facilities (entrances, seats, and toilets) necessary to comply with the Group Areas Act.[20] It was later announced that a maximum of 750 nonwhites would be admitted to the larger events, with only 150 to be admitted to events like tennis and cricket. In addition, nonwhite tickets would cost more than white tickets.[21]

By the beginning of March, it was announced that the following countries would be represented by full or partial teams: Britain, New Zealand, Austria, West Germany, Holland, Italy, Belgium, Greece, Switzerland, Denmark, France, and the United States (the latter two were to be represented in sports other than those that had prohibited sending teams).[22]

On March 3, SAN-ROC called on West Indian and African nations to boycott the 1970 Commonwealth games to avoid competition with nations that sent teams to the South African games.[23] Kenya immediately agreed, and Abraham Ordia, president of the African Supreme Council, said that Nigeria would probably do the same.[24]

With these announcements, the retreat of the European nations that had accepted invitations began in earnest. The *Star* [Johannesburg] reported that the West Germans were reconsidering in light of what might happen to the Munich games.[25] The *Eastern Province Herald* [Port Elizabeth] reported that the American embassy in South Africa denied permission to two American citizens working for the Department of State to compete in the games. The Soviet Olympic committee protested to the IOC about the games and called on individual nations to boycott them.[26] The Netherlands withdrew its team on March 10, becoming the first to withdraw after accepting the invitation.[27]

The British Olympic swimming captain, Tony Jarvis, said of the British athletes still scheduled to go:

> I deplore the attitude of our competitors who are going. It is nonsense for them to say they disagree with apartheid and then accept "to see for themselves.". . . There is too much hypocrisy in sportsmen's minds and too few principles.[28]

This, among other factors, probably convinced Olympic silver medalist, Lillian Board, not to go to the South African games. She had said that she was looking forward to returning to the land where she had been born but felt that her participation might jeopardize future athletic contests for Britain.[29]

Belgium became the second nation to withdraw on March 12; Italy followed four days later. The Italian withdrawal was the result of a threatened Kenya boycott of events in Italy later in March. A Kenyan official said, "I am glad Italy has seen the light."[30]

On the same day, the Supreme Council announced that if West Germany sent a team to South Africa, all African nations would boycott the Munich Olympic games.[31] West Germany hastily withdrew its team, once again demonstrating the growing power of the African nations when they acted from a unified position. It also showed the continued —and growing—influence of SAN-ROC, which had virtually instructed the Supreme Council on each step it took.

On March 21, U Thant, the secretary-general of the United Nations, called on all nations to break their sports links with South Africa.[32] But all nations did not respond, particularly Britain and New Zealand.

In New Zealand, Deputy Prime Minister Marshall said that the government should not interfere in sports and, thus, should not stop athletes from New Zealand who wanted to go to the games.[33] Prime Minister Holyoake confirmed this view, even after protest marches in Wellington, Aukland, and Hamilton.[34] However, national champion Davis Norris did refuse to go "on moral grounds."[35] The Anglican Bishop of Aukland, Bishop Gowing, condemned the very idea of sending a team from New Zealand, recalling the U.N. resolution of December 1968 to end all sports contacts with South Africa.[36]

British Minister of Sport Howell took a similar attitude to that of the New Zealand government: British athletes were free to go wherever they chose.[37] Ironically, it was reported later on the same day Howell made this blanket statement that the British government refused permission to three oarsmen to compete in Rhodesia.[38]

On March 26, the Supreme Council took particular note of the decisions of the leaders in New Zealand and Britain. In a clear reference to the 1970 Commonwealth games, it said that any white country that supported the South African games would bear full responsibility for the consequences. The SCSA press release stated that the games had been organized for only three purposes: to compensate for being excluded from Mexico; to consolidate the spirit of white supremacy; and to display the solidarity between white Western sportsmen and South Africa's racialist sports policy.[39]

Although only one athlete from Britain actually went to the games, the New Zealanders sent a full contingent. Throughout the debate on whether a team should go, New Zealand sports officials maintained that the athletes were going as individuals only—and not as representatives of New Zealand. But on the eve of departure, the team manager, A. O. Melville, said that it was a New Zealand team and that its members would wear official New Zealand uniforms.[40]

So the games—the white games, that is—were held. If they were to be honest with themselves, South African officials, both in the government and in sports circles, would have to admit that the games proved too costly in terms of South Africa's sports relations with other countries in general and with the IOC in particular. One last embarrassment for the South Africans was the fact that, after the government went to all the bother of persuading the Bloemfontein city council to drop its ban on nonwhite spectators, out of the first ninety thousand tickets sold, only three hundred were purchased by nonwhites.[41] Perhaps this was the best reflection of nonwhite opinion toward sports events run on racial lines.

THE IOC MEETING IN WARSAW

As the Warsaw meeting of the IOC neared, Avery Brundage predicted that South Africa would be expelled from the Olympic movement. Reg Honey was not ready to accept this:

> We have a strong case because we have never broken an IOC rule. It is not the President's duty to prophesy the outcome of a meeting before it is held. . . . He has no right to prophesy at all. . . . For the President of the IOC to make such a prediction . . . is not only a disgrace, but typical of the IOC's misconception of power. South Africa has never broken an IOC rule. There is no possible reason why we should be expelled, except for political reasons. . . . The IOC should act legally,—which is something they have not done for the past 20 years. The IOC is a farce today, as they do whatever they want and break their own rules every day.[42]

No one has ever accused Honey of not being aggressive.

The *Sunday Times* [Johannesburg] referred to the upcoming IOC session as "the Battle of Warsaw" and said that the best thing that could happen from South Africa's point of view was a postponed decision.[43] This was exactly what happened in Warsaw; the final decision on South Africa was put off until the meeting in Amsterdam in May 1970.[44]

An indication of what might happen in Amsterdam came at the general assembly of the National Olympic committees in Dubrovnik at the end of October. The NOCs voted to expel South Africa from the Olympic movement by the overwhelming vote of forty-six to six, with eight abstentions.[45] Of course, this vote was not binding on the IOC.

SOUTH AFRICA'S POSITION IN THE INTERNATIONAL FEDERATIONS

South Africa continued to have problems with the international federations throughout the year.

Football

In March, Dave Marais announced that the International Football Federation (FIFA) had rejected FASA's invitation to send an investigating commission. He also said that Stanley Rous, the FIFA leader, told him FIFA would veto FASA's proposed Southern African Soccer Federation (proposed in 1968).[46]

Later in the year, FIFA did grant permission for FASA to stage an interracial football match in Swaziland. The match was to take place on August 31 between the white Highland Park team and the black Orlando Pirates and was to be part of Swaziland's first anniversary celebration.[47] Two weeks before the match was to take place, however, South African Minister of the Interior Muller announced that he would withdraw all passports for those involved if the organizers went on with the match. He said that he could not allow South African athletes to do outside the country what they could not do inside the country.[48]

The *Times* of Swaziland accused the South African government of coming dangerously close to interfering with the rights and affairs of Swaziland, while Dave Marais warned that South Africa would be isolated in all sports within two years unless it changed its policy.[49] (Muller had also forced the cancellation of an interracial boxing match in Swaziland several days after the football ban in late August. He again had threatened to withdraw passports if plans went through.)[50] There could be no doubt that the government's decision on the football match, after FIFA had given its special permission, would seriously damage FASA's chances of having its suspension from FIFA lifted.

Judo

In March, the International Judo Federation refused South Africa's white Judo Association's bid for membership. The South African body was not a member of the regional federation, the African and Malagasy Judo Union (it had been denied membership in that body because of racial discrimination in South African judo), and, therefore, not eligible for membership in the International Judo Federation.[51]

Weightlifting

In June, SAN-ROC wrote to Oscar State, secretary-general of the International Weightlifting Federation (FIHC), expressing concern that Wally Holland, a lesser FIHC official, had become a one-man investigating team to South Africa. (The original plan was for a three-man team, but South Africa refused to grant visas to the three men picked. The South Africans then invited Holland to come himself.)[52]

Holland went to South Africa in July. While there, he predicted that South Africa's chances for remaining in the FIHC were about fifty-fifty. He also said that there could never be nonracial lifting in South Africa and, therefore, suggested that the two bodies form a joint committee with a white chairman. Holland said that this plan had been approved by the minister of sport.[53]

In his own report of October 1968, Holland had proposed that the SAAWLU (the white body) be tested: it had nine months to open its membership to all, with equal representation on committees and no separate registers, and it had to stage a nonracial championship.[54] Clearly, the SAAWLU had not complied with either of these tests by the time Holland arrived nine months later.

When the full FIHC met in September, South Africa was suspended by a substantial vote of twenty-seven for suspension, nine opposed, and two abstentions.[55] This suspension brought great satisfaction to SAN-ROC, which, with the exception of the IOC, had fought hardest to get South Africa out of the FIHC. It had taken twenty-three years.

South African teams became the virtual hostages of two socialist governments in two world championship events. In September, Hungary refused to grant visas to South Africa for the world modern pentathalon championships in Budapest. This action was contrary to the orders of the International Pentathalon Association, and Australia withdrew in protest.[56] In November, the International Gymnastics Federation claimed that it was up to Tito to hold the world championships in Yugoslavia, with or without the South Africans.[57]

Tennis

The story in international tennis was entangled in 1969. The South African government granted the honorary-white status to the Iranian Davis cup team for its series in South Africa.[58] While in South Africa, the Iranians had agreed to play against a nonwhite team, but the white SALTU refused to allow this. (It was not known whether the government influenced the SALTU decision.)[59]

Basil Reay, the leader of the International Lawn Tennis Federation (ILTF), visited South Africa in April. While there, Reay attempted to get the nonracial Southern African Lawn Tennis Union to affiliate to SALTU. In what the *Post* [Natal] called an "astonishing meeting," Reay admitted that the offer was neither attractive nor in accordance with international tennis laws. The nonracial body refused on the grounds that "it's not administration we're after. We want to play with them [whites]."[60]

Earlier in the week, Reay had told a SALTU official that South Africa's chances of remaining in the Davis cup competition were weak because Poland and Hungary had already announced that they would refuse to play against South Africa in the second round of the European zone Davis cup. Reay said that something would have to be done.[61]

Reay did do "something" when he published the agenda of the meeting of the Davis cup nations for July: South Africa was not scheduled. Reay said that the motion for discussion was received too late: "Under the rules, the motion should have been received not later than March 31. But it was not posted until that date and received on April 3rd, too late for inclusion."[62] There were many indications that Reay had pulled off something that did not sound quite right. During the week of April 6, well after the deadline, Reay addressed a SALTU meeting:

> And if the vote goes against South Africa at the annual meeting of the Davis Cup nations in July, particularly among those countries

playing in the European Zone Section, then South Africa will be forced to withdraw.

But if the motion for discussion had not been received on time, and, thus, could not be discussed, why should Reay have talked about such a discussion a week after the deadline had passed? A week after his address to SALTU, the *Sunday Tribune* [Durban] quoted Reay: "It's all a very tricky problem and I don't know the answer. We are trying to sort it out."[63] Reay was successful. The *Star* [Johannesburg] reported that he was going to present a "remarkably favorable report" on tennis in South Africa at the ILTF meeting in July.[64]

As the meeting neared, the opposing sides began jockeying for position. Both Poland and Czechoslovakia withdrew from the Davis cup competition rather than play against South Africa.[65] Sweden announced that it would attempt to make the ILTF ruling on race more explicit, while the ILTF maintained that it wanted a more general statement.[66] The South African National Lawn Tennis Union (nonwhite) was given voting status in SALTU. SALTU spokesman Chalmers said that he hoped this would lead to stronger bonds between the races in South Africa.[67]

At the end of June, Arthur Ashe, the black American tennis star, dramatically announced that the South African government had refused to grant him a visa to compete in the South African championships for 1969.[68] This was the beginning of another story that would be continued later in 1969 and become a full-scale crisis in 1970; but, for the moment, it appeared that this June announcement, made only days before the ILTF's meeting, would further harm South Africa's chances of remaining in the ILTF and the Davis cup. SAN-ROC made one final appeal to all ILTF members to ignore Reay's report if the South Africans discriminated in any way.[69]

Reay, however, was not ready to accept all the damaging news without trying to help the South Africans. He said, "It would be a tragedy for South African tennis and world sport if the SALTU were kicked out of the ILTF—that is my official and frank opinion."[70] The South Africans prevailed at the meeting. When the newly elected ILTF president, B. A. Barnett, was asked what the main achievement of the ILTF meeting was, he answered, "the retention of South Africa within the ILTF."[71]

It has been shown that, throughout the history of the extension of apartheid into sports, South African sports administrators had frequently made promises for reform before international federation meetings, presumably in the hope of retaining membership; but these promises were never made after the meetings. The tennis case changed this. At the end of July, Alf Chalmers, the head of SALTU, announced that nonwhite players could be on the South African Davis cup team if they qualified and—more important—that the government had agreed to this.[72] In fact, mixed trials were later held in private for the women's team, although no nonwhites qualified.[73] This did seem to be a major breakthrough. In addition, SALTU accepted Ashe's application to play in the 1970 South African championships and asked the government to grant him a visa—this in spite of the fact that Minister of Sport Waring had said he would not be granted a visa because of his anti-South African statements.[74] But by the time this was announced in December, a new element in South African politics had arisen—the Verkramptes and the calling of an early election for 1970.

TRADITIONAL RELATIONSHIPS

The traditional relations that South Africa shared with the United States, Australia, New Zealand and Britain came under close scrutiny in 1969.

The United States

The United States first felt the bite of the growing boycott movement against South Africa when Kenya, with its team of Olympic stars, withdrew from the U.S./U.S.S.R./Commonwealth track meet in Los Angeles, scheduled for July 18 and 19. The Kenyans were not allowed to run because they would have competed against athletes who had taken part in the South African games.[75]

A month later, Lee Evans, the black American track star, announced that black athletes would not compete with British athletes until they agreed to boycott events with South Africa. Evans said, "We want our African brothers to know that we are completely behind them. We are very aware of the sufferings of our black brothers in South Africa."[76]

Australia

In Australia, the formation of CARIS (Campaign Against Racialism in Sport) signaled a new stage in the movement for nonracial sport. The formation of CARIS was influenced by Dennis Brutus' tour of Australia. Before Brutus arrived, the South African ambassador to Australia actually asked the Australian department of external affairs to keep Brutus out of the country.[77] Brutus called Australia the number one "open" supporter of South Africa in sport. By open supporter, he was referring to the fact that New Zealand and Britain had given their support behind the scenes, while the Australians had given theirs openly.[78]

The secretary of the Commonwealth Games Federation warned Australia that its case for holding the 1974 Commonwealth games in Melbourne would probably be lost if it went on with plans to send a swimming team to South Africa; pressure from the African members of the Commonwealth would be too great.[79]

New Zealand

The controversy in New Zealand was focused on the scheduled 1970 All-Blacks tour of South Africa.

In March, George Nepia, a former All-Blacks star in the 1920s and a Maori, announced that he would lead a contingent of Maori supporters that would follow the All-Blacks in South Africa. CARE warned Nepia that Maoris would either be denied visas or would be humiliated when they got to South Africa.[80] The consul-general from South Africa assured New Zealanders and the Maori council that all New Zealand supporters of the All-Blacks would be welcomed in South Africa, after they were granted visas—an ambiguous statement which did not really state whether any Maoris would receive visas.[81]

Later in March, the Maori council, which had decided to back the tour, defended its decision on the grounds that nonwhite South Africans would view the arrival of Maoris as a tremendous advance.

On the same trip that took him to Australia, Dennis Brutus made an extensive speaking tour of New Zealand in April. In order to increase awareness of the issue, CARE published *An ABC of Racial Sport* in April, which among other things, pointed out that, earlier in the year, the New Zealand squash team had sent home its nonwhite coach before entering South Africa.[82] Thus, New Zealand had yet to send a nonwhite player to South Africa in spite of the many assurances made by New Zealand sports officials that they would never again send a racially selected team to South Africa.

The April 3 New Zealand *Listener's* editorial called the Maori council "myopic" and "parochial." It pointed out that after the tour was over, Maoris would not be allowed to stay in or return to South Africa with the same status they would have for the tour. It accused the New Zealand government of accommodating apartheid.[83]

During the tour, CARE was joined in its opposition to the tour by a new group, HART (Halt All Racialist Tours). Both groups constantly questioned whether Maoris would ultimately be allowed on the team. In response, Minister of Sport Waring repeated that Maoris would indeed be welcome—as they always had been.[84]

One week later, on September 9, a major development began in South Africa. At the Transvaal National party congress held in Pretoria, a resolution in support of Vorster's sports policy (as stated in his speech of April 11, 1967) was presented. Albert Hertzog, who was a cabinet minister at the time the policy was announced, led a group of ten who voted against the resolution of support. Hertzog was especially upset about the Maoris and said, "They will sit at the table with our young men and girls, and dance with our girls." He suggested that if Vorster wanted him out of the party as a result of his convictions, then he should put him out.[85]

One week later, the prime minister called for an early general election in 1970 because he feared that people would think the country was splitting on the issue. He said, "Nothing can ever damage us more than if the outside world were to get the idea that there is not a strong Government in power in South Africa."[86]

A *Star* [Johannesburg] editorial commented:

> What South Africa's sport policy now seems to amount to is that an off-white member of a visiting team is acceptable provided that nobody says anything about him. And that, nowadays, is a very tall order indeed.[87]

Government statements regarding the admission of Maoris became more guarded. When Jaap Marais challenged Vorster to expel him from the National party because of his support of Hertzog's policy, Transvaal National party leader Ben Schoeman said that one Maori coming to South Africa would not signal the end of civilization; however, Schoeman refused to answer when asked if five Maoris would end civilization in South Africa.[88]

The picture became more clouded with the election for the Colored persons' representative council on September 25. The six hundred thousand Coloreds who voted in the election gave a substantial victory to the anti-apartheid Labour party, dealing the National party an overwhelming defeat. The victory for the Labour party was more of a moral victory than a practical once since the government, with the power to select twenty of the sixty members of the council, still had control.[89] This election caused a blacklash among the Verkramptes, and the government's new reserve was reflected in Minister of the Interior Muller's speech the next day. Muller said he saw no problem with admitting a "certain number of New Zealanders with Maori blood," but that he would take action against a "massive influx of foreign non-white spectators."[90]

On October 25, Hertzog led a thousand delegates from 125 constituencies in South Africa and South West Africa to Pretoria, where they formed the Herstigte Nasionale party (the Reformed National party).[91] The threat to Vorster's sports policy became a much more serious matter with the formation of the HNP.

In New Zealand, HART activists, now more alarmed about the potential fate of the Maoris, led five hundred demonstrators in protest against the tour. HART also cabled U Thant at the U.N. concerning New Zealand's disregard for U.N. resolutions on South African sport.[92]

That HART's increased concern was justified was proven in late November when South African Minister of Information and Immigration C. P. Mulder said that South Africa would decide if the All-Blacks were acceptable after the composition of the team was announced.[93] It was obvious that the South African government was attempting to play down its outward policy as a result of the challenge by the Verkramptes.

On December 6, a group called Te Ragatahi met with the Maori council in Wellington to ask that it withdraw its support of the All-Blacks tour in light of the emergence of the Verkrampte backlash in South Africa. Te Ragatahi represented a major cross-section of Maoris, including the New Zealand Federation of Maori Students, the Maori Women's Welfare League, the Maori Organization for Human Rights, the Ratana Youth Movement, the Maori Graduates' Association, and the Maori section of the Wellington diocese.[94] The pressure against the All-Blacks tour was growing daily. HART had even initiated a petition calling for the government to intervene in December.

Rugby was not the only sport in New Zealand to be affected by the pressure. Ces Blazey, head of New Zealand athletics, announced the withdrawal of an invitation for the SAAAU to send to team in 1970. Blazey said this was done out of the fear that New Zealand would not be allowed to participate in the 1970 Commonwealth games if it allowed the South Africans to come. In Aukland, CARE praised the decision and said it hoped that the Rugby Union would follow the lead of the athletic association.[95]

GARY PLAYER AND PAPWA SEWGOLUM

The Verkrampte phenomenon also took its toll in golf. In November, Gary Player finally broke his long-standing support of government policy and requested that Papwa Sewgolum once again be allowed to play in South Africa.[96] However, the reaction against what he said in South Africa caused him to change his mind two days later. Player said:

> The Government of South Africa, rightly or wrongly, has decided on a policy of separate development. This is the law, and whether one is white, black, brown or brindle, one has to obey it.[97]

He also said that the policy was intended "for the betterment of all races."[98]

In December, the government ruled that if a white golf course was used for a nonwhite championship, whites could not enter the clubhouse (even though nonwhites were not allowed to use it) for the duration of the tournament. As of December 1969, there still was not a single nonwhite championship course in all South Africa.[99]

SOUTH AFRICAN SPORTS RELATIONS WITH BRITAIN

South Africa's relationship with England was, by far, the most extraordinary one in 1969. Traditionally, England had been South Africa's top rival in sports. But tradition became unimportant for this relationship in 1969, despite the fact that traditionalists fought desperately against this. In the end, their fighting proved ineffective against the new sports weapon: the direct action pressure group.

Netball

In January, the All-England Association withdrew its invitation to the South African Women's Netball Association because its team was not representative of the population.[100] This was the only time in 1969 that the English-South African controversy did not center, either directly or indirectly, in cricket relations.

The D'Oliveira Affair

In spite of all that had happened in the D'Oliveira affair in 1967 and in 1968, and, in spite of the fact that a survey conducted by Market Research Africa showing that 61 percent of the South Africans still opposed nonwhites from overseas competing with whites in South Africa had just been released, the MCC unanimously voted in January to go ahead with the 1970 tour.[101] Dennis Brutus warned, "This is by no means the end of the matter."[102]

In South Africa, there was an announcement made simultaneously with that of the MCC that the white South African Cricket Association (SACA) would hold discussions on matters of common interest with the nonwhite South African Cricket Board of Control (SACBC).[103] This was, it could reasonably be assumed, planned to soften the expected criticism of the MCC decision in Britain.

Discussion of the tour died down until a number of serious disclosures were made in April. The first was that Lord Cobham, an MCC member, had been told by Prime Minister Vorster in March 1968 that D'Oliveira would not be allowed to come to South Africa as a member of the British team. Cobham told MCC President Gilligan and MCC Treasurer Allen what Vorster had said.[104] Sir Alec Douglas-Home also advised the MCC not to press South Africa for a decision on D'Oliveira before the selections were made. He had also met with Vorster at about the same time that Cobham did. The MCC chose to follow the advice of Douglas-Home.[105] *The Times* [London] condemned the MCC for withholding this vital information.[106]

The disclosures made a mockery of Vorster's reason for not allowing D'Oliveira to come. Vorster claimed that he was unacceptable because he was a political choice for the team in September 1968. These disclosures proved that the method of selection had nothing to do with Vorster's decision.

It was also revealed that the South African Sports Foundation had offered D'Oliveira £40,000 to coach nonwhite cricket players in South Africa provided that D'Oliveira had made himself unavailable for the tour of South Africa *before* the selection of the British team was announced.[107] At first, the Sports Foundation denied it had made the offer.[108] However, after D'Oliveira wrote a full-page story for the *Sunday Times* [London] detailing the offer, Frank Waring admitted that the offer had been purely a business deal and not as a bribe.[109] Waring's statement left many skeptical, including British Minister of Sport Dennis Howell, who was also very critical of the MCC.[110]

Despite the new information, a poll conducted by the *Daily Sketch* [London] showed that 77 percent of the British people still favored the tour. H. Doughty said, "If the tour is cancelled it will be another victory for the vicious, pharisaical leftist meddlers who are dedicated to the destruction of the British way of life."[111]

Minister of Sport Howell, in an address in Parliament, pointed out: "There is no evidence that the continuing contacts with South Africa are having any beneficial or civilizing effect upon the administration there."[112] On the other hand, D'Oliveira defended the honesty and integrity of the MCC while calling for continued sports contacts with South Africa.[113] Predictably, the MCC chose the latter course and confirmed the tour.[114]

On May 15, SAN-ROC held a public meeting in London to discuss various ways to get the cricket tour called off. The first step, it decided, would be to disrupt the Wilf Isaacs cricket team tour of England during the summer.[115]

The one person who probably could have helped more than any other in getting the tour cancelled was D'Oliveira himself, but he steadfastly refused to change his attitude on the tour in the face of tremendous pressure from nonwhites. In June, eleven Cape Coloreds, then living in Britain like D'Oliveira, publicly condemned him for not taking the lead in the fight against apartheid in sport. They called his attitude "unthinking" and "insensitive."[116]

Early Demonstrations

The Wilf Isaacs team arrived in Britain in early July. Led by the Young Liberals, protests began on July 6 with the start of the tour at Basildon. The next day, protestors dug a forty-five-yard-long trench across the Oxford University cricket field in preparation for the match there on July 9.[117] At the match itself, fifty demonstrators ran onto the field and help up play for more than forty minutes.[118] The official statement of the protestors maintained that the South African team had been sent as "an ambassador of apartheid to test the reaction of the British public toward racialism in sport. It is a trial run for next year's official tour of this country."[119]

The same demonstrators were at the Davis cup match between South Africa and Britain a week later at Bristol, where there was a fake bomb threat.[120] One of the leaders, Peter Hain, said, "This is only the beginning."[121]

The *Sunday Tribune* [Durban] of July 20 described the main organizers at Bristol as a group of South African exiles made up of three communists and an anarchist. The story, almost prophetically, focused on Peter Hain as the most dynamic leader of the group and recalled his life in South Africa.[122]

When Wilf Isaacs returned to South Africa, he said that the protestors were well organized and had a large following. He went on:

> Some of them are definitely paid. Their tactics were usually to insult the biggest player on the team . . . or myself, in the hope that we would retaliate.

> Their behavior was disgusting. I was spat on. They were very crude and their language was filthy. Some of them are drug takers.[123]

In August, it was reported that SACA had asked Basil D'Oliveira to join its team for the 1970 tour. As quickly as this story broke, it was denied by SACA spokesman, Dave Bursnall, who said, "The team won't be a multi-racial one."[124]

STST

The formation of the Stop the Seventy Tour (STST) committee was formally announced on September 8.[125] It held its first press conference two days later. Louis Eaks, national chairman of the Young Liberals, made the opening address. He said, in part:

> The era of petitions and reasoned debate has been rejected by those responsible for sport. . . . Our action is a response to this morally indefensible policy of apartheid in sport. . . . Is there any justification for importing racialism into this country? . . . We are not committed to a programme of non-violent civil disobedience to disrupt the 1970 South African Tour. . . . We have asked the MCC on numerous occasions to take a reasoned stand against apartheid in sport. It is they who will be responsible if Lords becomes the Ulster of the sporting world next summer.[126]

(Lords is regarded as the mecca of world cricket, much as Madison Square Garden is regarded as the mecca of world basketball.) Peter Hain added, "We are fighting British collaboration with racialism in sport. We are confident of winning."[127]

The South African newspapers reacted to the formation of STST with great alarm. The front-page headlines of the various newspapers for September 11 read:

> "Lords 'Ulster of Sport.' " *Cape Argus* [Cape Town].
> "Springbok Tour Chaos Warning." *Star* [Johannesburg].
> "Bodies Unite to Attack Bok Tours." *Rand Daily Mail* [Johannesburg].
> "Paper Supports Anti-South Africa Move." *Daily News* [Durban].

The last headline referred to an editorial in the *Guardian* [Manchester] calling for the cancellation of the tour.[128]

Peter Hain addressed the Liberal party assembly on September 20 and answered accusations that his group was introducing politics into sports by saying that it was the South African government that had done this. Hain said that, after twenty years of dialogue, apartheid had only been expanded.[129]

In a page-one story in the *Christian Science Monitor* [Boston], Dennis Brutus described the dangers of the tour:

> There is a very real danger of race relations in Britain being poisoned to a large extent if there are going to be pro and anti-South African factions clashing. I think this tour may well go beyond the field of sport and enter the whole area of community relations.[130]

In early October, Peter Hain received a registered letter from the South African minister of the interior stating that Hain's right as a British citizen to enter South Africa had been withdrawn. The letter was especially curious, since Hain had not planned to go to South Africa. He said, "I took this as something of a compliment: at age 19 one hardly expects one's presence to be construed as a danger to the security of a state!"[131]

The South African Rugby Tour of Britain

By October, interest in the South African rugby tour had swelled, and STST decided to take advantage of it by expanding its activities. Oxford University, the site of the first match, officially disassociated itself from the tour. But the Rugby Union announced that the match would be held anyway.[132]

On October 19, Minister Howell said that he felt the 1970 tour should be cancelled.[133] This added to the momentum that STST had picked up, as did the event of October 24 when protestors ruined the playing field at Oxford with weed killer, spelling out, "Oxford Reject Apartheid." Officials immediately called off the match but hoped to find another location for it.[134] Peter Hain told what this meant to his movement: "The calling off of the Oxford match was absolutely crucial to the fantastic growth in momentum of the campaign at this vital period just before the tourists were to arrive."[135]

The South African press sensed the growing importance of the rugby tour as the day of the team's departure neared. *Die Volksblad* [Bloemfontein] commented: "Every international sports success of South Africa is a blow against our sports and political enemies.[136] *Die Burger* [Cape Town] said that the rugby team had an extraordinary responsibility to influence British public opinion.[137]

Home Secretary James Callaghan of Britain refused to intervene in the matter after STST leaders warned that the movement had grown so large that they could no longer be responsible for what happened.[138] Prime Minister Vorster said that South Africa would not interfere in any way with any touring teams, and he hoped the Springboks would be treated in the same way by Britain.[139]

The South African team held a press conference upon arriving in London. Corrie Bornman, the Bok manager, said, "It's a free country. They can demonstrate if they want. We are here to play rugby."[140] Dawie de Villiers, the team's captain, commented, "We have come to play rugby and not worry about politics."[141] But it was not to be. STST held its own press conference that day and announced that it would stage a demonstration at every match.[142]

By the end of October, the Irish Anti-Apartheid Movement had also joined the campaign against the rugby tour (matches were scheduled for Ireland in January), calling for the cancellation of the matches in Ireland:

> It is also naive of the Irish Rugby Football Union (IRFU) to pretend that to accept an all-white team in Ireland has nothing to do with accepting racialism. . . . The IRFU cannot get away from the fact that in South Africa the playing of matches against all-white teams is regarded, by white and black, as an agreement with segregation.[143]

By November 4, the Irish AAM had sent off letters to thirty-four rugby clubs, forty-four potential players, and Prime Minister Lynch, and it had printed sixty thousand leaflets.[144] Its preparation was to pay large dividends when the South Africans arrived in January.

The day before the first match of the rugby tour (this was the match that was going to replace the cancelled Oxford match; the site of the game was not announced until late in the night before the match so the demonstrators could not prepare for it), Prime Minister Vorster virtually set up the case for STST:

> It is not for you to say how we should play sport in South Africa. The particular sporting relations as far as the Springboks are concerned, and Britain on the other hand is concerned, is sporting relation of white South Africa with Britain. That has been accepted all along.[145]

That was exactly what STST was protesting. *The Times* [London], however, ran an editorial from the viewpoint that the majority wanted the tour, so it should go on as planned.[146]

The first match was held at Twickenham. There were five hundred police and a thousand demonstrators; the *Guardian* [Manchester] reported that the match could never have taken place without police protection and that the rugby supporters cheered whenever police manhandled a demonstrator. The demonstrations had another effect: the stands were only 25 percent filled.[147]

The *New Statesman* [London] ran a cover story entitled, "Apartheid Is Not a Game," which claimed that in the ninety years of competition with South Africa, "their racial ideas have made more headway with us than ours with them."[148]

The tempo picked up for the second match: a thousand police battled with between fifteen hundred and three thousand demonstrators (depending on whose estimate you believe). Eight demonstrators were hospitalized and one policeman suffered face lacerations.[149]

In a November 9 editorial, *Die Beld* said:

> We have all become accustomed to Britain becoming a haven for all sorts of undesirables from other countries. Nevertheless, it is degrading to see how a nation can allow itself to be dictated to by this bunch of left-wing, workshy, refugee long hairs who in a society of any other country would be rejects.[150]

Arthur Coy of SACA announced that he was trying to arrange for a nonwhite overseas cricket team to come to South Africa to play against its nonwhites.[151] This news did nothing to soften the resolve of STST. (The proposed nonwhite tour never took place.)

Before the third match took place, British Minister of Sport Howell condemned those who ignored the political aspects of sport.[152] It was reported on the same day that the demonstrations were boosting the stock of the Hertzog Verkramptes in South Africa.[153] The third match was the first leg of a swing through Wales, and four hundred peacefully demonstrated at Newport, where the Boks lost for the second time in three matches.[154]

In South Africa, it had been reported that SACA had established a trust fund for nonwhite cricket. Hassan Howa, vice-president of the SACBC, rejected the offer "as a bribe to keep us quiet on the real issue, which is our drive to have our cricketers recognized and given a chance for selection for a Springbok side."[155] By all indications, SACA's offer was another attempt to soften the resolve of the demonstrators.

However, what took place at the fourth match at Swansea ended all chances for such hopes on the part of SACA. The demonstration turned into a bloodbath as police and stewards (men who volunteered to help the police control the demonstrators) collided with the demonstrators.

Most of the British newspapers agreed with Peter Hain that the police and stewards used far too much force. In reading the more than a hundred individual statements from demonstrators who had been caught in the middle, it was easy to see why the normally conservative press took Hain's side. Hugh Geach, STST's secretary, described how he had been carried off the field by his genitals and then thrown into a group of rugby enthusiasts who beat him. Home Secretary Callaghan recommended that no more stewards be used and ordered the constables at all remaining match sites to meet with him. The final results of Swansea: fifteen hundred demonstrators, a thousand police, two hundred stewards, sixty-seven arrests, and ten policemen injured.[156] These did not read like normal sports stories with normal statistics, but, then, this was not a normal game. An editorial in *The Times* [London] was highly critical of STST, claiming it was responsible only for deepending prejudice in Britain.[157] To some extent, Peter Hain agreed in that he said that before Swansea the issue was that of a racially selected team; however, after Swansea, the issue became the social cost of the tour for Britain itself. He maintained that it was not STST that was responsible, but the sports administrators who allowed the tour to go on.[158]

The next match was peaceful, with only 150 demonstrators gathering at Ebbw Vale. The group was led by the Gwent Socialist Charter.[159] But the controversy raged on: Prime Minister Lynch of Ireland announced in the *Dial* that he would not receive the Springboks in Dublin because the team had been racially selected.[160] (Earlier in November, the administrative council of the Irish Labour party called on the IRFU to cancel the Irish segment of the tour.)[161]

MPs in Northern Ireland appealed successfully for the scheduled match in Belfast to be called off because of the fear of violence.[162]

Enoch Powell said the British government should not interfere with the tour and called the behavior of STST demonstrators cowardly, cheap, and nasty.[163]

While there were many accusations being made against STST, it is instructive to examine its "Confidential Briefing on Twickenham." The memorandum, which was never publicly released and, therefore, not meant to convince the public of anything, gave specific instructions to demonstrators about nonviolence:

> Punch-ups outside the ground do not achieve anything positive—non-violent militancy inside does. . . . *At all times, refrain from* provoking violence; if you are pulled free, do not resist, but do not help either—get carried off.[164]

There were three thousand demonstrators at Twickenham: two thousand inside and another one thousand outside. The match was held up for ten minutes when more than 100 ran on the field. There were 22 arrests, and 191 were ejected from the stadium. Peter Hain called this STST's biggest success so far.[165] He changed his mind after the next match at Manchester where there were seven thousand demonstrators and two thousand police. One hundred and fifty were arrested. As a result of the many demonstrations, the Labour party's national executive called for an end to all tours with South Africa.[166]

At this point, STST and SAN-ROC petitioned the MCC to call off the 1970 tour since it would be much easier for demonstrators to invade a cricket field than a rugby field. MCC spokesman Jack Bailey replied that the tour would go on as planned.[167]

There were ninety-eight arrests at the next match at Aberdeen, where a thousand took part in the demonstrations, including MPs and local councilors.[168] Beatle star John Lennon paid the bail for those arrested.[169]

After the Aberdeen match, STST received a major boost when more than a hundred Liberal and Labour MPs sent a letter to the MCC saying they would join the protestors if the tour went on in 1970.[170]

In Edinburgh, more than seven hundred police were called in for the match there after fifteen hundred had marched in protest the night before the match was to take place. The Springboks lost the first test match.[171]

The match at Cardiff was the first where barbed wire surrounded the field for protection. More than two thousand peacefully demonstrated there. On the sixteenth, the South Africans played the Combined Services at Aldershot, where there was a small demonstration outside.[172]

In the meantime, the campaign against the upcoming rugby tour in Ireland had gained more momentum. The Irish Post Office Officials Association announced that it would go on strike if the tour was allowed to go ahead.[173] On December 10, the Irish AAM held a press conference. Dennis Brutus spoke there, disclosing plans, as well as an impressive list of Irish citizens supporting the AAM position.[174]

Nevertheless, the MCC voted unanimously to go ahead with the tour. The leader of the protesting MPs said the decision could only be regarded as a condonation of racialism in sport.[175]

Whether consciously or not, Basil D'Oliveira again helped the MCC cause with a story he wrote for the *Sunday Times* [Johannesburg]:

> I want to play against South African cricketers wherever I am invited to do so. . . . I believe in demonstrations. . . . I use my cricket to demonstrate how a non-white can live and behave. I am a miserable failure unless I am proving that the colour of a man's skin should not decide which cup he should drink from. . . . The thing we non-whites want most of all is freedom. And that means freedom to do what we want to do within a normal society, and that means playing and watching sport with whom and where we choose. If we are going to deny that choice to some who may not agree with us are they likely to help us achieve that right for ourselves? . . . I believe that all who abhor apartheid, and surely none

> can despise it more than I do—should register their protest. But equally I believe that it will be the steady, determined and sincere expression of disgust which will bring about the change. The acts of vandalism and violence will succeed only in turning against us those whom we are trying to impress and those whose help we need.[176]

However, the fear of isolation was taking its toll on South African sports administrators. In mid-December, Jack Cheetham of SACA announced that the 1970 cricket team would be chosen on merit at the same time that Alf Chalmers announced his support of Arthur Ashe's visa application.[177]

John Arlott, a persistent critic of South Africa's sports policy, hailed Cheetham's decision, as well as what he felt provoked it: "The demonstrators, by their action against the Rugby Tour, have in a few months achieved more than the cricket officials have done by fifteen years of polite acquiescence."[178]

Cheetham was joined by Chalmers from tennis and officials from South African athletics and weightlifting in deciding that future touring teams would be chosen on merit. It is worth taking note of which sports these developments occurred in: cricket, in which the 1970 tour had become doubtful; weightlifting, which had just been suspended from the international federation; athletics, in which the 1970 tour of New Zealand had just been cancelled; and tennis, which was potentially riding on the fate of Arthur Ashe's visa application. All of these cases suggest that it was the fear of isolation, and not bridge building through continued sports contact, that led to changes in apartheid sports.

It was, however, entirely another matter as to whether the South African government would allow such policy changes. Both *Dagbreek* [Johannesburg] and *Die Vaderland* [Johannesburg] were up in arms over the new policies, accusing the sports administrators involved with deliberately choosing to make their announcements at a time when the cabinet was on vacation. They predicted that the new policies would be repudiated as soon as the cabinet returned in January.[179]

But in Britain, all eyes were focused on the Twickenham match of December 20, which still loomed importantly for STST. The day began when an STST supporter, Michael Deeney, highjacked the Springbok bus, which he apparently did not know how to drive. As a result, he rather gently crashed into a post office van. The South African players on the bus rewarded him with a broken jaw.[180] The demonstration itself was a tremendous success for STST: five thousand people were peacefully led by the bishops of Southwark, Woolwich, and Stepney, as well as Methodist leader Lord Soper.[181]

Shortly after the match at Twickenham, Dannie Craven, the South African rugby chief, called for the tour to be ended unless there was better protection. Peter Hain replied, "We welcome that the tour should be stopped and suggest to Dr. Craven that he make every endeavor to have his boys home, safe and sound, by Christmas."[182] Hain also decided to change STST's strategy: since they were no longer able to penetrate the playing fields because of the barbed wire and the police, STST adherents would follow the South Africans wherever they went, on and off the fields.[183]

As the Irish segment of the rugby tour approached, Irish Prime Minister Lynch announced that he could not cancel the matches in a free country.[184] Then the Transport and General Workers Union joined the Irish Congress of Trade Unions in a boycott of the tour (this meant that no services would be provided during the tour), and divinity students of five orders led a fast outside the IRFU offices.[185]

As 1969 came to a close, it must have seemed to the South Africans that things would have to get better in terms of their sports situation. They could not know that 1970 was going to be even worse.

JANUARY-MAY 1970

The first five months of 1970 were devastating in terms of South Africa's international sports relations. From South Africa's side of the story, almost all developments through April were to some degree, affected by the general election. The pressure from the extreme right-wing Verkramptes resulted in a hard line on a number of issues until the election was over; however, by that time it was almost too late for South African sports.

In January, the government refused to allow Arthur Ashe, the black American tennis star, to compete in South Africa. This led to South Africa's suspension from the 1970 Davis cup. The rugby tour of England

and Ireland was completed in January, but only after tens of thousands had demonstrated against it as a prelude to the 1970 cricket tour. From January through May, intense pressure built up at the highest levels, including the prime minister and the leader of the opposition, who took predictably opposite stands on the merits of the tour. It was finally cancelled at the insistence of the government.

Within South Africa, the Japanese-Chinese controversy and the case of Papwa Sewgolum were once again in the news, and the nonwhite South African games were finally held in relative obscurity. There were further controversies in golf, rugby, and other athletics.

Internationally, in addition to England, South Africa became entangled with no fewer than twenty other nations over its sports policy. South Africa was banned from three international championships. Its sports relations were twice the subject of debate at the United Nations. But the ultimate international blow was South Africa's exclusion from the Olympic movement in May. By that time, the line-up of nations for or against South Africa in sports was drawn almost strictly along racial and political lines.

In addition to all the pressures that had built up over the previous eleven years, the events of the first five months of 1970 opened the floodgates of public criticism of South Africa's sports policy inside South Africa among white sportsmen and officials. What the threat of international sports isolation could not quite do, the fact of that isolation did.

SOUTH AFRICAN SPORTS RELATIONS WITH BRITAIN

In his New Year's speech, Prime Minister Vorster dashed whatever hopes the sports officials who had spoken out in December in favor of teams chosen on merit had when he announced that no multiracial teams from South Africa could tour overseas.[186] Peter Hain commented:

> If the MCC ever needed a final prod in the back, then Mr. Vorster's predictable announcement that apartheid would remain firmly within sport must surely have done so. The MCC cannot honestly go ahead with the tour.[187]

The MCC and East Africa

The MCC had been scheduled to send a team to tour Kenya, Uganda, and Zambia in early 1970. On December 31, 1969, SAN-ROC called on those nations to cancel the tour in light of the MCC's decision to go ahead with the South African tour.[188] A week later, the tour had been cancelled.[189] Masinde Muliro, the Kenyan minister responsible for sport, explained:

> I find myself in a very embarrassing position to see Britain inviting South African rugby and cricket teams, and then sending the same British sides on tours to Commonwealth African countries. As long as the MCC has been playing matches with South Africa, I do not want to see the MCC playing in Kenya.[190]

The next day, Mayor Isaac Lugonzo of Nairobi called for a Kenyan boycott of the Commonwealth games since some of the participants had competed with South Africans.[191]

The Rugby Tour in Ireland

The Springbok rugby team went to Ireland for its most difficult test of the tour. The difficulty was no longer measured in sports terms, but in political terms. The Irish AAM had sponsored a declaration of protest by 150 prominent MPs, trade Union officials, educators, clergy, and councilmen.[192]

When the team arrived, the unions blocked out the press at the airport and also cut off telephone service at the hotel where the team stayed as demonstrators chanted in the street throughout the night.[193]

The Fine Gael party condemned apartheid but said that the tour should not be interfered with in any way.[194] Hugh Byrne, the leader of the Fine Gael party, had a reception for the Springboks in the Dial in the face of two hundred demonstrators clashing with police outside.[195] The *Irish Press* [Dublin] condemned such street politics and warned what might happen at the Lansdowne Road match against South Africa.[196]

That match was, indeed, something to see. Bernadette Devlin, the controversial MP, led more than ten thousand demonstrators. The playing field was surrounded by barbed wire as the South Africans failed to win an unprecedented third consecutive test match.[197]

After the match, twelve police were hurt and three demonstrators hospitalized outside the Springbok's hotel in Dublin. Bernadette Devlin charged the police with brutality against the demonstrators.[198] Police were forced to allow her to enter the hotel since she was an MP. Once inside, Devlin cornered Springbok team captain, Dawie de Villiers, and explained to him what the protests were about.[199] This was surely the most frustrating segment of the tour for the South Africans.

In London, Omar Kureishi, Pakistan's leading cricket commentator, warned Britain that Pakistan, India, Ceylon, and the West Indies would break off cricket relations with Britain if the South African cricket tour was not cancelled.[200] Commonwealth race relations were clearly in jeopardy as a result of the tour. On the same day, STST announced that twenty-three unions in Britain had given their support to STST's objectives in its campaign.[201]

In South Africa, Hassan Howa, a leader of nonwhite cricket, called SACA's financial offer to help nonwhite cricket in South Africa a betrayal: "Two-thousand years ago it was 30 pieces of silver and in 1969 it's R50,000 for a betrayal."[202]

STST and the Cricket Grounds Attack

On January 20, there was a bold indication of what might be ahead if the cricket tour was allowed to proceed: eleven country cricket grounds were attacked and vandalized during the night in what was obviously a well-planned action. Peter Hain denied that STST had anything to do with the raids, but Louis Eaks, chairman of the Young Liberals (one of the groups working with STST), said his group was responsible.[203] British Minister of Sport Howell called the actions "lunatic" and said they could "not possibly be justified under any circumstances and I utterly condemn such conduct."[204]

The End of the Rugby Tour

As the rugby tour came to a close, two events in South Africa cast further doubt on the possibility of the cricket tour taking place. First,

Arthur Ashe was denied a visa to enter South Africa, starting another worldwide protest against South African sports policy. Second, the SACA barred the multiracial international cricket Cavaliers from entering South Africa.[205] This brought on more protests.

However, it was still what STST had itself accomplished that worried the MCC most. *The Times* [London] estimated that STST had brought out more than fifty thousand protestors for the rugby tour, with more than four hundred arrests.[206] Peter Hain commented:

> Our chances of stopping the tour are 100 percent. If it does begin, I think we shall send the tourists back within a month. Official Coloured groups, including West Indians, Pakistanis, and Indians all pledged support of demonstrations vs. cricket.[207]

In an important development, British police spokesmen came out against the tour at the end of January. Inspector Reg Gale, chairman of the Police Federation, said, "Anything which throws an extra load on the police we can certainly do without."[208] Another spokesman said:

> We are certainly concerned at the burden on the police and at the public disorder which accompanies these tours. Already a great number of policemen have had to be diverted from other work—largely at public expense— . . . to cover Springbok tours, and I understand the cricket tour will be much more difficult to deal with.[209]

With the rugby tour over, Corrie Bornman, manager of the Springboks, finally said what he had obviously been holding in for a long time:

> The last three months have been an ordeal to which I would never again subject young sportsmen. . . . I would be a fool to deny that this awful undercurrent didn't affect the team and their performances. . . . Naturally, most of the players are not too keen to return to England. Can you blame them?[210]

The 1970 Cricket Tour

At that very moment, SACA officials were in London conferring with the MCC. They decided that the tour would go on as planned.[211]

With his players safely home, Prime Minister Vorster lashed out at the demonstrators: "It is not their [sports lovers'] faults that communists and hooligans were allowed to interfere with players in a way which one does not expect in a host country."[212]

Frank Cousins, chairman of the Community Relations Commission, warned Home Secretary Callaghan that the nonwhite population of Britain would be seriously disturbed if the tour was allowed to go on,[213] but a public-opinion poll, conducted by the Opinion Research Center for the *Evening Standard* [London], confirmed that the British public did, in fact, want the cricket tour to proceed. A full 62 percent agreed the MCC was correct to issue the invitation, while 48 percent felt it was the demonstrators who had brought politics into sport.[214]

The two most important figures in British politics took positions on the tour in February: Conservative party leader Edward Heath said the tour should not be cancelled;[215] Prime Minister Wilson announced that he would not attend the tour and doubted the wisdom behind it: "Once the South Africans had said that they were not taking a player we wanted to send, I would have rather thought that put them beyond the pale of civilized cricket."[216]

On February 9, the 285,000-member National Union of Public Employees came out in opposition to the tour.[217] If it was true that the majority of British citizens wanted the tour to go on, there could be no doubt that the forces opposing the tour were growing. More important, while the demonstrations against the rugby tour were primarily led by the young, more and more establishment figures were joining them by February. This would be a key to the eventual cancellation and had a strong effect on the MCC's decision in mid-February to reduce the tour from eighteen weeks, with twenty-eight matches on twenty-three grounds, to eleven weeks, with twelve matches on eight grounds.[218] It was also announced that Lords was to be completely surrounded by barbed wire. Peter Hain said, "This seems to be the first round to us."[219] The Reverend David Sheppard predicted, "Today's decision means the tour will take place under siege conditions."[220]

Shortly after announcing its decision, the MCC published an official document, detailing its reasons for going ahead with the tour. Among the reasons were:

1. The MCC deplores apartheid.
2. The MCC's responsibility is for the long-term well-being of cricketers.
3. The MCC is encouraged to learn that SACA would choose its team on merit (although it stated that no nonwhites were qualified).
4. SACA does not endorse apartheid in sport.
5. The MCC would not opt for expediency and cancel the tour in face of illegal acts by a small minority of the British public.[221]

While not doubting the MCC's sincerity, its naiveté was another matter. Eight nonwhite cricket nations had all but said they would not compete with the MCC if the tour went on; therefore, the MCC's judgment of what was in the long-term interest of British cricket was, at best, doubtful. In view of Prime Minister Vorster's New Year's speech, it is also difficult to comprehend how the MCC thought that SACA could choose its team on merit. While it might have been true that SACA did not *endorse* apartheid in sport, neither had it ever *condemned* it. Finally, as for the small minority opposing the tour, the MCC must have realized that it was no longer such a small minority.

On March 7, STST held a national conference in London to discuss racism in sport and to plan its strategy for the 1970 tour. The conference was closed to the public, and security precautions had been taken so that the meeting could not be infiltrated by those opposing STST. That those precautions were not adequate was immediately brought to the attention of all when an older member of the MCC occupied the speakers' table, saying he was adopting STST's tactics to let them know the MCC's point of view.

Although the incident itself was amusing, it changed the mood of the meeting as paranoia that the meeting had been further infiltrated set in. Many stories circulated about conspiracy charges being brought against the organizers. Therefore, there was little, if any, organizing done at this meeting. What the meeting did was to point out the diversity of opinion within STST. Some, mainly older delegates, opposed the tour but refused to condone direct action; others, mainly the younger delegates, not only favored direct action, but violent direct action (such as had taken place in the January raids of the cricket grounds). But the vast majority of the five hundred delegates present favored nonviolent direct action. Commenting that it would be foolish to take violent actions now that STST had become such an important national movement, Hain announced a fourfold strategy for it:

1. To get the tour cancelled before it began, rather than after it started, as some wanted.
2. To lobby for Afro-Asian support (this job was delegated to SAN-ROC).
3. To get unions to "black" the tour (there was strong union representation at the conference).
4. To alert the community to the danger to race relations in Britain if the tour went on (there was also strong representation of non-white groups at the conference).[222]

Two weeks later, the West Indian Campaign Against Apartheid Cricket was formed. Its spokesman, Gary Burton, said:

> We cannot guarantee the safety of any MCC player participating in this tour should they come to the West Indies in the future. Our object is to call on every black player to refuse to participate in the tour and emphasize that their participation would be an insult to every black player.[223]

As if to prove what was happening to race relations in Britain, Peter Tombs, leader of the Anti-Demonstration Association, warned:

> These West Indians come to this country as guests and they had a bloody cheek to say the least. They are in Britain on sufferance and must behave themselves. We are becoming so overwhelmed by the colour question in this country that we are allowing these people to dictate to us.[224]

In the meantime, the chief constable of Lancashire, William Palfrey, proved that the fears of the STST organizers were not completely unwarranted: he warned protestors that they would be indicted in higher courts for conspiracy.[225]

It was announced on April 4 that a group of two hundred people in favor of the tour would travel with the South Africans to "stamp out demonstrations before they start."[226]

Just as things were beginning to look bleak for the demonstrators, more support began to show. The Pakistan Board of Control for Cricket came out against the tour and told its players on English teams not to compete with the South Africans.[227] The Association of Cinematography, TV and Allied Technicians urged its fourteen thousand members not to cover the tour.[228] John Arlott, the most prestigious British cricket commentator, who had covered every British test match for the BBC since World War II, announced that he would not cover the 1970 tour.[229]

That night, Prime Minister Wilson, in a televised interview, said he hoped people "would demonstrate against the South African cricket tour. Everyone should be free to demonstrate against apartheid." He called the MCC's decision ill-judged.[230] This speech was a major turning point in terms of who was going to support the demonstrators.

Conservative MPs condemned Wilson. Stephen Hastings spoke out:

> The Prime Minister's words can be interpreted as a direct encouragement to lawlessness. Any uncertainty about the Government position or the Prime Minister's position could lead to a breakdown of law and order abhorrent to most people and an intolerable burden on the police. As a result of that broadcast, this uncertainty is virtually complete.[231]

Shadow Chancellor Ian Macleod called Wilson's statement an utter act of irresponsibility. He went on:

> The silent majority will go unrepresented unless people of all parties speak now for them. . . . But there can be no respect for a Prime Minister who deliberately encourages a minority whose declared object is to stop the majority from enjoying their lawful pleasures.[232]

Shadow Home Secretary Quintin Hogg warned that if anyone was hurt in the demonstrations, Wilson and Callaghan would be largely responsible.[233] Although Peter Hain pledged that there would be no violence by STST militant demonstrators, this made little difference; the issue of law and order was clearly to be an important one in the upcoming British election.[234] Any tour disruptions would almost surely be to the advantage of the Conservative party. (The South African election had just been concluded by the time Hogg and Macleod spoke, with Vorster soundly defeating the Verkramptes but receiving unexpected opposition from what is known in South Africa as the left.)

But the controversy was merely warming up. Archbishop of Canterbury Ramsey warned that the tour was placing an increasing strain on race relations in Britain.[235] The MCC then showed one of the greatest problems when it started a fund-raising drive for £250,000 to cover the costs of policing the cricket grounds during the tour.[236]

In a period of eight days at the end of April, STST had five major coups. The British Council of Churches called on its six million parishioners to boycott the tour.[237] On the next day, the general secretary of the Trades Union Congress, Vic Feather, urged TUC's nine million members to boycott the tour.[238] What was undoubtedly the most significant of the five coups was the announcement by the Supreme Council that its thirteen Commonwealth members would boycott the Edinburgh Commonwealth games in July if the tour went ahead as planned.[239] SAN-ROC had done its job well at the March meeting of the Supreme Council (Chris de Broglio and Wilfred Brutus represented SAN-ROC). The prospect of an all-white Commonwealth games was an ominous one, not only for sports but for Commonwealth relations in general. Sandy Duncan, the secretary of the organizing committee of the games, said that they would be held anyway.[240] Alex Ross, chairman of the British and Commonwealth Games Federation, flew to Lagos to meet the SCSA's Abraham Ordia, the leader of the Supreme Council for Sport in Africa. He reported that the African countries would indeed boycott the games.[241]

Granada television announced that it would not broadcast any of the cricket matches because it felt that "it would be wrong to present these matches as entertainment."[242] This was followed by the television technicians in London calling on the BBC to cancel its contract with the MCC for the rest of the matches.[243] It was announced on April 26 that the Queen would not attend any of the cricket matches.[244] The blows to the MCC were coming in rapidly at this point, but it still did not budge.

The issue of potential damage to race relations in Britain was again raised, this time by the Association of Community Relations Officers, which called for the tour to be cancelled.[245] Peter Hain and the National Council for Civil Liberties called for a pledge from the police that they would not single out nonwhite protestors and intimidate them.[246]

Prime Minister Wilson reaffirmed his stand on demonstrating against apartheid, but added that he hoped the MCC would cancel the invitation so that demonstrations would not be necessary. Edward Heath, in turn, reaffirmed his opposite stand and said he was glad that the South Africans were coming.[247]

With tensions in Britain rapidly rising, both the *Guardian* [Manchester] and the *Observer* [London] suggested that the MCC cancel the tour. The *Observer's* political analyst warned that if the tour did go on, there would be mass violence from right- or left-wing extremists. This would occur at the time of the election and would certainly damage Wilson's campaign in which law and order had become the main issue, largely due to the tour.[248] In a poll conducted by the Opinion Research Center for the *Sunday Times* [London], 55 percent of the British public thought that Wilson's stand was wrong, while only 33 percent thought that he was correct.[249]

In South Africa, leading cricketer Peter Pollock, said:

> I see these demonstrations and riots as part of a Communist-inspired idea to smash the vital links which have for years forced the Western nations firmly together. . . . A principle is involved and any measure of success for this kind of defiance would see the idea spreading far beyond the realms of sport.[250]

In order to blunt such criticism and appeal to the masses of the British public who did not want to join direct action demonstrations, a group of respected British citizens, led by Conservative MP Sir Edward Boyle, Labour MP Reginald Prentice, and the Bishop of Woolwich, David Sheppard, formed the Fair Cricket Campaign (FCC). The FCC, which said that it would lead massive peaceful demonstrations, feared that the tour would lead to uneasy racial relations in the Commonwealth.[251]

Of the FCC, Peter Hain said:

> We don't see this as a split. It is putting into organized form a difference in tactics which has always existed between more moderate demonstrators and militants over direct action. It will bring out people who would not want to be associated with us.[252]

Things were happening rapidly in May. By May 15, India, Jamaica, Trinidad, Guyana, and Barbados had announced their intentions to withdraw from the Commonwealth games if the tour began.[253] The government of Pakistan cancelled a fourteen-match tour of Britain.[254] Malaysia and Singapore expressed their concern over the tour.[255]

Alex Ross of the Commonwealth games met with the MCC to attempt to get it to reconsider, without success.[256] To make matters worse, the MCC announced that its new president was Sir Cyril Hawker, who was also chairman of the Standard Bank of South Africa.[257] At the same time, the MCC also wrote a letter to all members asking for volunteer stewards to help the police at the matches.[258]

Another public opinion poll in early May, conducted by the *Daily Mail* [Johannesburg], showed that 53 percent were in favor of the tour, with only 28 percent opposed. Eighty-two percent of those surveyed opposed demonstrations.[259]

Such was the climate that led to an emergency debate in Parliament. Callaghan said that, although the police could certainly cope with the demonstrators, race relations in Britain would be so seriously damaged that the MCC should call off the tour immediately.[260] Philip Noel-Baker, in his last speech in Parliament, said that the tour could wreck the entire concept of the Commonwealth.[261] Minister of Sport Howell pointed out that twelve of the eighteen nations scheduled to compete in the Commonwealth games had already withdrawn, three more were unsure whether to participate, and only three (all white) were definitely playing.[262] William Hamilton (Labour) and David Steel (Liberal) called on the government to cancel the tour.[263]

Conservative MPs pointed out that it was completely hypocritical to have military, economic, and political ties with South Africa and to then cut off sporting ties. Boyd-Carpenter reminded his fellow MPs that the British and South African navies were at that moment conducting joint exercises.[264] There was no vote taken, but the government put all responsibility squarely on the shoulders of the MCC.[265]

An editorial in the *Star* [Johannesburg] commented that it was sad to see the British Parliament "scrape the very bottom of the barrel of emotionalism." The same editorial called STST the best friends the Verkramptes had because it was causing a severe backlash in South Africa itself.[266] An editorial in the *Rand Daily Mail* [Johannesburg] said that the only way that the tour could take place would be if the SACA made a clear repudiation of apartheid in sport.[267] No such repudiation was forthcoming.

In Britain, reactions to the debate and the prospect of demonstrations continued to be mixed. The Anti-Demonstration Association announced that it would photograph the demonstrators and give the pictures to the police.[268] Conservative MP Joseph Hiley said, "One can see the sinister head of the extreme left, the communists, behind what is happening today. It is a mistake to give way to the clamour of the left-wingers."[269] But the *Sunday Times* [London] finally came out against the tour in an editorial the day after South Africa was expelled from the Olympic movement.[270] The Police Federation's journal, *Police,* realized that "there is a great deal of uneasiness . . . over the question of police being employed as paid henchmen to separate the opposing factions during the forthcoming tour."[271] The Inner London Education Authority decided that none of its facilities could be used for the tour.[272]

With the tour virtually collapsing, the MCC announced that it would call a full meeting, presumably to cancel the tour. But on May 18, there was an important leak: the MCC had paid a £50,000 premium on an insurance policy that would pay it £250,000 if the tour was cancelled by the South African government, the British government, SACA, or by mass disturbances *after* the tour began.[273] The idealistic arguments the MCC used about its concern for the well-being of cricket suddenly took on a hollow ring.

When the MCC cancelled all appointments for the day of its meeting, including one with a deputation of MPs opposed to the tour, the *Evening Standard* [London] interpreted it as a sure sign that the tour was off and even ran such a headline on the night of the meeting.[274] An opinion poll conducted by Social and Community Planning Research showed a dramatic shift of opinion: 58 percent wanted the tour cancelled, a shift of 30 percent in less than two weeks, and 62 percent now approved of demonstrations against the tour.[275]

The MCC no longer had to fear losing face by cancelling the tour: the IOC had expelled South Africa, the British government opposed the tour, and the British public had joined the government in its collective opinion. However, the MCC, in an astonishing move, voted for the tour. There was a vague promise that there would be no more tours unless they were multiracial, and the date of the first test match at Lords was changed because it was the same day as the election.[276]

Hundreds of police said that they would refuse to work at the cricket grounds as a result of the MCC's decision.[277] As the crisis deepened, all the British newspapers reported that the MCC's decision would substantially help the Conservative party.[278]

From the time that the Fair Cricket Campaign had been organized, Peter Hain and STST had been quiet, apparently hoping that the swing in public opinion would force the MCC to change its mind. But with the May 19 decision, Hain's patience was worn out:

> We intend to press ahead with renewed attempts to stop this racialist spectacle. Demonstrations and disruptions will be staged at every match. In the coming months we shall see the greatest show of opposition to the tyranny of apartheid ever in Britain.
>
> How can the Council claim to be in favour of multi-racial cricket and yet proceed with a blatantly racialist tour? The hypocritical attitude is an arrogant insult to Britain's coloured community.
>
> While British cricket equivocates and appeases, white South Africans will be laughing. Mr. Vorster will enjoy the spectacle of disorder in Britain.
>
> Our prime aim is to get it [the tour] cancelled. I don't think the tour is on yet. There are a number of pressures which still could be exploited and which could be built up.[279]

THE CANCELLATION

Hain was not alone. Home Secretary Callaghan invited the MCC to meet with him to discuss the potential problems of the tour. Callaghan met with Maurice Allom, MCC chairman, and S. C. Griffith, MCC secretary, for three hours and offered them a face-saving device by announcing that the government was willing to take the blame for the cancellation of the tour and it might defray some of the costs for the cancellation.[280]

The government gave four reasons for what amounted to a request for cancellation:

1. If the tour was allowed to go on, it would destroy the Commonwealth games.
2. The tour would have a serious effect on race relations in Britain.
3. The tour was having a divisive effect on society in general in Britain.
4. The tour was having a serious effect on Commonwealth relations in general.[281]

Of the entire situation, Callaghan said:

> A body as responsible as the Cricket Council would think very carefully before it refused to consider a request by the Government on the grounds of broad public policy. I have not the power to stop the tour and, if I had, I would not use it. It would be monstrous for a Government to get involved in such a procedure. If they [MCC] want the Government to carry the can, then at this stage we are quite prepared to do it.[282]

Despite what Callaghan termed "monstrous," the government had, in fact, become involved in such a procedure. It was merely a formality when the MCC cancelled the tour the next day:

> The Cricket Council today considered the formal request of Her Majesty's Government to withdraw the invitation to the SACA to tour the United Kingdom in 1970 contained in your letter of May 21, 1970.
>
> The Council were of the opinion that they had no alternative but to accede the request and are informing the SACA accordingly.[283]

The official reaction in South Africa was predictable. Minister of Sport Waring said, "It amounts to bowing down to irresponsible elements that manifest a total disregard for sport and the rights of others.[284] Minister of the Interior Marias Viljoen said:

> We know, of course, that the people behind the Olympic decision are the same Communist-inspired and Communist-paid agents who are behind the agitation in England to wreck the cricket tour. The attitude of the Nationalist Party is clear on this issue—we shall not budge. To bow to this anti-white dictatorship will offer no real solution.[285]

And this from Prime Minister Vorster in a speech made in Rhodesia:

> Any lawyer will tell you that if you once pay a blackmailer you will have to meet increased demands as time goes on. For a Government to submit so easily and so willingly to open blackmail is to me unbelievable.
>
> It is not cricket or sport that loses, but the forces of law and order. . . . This particular cricket relationship between South Africa and Great Britain was a relationship of the MCC with white South Africans.
>
> Even in previous years, when there was nothing against it whatsoever, Britain did not include coloured players when sending a team to South Africa, because they recognised the particular sporting relationship which existed between the countries. . . . As far as the long-term outlook is concerned, I am not despondent at all because, as I have said, it is not sport that has suffered a momentary defeat . . . at some time somebody has got to climb down. I am firmly on the ground, and I do not see that I can climb down.[286]

The South African press generally supported Vorster's position. The *Natal Mercury*'s [Durban] editorial on the decision charged: "Mr. Harold Wilson and his cabinet colleagues emerge from this black day for cricket as men who were bold enough to wound but lacked the courage to kill cleanly."[287] The *Sunday Express* [Johannesburg] and the *Sunday Times* [Johannesburg] both blamed Wilson's government for supporting the demonstrators and, thus, increasing the support for their cause.[288] The *Star* [Johannesburg] regretted that the tour had been called off but felt that, in the long run, the decision would benefit the relations between the two countries as the wounds would heal quickly with the MCC on South Africa's side.[289]

The most interesting reaction from the South African press was a call for a national sports conference by the *Rand Daily Mail* [Johannesburg]. The conference would be designed to redirect South Africa's sports policy so that South Africa could continue to compete internationally.[290] The idea for such a conference quickly caught on with many South African sportsmen and sports administrators in an unprecedented level of calls for a change in policy.

In Britain, the Conservative party was ready to seize the government's action as a crucial election issue. MP Quintin Hogg called the whole operation "a classic illustration of the inability of this Government to preserve freedom in this country, or to maintain law and order."[291] Reginald Maudling, the deputy leader of the opposition, flatly condemned the government:

> The Government used their full authority to force a group of British citizens to abandon an activity which was peaceful and lawful and would have given enjoyment to thousands of their fellow citizens. The Government acted under the pressure of threats from abroad and at home, the one amounting to blackmail, the other including threats of violence.
>
> It was a clear concession to those who advocate force and intolerance in our society. For theirs was the victory; and the defeat went to those who were going about their lawful pursuits.[292]

The leader of the Support The Seventy Tour group, John Jackson, said that the tour was not called off by the MCC but by a weak government, whose support for the demonstrators "makes the triumph of the campus bums over democracy a major election issue."[293] (The government's decision on the tour did, in fact, become a major election issue, although its impact on the defeat of the Labour party is beyond the scope of this study.)

The reactions of those who had opposed the tour were not of joyous victory but of commitment to future action and progress toward non-racialism. Peter Hain hoped

> people will regard this as a beginning, not an end, an example for protest movements in Britain of what you can do with direct action

> and militant non-violence. . . . We want to see a broad anti-apartheid militant movement. We've got the immigrant groups working with us, and this has never happened before.[294]

A leader of one of the West Indian groups, Jeff Crawford, said, "I would hope that the momentum we have gained for the fight against racialism will go on in Britain."[295] Brutus commented that "the way is open to real progress toward non-racial cricket in South Africa."[296] David Sheppard of the FCC added:

> This decision is a victory for reason. It is not a surrender to intimidation or blackmail. By its decision, the Cricket Council has commited itself firmly to the principle of non-racial cricket in the future.[297]

The case of British-South African sports relations provides a dramatic example of how a sports issue can have critical political and racial effects, both domestically and internationally. The extraordinary concern is demonstrated by the number of groups in England formed solely to confront the cricket issue: the Anti-Demonstration Association and the Support The Seventy Tour groups for the relationship, and STST, the FCC and the West Indian campaign against; by the number of groups already formed that became involved: the British AAM, the Irish AAM, SAN-ROC, and the Supreme Council for Sport in Africa, all opposing, of course, the direction chosen by the MCC; by the community relations groups that protested the potential effects of the tour; by the involvement of the unions and the churches in opposition to the tour; by the actions of the nonwhite cricket-playing nations opposing the tour; by the effects on elections in both South Africa and England; and, finally, by the fact that the ultimate decisions in all cases were made at the highest levels of the South African and British governments and not by the sports authorities themselves.

THE ARTHUR ASHE AFFAIR

In another story of politics, race, and sport conducted at the highest levels of government, Arthur Ashe, the black American tennis star, was denied a visa to enter South Africa to play in the national championships. Almost immediately after this was announced in South Africa on January 27, all leading South African sportsmen and officials (with the most notable exception of Arthur Coy of the SACA) expressed dismay over the decision and predicted that it would lead to further exclusion in world sport.[298] The *Star* [Johannesburg] called it a pathetic decision, and reactions from around the world immediately condemned the decision.[209]

A United States Department of State spokesman said the decision would damage "correct" United States-South African relations.[300] George Hauser, the head of the American Committee on Africa (ACOA), called the decision "a dramatic demonstration of the commitment of South Africa to a racist position" and vowed that the ACOA would fight to have South Africa excluded from all sports bodies.[301]

To counter the criticism, the South African ambassador in Washington, D.C., claimed that Ashe had to bear "a share of the responsibility of depriving South African nonwhites of the opportunity of taking part in the Olympics."[302] He apparently expected that the public would believe Ashe had been denied a visa because he had previously hurt nonwhite South Africans.

Ashe himself was reluctant to talk: "The issue is so politically hot and volatile that I do not want to shoot off my mouth."[303] He added:

> I thought that I was doing South Africa a favor. I bent over backwards to be nice to them—to the extent that some of the black militants back at home think I'm nuts.[304]

Alastair Martin, president of the United States Lawn Tennis Association (USLTA), called the decision "a clear case of racial discrimination and the rules of the ILTF prohibit this" and warned that USLTA would take vigorous action to have South Africa expelled from the ILTF.[305]

South African Minister of Sport Waring blamed Ashe's general "antagonism toward South Africa" for the decision and said that Ashe's real motives were political.[306] *The Times* [London] and the *Guardian* [Manchester] both blamed the decision on the upcoming election in South Africa, meaning Vorster did not want any more criticism of his outward policy.[307]

In general, however, the decision had the opposite effect in South Africa. Herstigte (Reformed) National party MP, Louis Stofberg, said the government was in deep trouble over its sports policy. He added:

> On the one hand the Government says Ashe will be welcomed in a mixed US Davis Cup team, but on the other hand he will not be allowed into the country because of his political enmity towards South Africa. Why should he exhibit a different political attitude as a member of a team? Why does his political attitude serve as a reason for his exclusion in one case, but not in the other?[308]

In the midst of all the athletes and politicians condemning the Ashe ban came two supporting statements. The first was that of Margaret Court, the women's tennis star:

> I love South Africa. I have many friends there. Of course, I will keep on going to play. It is a tragedy that politics has come into sport—but if you ask me, South Africa has the racial situation rather better organized than anyone else, certainly much better than the United States.[309]

Britain's reigning Wimbledon champion, Ann Jones, asked:

> But who are we to judge? The racial situation in both the United States and Britain is difficult. It is not easy to offer easy solutions. I would not support a boycott against South Africa because of this act. I would continue to play against South Africans or in South Africa in the hope of an improvement in the situation.[310]

The Ashe affair had introduced the issue of apartheid in sport to the general public of the United States for the first time (those involved in the 1968 movement had been a relatively small segment of the population). The South Africans who had competed most regularly in the United States were the golfers, particularly Gary Player and Harold Henning.

Player was probably aware of what might happen to him if Ashe was banned when he asked Minister for Planning Carel de Wet to admit Ashe and to drop the renewed ban on Papwa Sewgolum ten days before the decision was announced.[311] Two days after the decision, the United States Department of State asked Harold Henning to leave the U.S. tour for his own protection. Henning had already been threatened by phone.[312]

Harry Edwards, the 1968 leader of the OCHR, wrote to Secretary of State William Rogers:

> The regrettable situation surrounding the case of Mr. Arthur Ashe gives even more immediate urgency to call for the banning of South African athletes from this country. So long as the Union of South Africa continues to exclude black Americans from participation in athletic contests within its political boundaries . . . it is unjustifiable that South Africans should be allowed to participate in this country.[313]

In March, Ashe himself said he feared for Player's life.[314] In spite of constant threats, however, Player was only minimally harrassed when he played. One such incident occurred in April when John F. Williams, the director of the model cities program in San Diego, followed Player around the course in the Tournament of Champions. Williams wore a shirt that said, "No Ashe, No Player." Player was, as usual, accompanied by the local police.[315]

It was not until Oliver S. Crosby, country director of the Office of Southern African Affairs of the Department of State, testified before the Subcommittee on African Affairs of the House Committee on Foreign Affairs that the full details of the Ashe affair were known. Crosby related the following sequence of events:

December 3, 1969: Minister of Sport Waring took exception to SALTU acceptance of Ashe's application, alleging that Ashe was going to South Africa to engage in political activity.

December 7, 1969: Secretary of State Rogers met Ashe in Paris and offered to help him obtain a visa.

December 15, 1969: On the same day, Ashe applied for the visa in New York; United States Ambassador Rountree met with the South African foreign minister in Pretoria on behalf of Ashe; and Assistant Secretary of State Newsom met the South African ambassador in Washington. It was pointed out in both Pretoria and Washington that Rogers had a personal interest in the case; the Department of State vouched for Ashe in that he wanted to go only to play tennis; the United States warned that a denial of the visa would harm relations between the countries. Rountree later met Prime Minister Vorster, who promised to give the matter careful consideration at a cabinet meeting.

January 27, 1970: Vorster and Foreign Minister Muller both personally told Rountree that the cabinet had unanimously rejected the visa application and that Ashe could come to South Africa as a member of the U.S. Davis cup team.[316]

Dennis Brutus of SAN-ROC testified before the same committee the next day (February 5). He told the committee he regretted that the United States did not act in accordance with the United Nations resolution of December 2, 1968, that called on all countries to break off sporting relations with South Africa. He went on:

> I do not desire their isolation. But as long as they do not play the game the way the rest of the world plays it, as long as they are guilty of allowing the sport to be dictated by the political and racial considerations, I believe they deserve to be excluded.[317]

In Wellington, the New Zealand Lawn Tennis Association was approached by Tom Newnham of CARE to support the move by the USLTA to have South Africa excluded from tennis competition.[318] On March 10, USLTA announced that it had called a special meeting of the Davis cup nations for March 23 in London to consider South Africa in light of the Ashe affair.

On the day of the meeting, Dennis Brutus testified before the United Nations Special Committee on Apartheid, which was holding hearings on race and sport, and proposed:

1. The U.N. directly approach Britain and New Zealand to stop their sports relations with South Africa.
2. The U.N. set up a coordinated program to ensure that South Africa be excluded from all world sports by the end of 1971.
3. All nations should follow Kenya's lead and break off relations with any nations that compete with South Africa.
4. The special committee should hold an international conference to coordinate the activities of all the pressure groups.

5. Pressure should be put on the United States to ban all South African athletes unless they make a stand against apartheid.[319]

He indicated that South Africa would not be allowed in the 1972 Olympics and this would be a strong point in the U.N.'s arguments. When the committee made its recommendations in April, it used virtually the same wording and proposals that Brutus had used in March.[320] Brutus was still the dominant figure in the movement for nonracial sport in South Africa.

At the Davis cup meeting itself, South Africa was excluded; members feared its inclusion would have endangered the competition because of boycotts and visa problems. Neither racial discrimination nor the Ashe affair was mentioned in the resolution, however. The United States, Malaysia, Uruguay, the U.S.S.R., and Australia voted for the resolution to exclude South Africa, while France and Britain voted against it. Australia's vote was apparently determined by the threat of losing the 1974 Commonwealth games.[321] The pressure continued to work its toll on those nations with traditional ties with South Africa, as well as those without them. (Two weeks before, Australia had decided to suspend athletic relations with South Africa.[322] This decision was reached after much controversy within Australian athletic circles over a proposed 1970 South African tour in which South Africa's athletes were not going to be allowed to wear the Springbok colors.)[323]

Donald Dell, the former Davis cup Captain and Ashe's lawyer, told the press after the London Davis cup decision:

> Emotionally, I'm sure Arthur is pleased with this result. Naturally, he made his request for a visa hoping that it would be granted so that he could win the South African Open Championship before a stadium full of whites. But if his request were denied, he thought that South Africa would have to be suspended by the Davis Cup nations. That was one of the very reasons why he applied to play. But he also wants to emphasize that he does not want individual South African players to be affected in the United States because of the situation. Cliff Drysdale and Ray Moore led the South African players' fight for Arthur.[324]

Ashe himself commented: "I would much rather have seen South Africa alter its attitude than have it banned from the Davis Cup."[325] South

African tennis players said they felt that the decision was inevitable, but they hoped they could continue to play as individuals with a minimum of harrassment.[326] SALTU head Alf Chalmers predicted that if South Africa gave "a bit," it would be readmitted to the Davis cup.[327]

Editorials in the *Star* [Johannesburg] and *Rand Daily Mail* [Johannesburg] pointed out that South Africa had been excluded from the Davis cup for racial and not political reasons.[328] The *Rand Daily Mail* [Johannesburg] agreed:

> Nothing could have illustrated more sharply the fact that it is racialism not politics, that is causing our isolation in sport than the decision of the ILTF to exclude South Africa from the Davis Cup competition while allowing Rhodesia to go on participating. . . . The point is that there is an essential difference between politics and racialism. The one concerns the general manner in which a country orders its political affairs; the other amounts specifically to a denigration of a portion of the human race.[329]

A good example of this denigration happened two weeks later when a member of the South African security branch forced Patricia Tam, a thirteen-year-old Chinese girl, to stop playing in a white school tennis tournament in East London, South Africa.[330] This action, combined with what had already happened to Ashe, resulted in the ILTF's excluding the South African national championship from the Grand Prix series of the ILTF.[331]

Several days after the ILTF decision, Ashe testified before the United National Special Committee. He told of signing notarized statements that he would not make any political statements about South Africa for a reasonable time. He said that the South African government either did not believe the statement "or did not want me because I am not white; I believe it was the latter.[332]

So, as with the cricket case, the ultimate negotiations in the Ashe affair were made at the top levels of the governments involved: for South Africa, the prime minister, the foreign minister, and the ambassador to Washington; for the United States, the secretary of state, the assistant secretary of state, and the ambassador to South Africa. Again, there was no pretense about sport being above politics.

There was one final tennis-related event in 1970: the South African team had not been excluded from the Federation cup (the women's equivalent of the Davis cup) and, as a result, Hungary and Czechoslovakia both withdrew to avoid playing against South Africa.[333]

SOUTH AFRICA'S POSITION IN OTHER INTERNATIONAL SPORTS

In addition to its problems in cricket and tennis, South Africa was excluded from four other—though relatively less important—international championships during the first five months of the year.

At the end of February, the Jamaican government refused to grant visas to the South African women's netball team to compete in the world championships being held in Kingston.[334]

In anticipation of the same thing happening for the world gymnastic championships in Yugoslavia, the South Africans themselves withdrew to avoid the confrontation in early March.[335]

In March, the International Amateur Cycling Federation refused affiliation to the South African Amateur Cycling Federation, thus making it ineligible for the world championships in England scheduled for August.[336] The most interesting note about this is that, for the first time, England voted against South Africa in this federation.[337] The *Star* [Johannesburg] reported that it probably voted this way because of a fear that STST would mobilize its forces to demonstrate at the championships. Its pressure was working even where it was not being directly exerted. J. C. Geoghegan, the spokesman for the South African body, said:

> Perhaps the most disappointing part of it all is the fact that we intended sending a multi-racial team. This decision is as much a slap in the face to our non-white cyclists as it is to us.[338]

However, Geoghegan's statement had that now all-too-familiar hollow ring to it, especially in light of Vorster's warning in January to sports administrators that they should not make promises to send multiracial teams overseas since they would not be able to keep such promises.[339]

As if to prove that those opposing South Africa's competition in international sport were attacking on every conceivable front, South Africa was excluded from the world tuna championships in the Bahamas in April.[340]

In a preelection speech, Prime Minister Vorster claimed that South Africa's exclusion from various international sports was part of an international communist plot to control the world. Vorster felt that this was their initial move for control of the Cape sea route.[341] As the election drew near, Vorster sounded more and more like Hertzog every day.

To show just how far things had gone with South Africa's traditional sports allies, the SAAAU attempted to arrange a tour of seven European countries, but by March, five of the seven had refused because of potential international repercussions.[342]

Without consulting Vorster, Minister of the Interior Lourens Muller did not grant a visa to a Japanese jockey who had wanted to compete in South Africa. The decision was later reversed without explanation, but the jockey refused to come. For his mishandling of the affair, Vorster dropped Muller from his cabinet in early May (after the election).[343] The affair was particularly embarrassing to the South Africans who recognized Japanese as honorary whites, not to mention major trading partners.

By the end of May, it appeared that the only potentially stable sporting relation that South Africa had was with New Zealand. The key to this was the scheduled All-Blacks tour of South Africa in 1970. CARE and HART were hard at work throughout the year in their collective attempts to break the relationship. In March, they sponsored a speaking tour of New Zealand by Dennis Brutus.

The Kenyan decision not to send its athletes to the pre-Commonwealth games trials in Christchurch jarred most New Zealand officials. Secretary of CARE, Tom Newnham, wrote to Masinde Muliro in March, suggesting that the decision was too strong and asking him to reconsider it.[345] (Kenya's reason for not sending its team was that its athletes would be competing with athletes who had competed against South Africans in the previous three years.) The New Zealand Athletic Association also tried to devise a way for the Kenyans to come: they apparently attempted to get Laurie D'Arcy, who had been to the South African games in 1969, to withdraw. D'Arcy refused.[346]

But the main concern of CARE and HART was the All-Blacks tour. In early May, a delegation of clergymen, trade unionists, and representatives of thirty anti-apartheid groups met with Prime Minister Holyoake and requested that he withdraw the government's backing of the tour. Holyoake agreed to submit the matter to his cabinet.[347] This appeared to be a breakthrough for the protestors, for the government of New Zealand had maintained that the tour was not its affair.

As the cabinet meeting was about to be held, the anti-tour forces seemed to be gaining strength: the powerful Federation of Labour was considering taking direct action, while the Labour party declared that it sincerely regretted the tour, especially noting that the United Nations had singled out New Zealand for violating the U.N. resolutions.[348] The cabinet met on the same day that the British Parliament was debating the cricket tour and came up with the same result: it was up to the responsible sports body, in this case, the New Zealand Rugby Union.[349]

By that time, the election had been held in South Africa, and Vorster was free to go ahead with his outward sports policy, that is, Maoris would be allowed to come as part of the New Zealand team.[350] Therefore, the New Zealand Rugby Union held trials at the end of May, and three part-Maoris and one part-Samoan were chosen. The *Guardian* [Manchester] reported that "all four are sufficiently European in appearance to satisfy Dr. Vorster, if not Dr. Hertzog."[351] Police had to remove demonstrators from the field where the trials were being held. One protestor soaked himself with gasoline, but the police reached him before he could set fire to himself. Protestors badly damaged the headquarters of the Rugby union in Aukland when a fire was started with a molotov cocktail.[352] The determination of the protestors was approaching that of the STST group in Britain. (The All-Blacks tour did, in fact, take place later in the year.)

THE NONWHITE SOUTH AFRICAN GAMES

The nonwhite version of the South African games was finally held in May in Soweto. The nonracial sports organizations in South Africa refused to participate, and many potential nonwhite spectators stayed away from the games because of their racial nature. With the IOC due to meet only two weeks after the opening of the games, the South Africans still insisted on using the Olympic symbols for the games.[353] It was not a wise decision.

The *Rand Daily Mail* [Johannesburg] reported that the nonwhite boycott of the games was tremendously effective; at some soccer matches, there were more players than spectators. Hassan Howa summed up the feeling of the boycotters:

> The Olympic Games take no notice of colour, race or creed. This is where the non-white Games, with their five-ring Olympic symbols, are wrong. And my Board's attitude toward them is that we will never accept Games where colour, race or creed are taken into account.[354]

The newspaper concluded that, despite the fact that the number of participants had doubled from the 1964 games, this particular version of the nonwhite games could hardly be termed a success.[355]

THE IOC MEETING IN AMSTERDAM

As for the IOC meeting in Amsterdam in mid-May, the feeling in South Africa was that it would be ruled ineligible for the 1972 Olympics but would not be expelled at that time.[356]

The agenda for the meeting and discussion on South Africa was to consist of a presentation of a list of charges by the African NOCs, to be followed by a defense by the South African delegation.

The African NOCs drew up their list of charges at the meeting of the Supreme Council in March in Cairo. In addition to the charges, the council voted unanimously to follow Kenya's lead to boycott any events in which athletes who had competed against South Africans during the previous three years were participating.[357]

There were eight basic points in the list of charges against SANOC:

1. Its policy was tied to that of the government, contravening rule 25.
2. It had never guaranteed membership in its affiliated national sports federations to nonwhites, contravening rule 24.
3. It practiced racial discrimination by not allowing nonwhites full and equal participation in the competitive and administrative activities of the committee, contravening rule 1.

4. It practiced racial discrimination by not allowing multiracial competitions and by not providing equal facilities and training opportunities for nonwhites, also contravening rule 1.
5. It had not complied with the Baden-Baden resolution.
6. The 1969 white South African games contravened the spirit of the Olympic charter.
7. It had used the Olympic symbols despite an IOC ban on such use.
8. Its affiliates were already suspended or expelled from nine international federations.

The African NOCs resolved that South Africa, in view of all the evidence, should be expelled from the Olympic movement.[358]

All reports at that time, however, indicated that South Africa was not going to be expelled. Those reports had been made before Frank Braun's presentation and assumed that he would make the same type of speech that he had always made in the past, that is, a speech marked by a moderate, compromising tone. Instead, the speech was most inflammatory:

> Our first submission is that the motion to expel the NOC of South Africa should never have been placed on the agenda. . . . No single article of the Charter was intended to withstand the rigors of litigation in law. Rules 1, 24 and 25, which are being used as the basis for the case against South Africa, are striking examples of the lofty ideals, the hopes and the prayers of Baron de Coubertin. . . . We of the South African NOC . . . have fought fairly and taken our defeats as gentlemen.[359]

In the world of the IOC, the name of de Coubertin is not one that is freely tossed about without absolute reverence. Thus, Braun's opening remarks immediately set off a reaction among the de Coubertin-worshippers. As for his remarks about defeats and gentlemen, Braun had a short memory, for, after each and every defeat, South Africa condemned the IOC.

Braun continued, referring to the post-Grenoble reversal of the decision to readmit South Africa in 1968:

> This shocking rebuff by the IOC was accepted gracefully by South Africa in spite of gross legal irregularities which were committed by the IOC in the handling of the Mexico Games issue.[360]

He quoted Avery Brundage's legal opinion on the matter and charged that it was the IOC that violated rule 1 by not allowing the South Africans to compete:

> It is not within the power nor was it ever contemplated by our founders, that the internal affairs of a member country . . . could be the subject of investigation, control or denouncement by the IOC, so long as it does not relate directly to, or effect the Olympic Games.[361]

It is difficult to believe that Braun thought South Africa's internal policies did not affect its Olympic participation and, therefore, the games themselves. He asked:

> Why must South Africa be the victim of a vendetta? . . . The driving force has constantly emanated from quarters which can least of all claim autonomy from their own governments and which have themselves not been free of repeated occurrences of internal strife.[362]

About SAN-ROC, he said, "If any sort of victory was scored in the process it went to the agitators of SAN-ROC in London, the self-appointed political fanatics."[363]

Braun then attempted to answer the charges posed by the African NOCs:

1. SANOC openly accepted Olympic principle 1, and no one is a Government appointee (he did not talk to the main point of government interference).
2. SANOC had never been asked for guarantees of admission of nonwhites to the national sports federations.
3. Unless the IOC remained neutral, it would have to investigate the situations in many other countries. He said that SANOC had certainly provided for nondiscrimination in terms of the Olympic games themselves. (Braun failed to mention the matter of no mixed trials and the failure to award nonwhites Springbok colors.)
4. No mixed competitions was the law of the country, he said, and claimed that nonwhites had more facilities than whites. (He did not

mention that there were also 400 percent more nonwhites than whites.

5. SANOC had indeed complied with the Baden-Baden resolution. (He did not mention that SANOC had never obtained a change of policy from the government, as demanded in the resolution.)

6 and 7. The Olympic rings used for the South Africa games were a part of SANOC's emblem and had been used for thirty years. He said that after he explained this to Brundage, Brundage gave his permission to use the rings. (Brundage denied this. But the damage was done; this last claim made Brundage turn against SANOC.)[364]

Braun concluded by referring to the possibility of exclusion:

> Could any purpose be achieved other than personal aggrandizement, chauvenistic [sic] aspirations and satisfactions derived from hatred? The relentless campaign against SANOC is purported to be inspired by the condemnations of racial intolerance in South Africa. Do the protagonists of this campaign against SANOC themselves display the degree of compassion and tolerance that they demand of South Africa? . . . The peace and friendship that the IOC has been able to create for the South African non-white and white athletes should not be endangered by exorbitant demands and threats of expulsion.[365]

It seems evident from the general tone of this statement that Braun was aware that South Africa had no chance to be readmitted for the 1972 games and was, perhaps, attempting to win back some government support by not offering any compromises. His tactics, however, may have been the direct cause of South Africa's expulsion (as opposed to mere suspension). All press accounts about the thirty-five to twenty-eight vote (with three abstentions) to expel South Africa expressed great surprise, with most blaming Braun's abrasive remarks for the result.[366]

Minister of Sport Waring claimed that it would be the Olympic movement and not South Africa that would suffer most as a result of the expulsion.[367] Frank Braun said, "Non-white sport has been set back 30 to 40 years and everything we have worked for is lost."[368] The implication was clear: all attempts for change over the years were for the IOC and not for the nonwhite athletes. If it was not clear enough, Braun added:

> In the past years a lot of money has been poured into sports to prove to the world that non-whites were also getting their fair share. Now there is no longer anything left to prove.[369]

Asked about SAN-ROC, Braun said, "The action of an organization which has so little respect for the rules and constitution of the IOC does not warrant comment."[370]

Rudolph Opperman, another member of the South African delegation, asked, "After ten years of humiliation, what do you expect? They [the Africans] won't be satisfied until they get a black Prime Minister."[371]

Abraham Ordia, who led the African group, put the decision in a more realistic perspective than Braun:

> It is nothing to be happy about. They are Africans–they are my brothers. I want to compete with them. I want to invite them to Nigeria. I want to invite them to the Pan-African Games. But for God's sake, let them change. If this were the medicine that will let them live, then this will not be in vain.[372]

Ordia even asked Avery Brundage to persuade Reg Honey to remain on the IOC.

With all the evidence and, seemingly, the majority of world opinion against South Africa, it would be reasonable to ask why the country was permitted to remain in the Olympic movement until 1970.

Perhaps the best explanation is that the IOC had been dominated by representatives from white member nations who did not oppose South Africa's continued good standing in the Olympic movement. The IOC, according to its own publication, *Olympism,* is a self-recruiting elite: membership on the committee is a result of election by existing IOC members. The statement, "It is customary to favour nationals of countries with a long Olympic tradition behind them" is reminiscent of the grandfather clause in the post-Reconstruction era of the South in the United States.[373] The custom was a convenient way of excluding representatives from nations that were colonies during the period when "a long Olympic tradition" could have been formed. In fact, the first two representatives from Africa were white men: Reg Alexander of Kenya and Reg Honey of South Africa.

De Coubertin commented on the nature of membership on the IOC, "The second characteristic of Olympism is that it is an aristocracy, an elite."[374] De Coubertin also said, "It is not sufficient to be an elite; it is also necessary for this elite to be a chivalry."[375]

During the 1960s, 61 percent of the representatives from nonwhite member nations of the IOC were admitted, but that meant only a minor change in the racial composition of the IOC. The representatives from the nonwhite countries had only 33 percent of the voting power on the IOC in 1970. To achieve their 67 percent control, it was necessary for eleven of the white nations represented on the IOC to have two or more representatives. Moreover, of the NOCs without an IOC representative (which, in effect, means they are powerless), only 12.4 percent were from white nations while 87.6 percent were from nonwhite nations.[376]

To the idealistic sportsman who might feel that such statistics are meaningless because sport and the Olympic movement are above politics and race, the results of the following survey should be instructive. The information was gathered in a survey completed in spring 1970 in which the NOCs were asked for their position on South African participation in the Olympics. (The country-by-country results are contained in the appendix.) Sixty-eight percent of the white nations were not opposed to South Africa's participation. However, 98 percent of the nonwhite nations opposed South Africa's participation without complete sports integration in South Africa.

Thus, it can be seen that the South African issue developed along rather strict racial lines. It is also intriguing to note the exceptions to the more or less strict racial groupings. The full 32 percent of the white nations who opposed South Africa's participation were from the socialist bloc, perhaps implying that their attempted alignment with the Third World extends into the world of sports. The only nonwhite country that did not oppose South Africa was Malawi. The implication of economic ties as a balancing factor for racial differences is well worth pursuing in another study.

In any event, it must come as a shock to the sportsmen to recognize the extent to which race and politics have become a part of the world of international sports. However, the 1970 world of international sport is a far cry from that envisioned by Baron de Coubertin at the turn of the century.

SOUTH AFRICAN REACTIONS TO INTERNATIONAL SPORTS ISOLATION

By the end of May, South Africa was close to a position of total isolation in world sport. In addition to being expelled from the IOC, it was either expelled or suspended in the following sports: table tennis, football (soccer), basketball, fencing, judo, volleyball, boxing, weightlifting, tennis (Davis cup), gymnastics, big game fishing, cycling, and netball. Later in 1970, South Africa was suspended in athletics and wrestling, as well as being banned from the world softball championship in Japan.

All the talk of bridge building had produced no clamor for change from South African sportsmen. Such was not the case with the isolation that was at hand in May 1970.

A page-one editorial in the *Rand Daily Mail* [Johannesburg] of May 23 called for a national sports conference to take action. Springbok cricketer Dennis Gamsy said:

> In my own mind, there is no question but that we should have mixed sport here. What has happened now is only the thin end of the wedge. If we turn back into the laager because of it, our position can only worsen, not only in sport but also economically.
>
> We are only four million whites in a continent of several hundred millions of blacks. If we go on the way we are, we could find ourselves being sacrificed to rid the world of one of its niggling problems.[377]

To demonstrate how deep the effect of the isolation went in South African sportsmen, one has only to look at the change in the attitude of Peter Pollock, the Springbok cricketer. Three weeks earlier, he had condemned the demonstrators and called them "communist inspired." He had worried that "any measure of success for this kind of defiance would see the idea spreading far beyond the realm of sport." At the end of May, Pollock was urging all sportsmen who wanted multiracial sport in South Africa to step forward and be heard. He said:

> It is my sincere belief that there is a growing body of sports opinion—which like mine, is not politically inspired—that echoes my

> sentiments. . . . I'm sticking my neck out all the way. I feel that the Government owes something to people who play sport in this country.[378]

Pollock was joined by his brother and Springbok captain Ali Bacher in calling for multiracial sport in South Africa.[379] MP Dave Marais announced that he would ask the government to set up a special commission to investigate sport in South Africa.

Alf Chalmers, the SALTU leader, called for a sports summit meeting to "formulate a policy for sport which must be agreeable to this country and to those outside. We must look for a happy medium."[381]

Frank Braun immediately criticized the idea of a sports summit meeting.[382] He was not, however, as imflammatory as Frank Waring, the minister for sport:

> As Minister for Sport on behalf of the Government I wish to advise that no such "conference" or commission is acceptable. I wish to make it quite clear at this early stage that the Government is in no way whatsoever going to be intimidated by the demands made for integrated multi-racial sport in South Africa. It is by now abundantly clear to all that sport is being employed by anti-South African political organizations to bring South Africa to her knees.
>
> Although in sport their demands are that we should have completely integrated sport in South Africa, in which whites and non-whites belong and play for clubs in mixed teams the ultimate objective is in fact for the political control of this country.
>
> The Government also rejects a policy which would allow white teams to compete with non-white teams, whether in South Africa or, as has been suggested, in neighboring territories, nor will it consider any form of mixed trials. . . . The fact that overseas competition is being withheld in so many directions does mean that there is an increasing onus on the Government to assist, where possible, in meeting this particular need to a greater extent in South Africa itself than it has been in the past. This applies to both white and non-white participants in sport.[383]

Two days later, Waring changed his mind about the summit and said it could take place, but without government participation.[384]

While there were moves for real changes in the minds of sportsmen and sports officials, Waring's statement made it absolutely clear that the government was not willing to relinquish its control over sport—and that is how the problem became a significant one in the first place. Minor changes have taken place since the period under study, but they in no way affected the basic extension of apartheid into sport. It is a complete extension and is a part of the whole of apartheid.

This is also realized by those who oppose apartheid in general and attack it through sport. The *Sunday Times* [Johannesburg], on the last day covered in this chronological study, aptly summed up the essence of that attack in an editorial:

> South Africa's critics have simply discovered that sport is the most useful weapon they have yet found with which to beat us and while it is the sportsmen who are the sacrificial victims—they are being ostracized and deprived of the right to participate in world sport—the main target of attack is the racial policy of South Africa or, to put it more precisely, the racial policy of the Nationalist Party.[385]

5
Summary and Conclusions

SUMMARY

In this lengthy description of the history of the extension of apartheid into sport, several distinct phases in that extension have been recognized.

Segregation in South African sport was a fact of life before the National party took over in 1948; it was enforced not by the government but by the sports authorities themselves. This continued to be the case throughout most of the first decade of National party control, although Dr. Donges laid down specific guidelines in 1956 as a result of several relatively small and insignificant protests of sports policy during that period. (The importance of table tennis could hardly be compared to that of cricket, rugby, football, tennis, or golf in South Africa.) But Donges' statement was not insignificant and became the basis of government sports policy throughout the period under study.

Another distinct phase began in 1959. During this period, white sports authorities accepted sports apartheid. The South African Sports Association (SASA) undertook two major campaigns in regard to touring teams from Brazil and the West Indies, and it was successful in both. The matter of South African sports policies was raised for the first time at the IOC (with Reg Honey adamantly denying any discrimination). Finally, the first sports protest group outside South Africa, the Citizens All-Blacks Tour Association (CABTA), was formed in New Zealand and undertook an unsuccessful protest against the exclusion of Maoris for the 1960 rugby tour of South Africa. The South African government was beginning to take a more active part by asserting its sports policy to counter SASA's effectiveness, while white sports authorities did little about it.

The Sharpeville massacre caused a dramatic change of mood in 1960. After Sharpeville, the world began to take notice of South Africa. With the increasing protest at home and abroad, the South African government openly began to suppress sports protestors by withdrawing their travel documents and by conducting police raids on their homes.

However, the South Africans knew that the IOC would now have to deal with the issue of apartheid in sport, and several face-liftings were undertaken to some degree before the 1963 Baden-Baden session.

The full-scale move toward compromises by the white sports authorities began in 1964. Sports officials said that they would give nonwhites a voice in the administration of sports (usually in the forms of whites representing them on the white sports bodies), financial aid, and the promise of international competition. Some pledges were even made that South African teams would be chosen on merit (all evidence indicates that the government would never have allowed selection on merit). Even if these promises proved true, it would still be difficult to imagine a team chosen on merit through segregated trials, not to mention that nonwhites would have begun at a tremendous disadvantage due to substantially inferior possibilities for training.

Several nonwhite groups broke away from the nonracial movement between 1964 and 1968 in order to take advantage of these limited concessions. It must be noted that all the concessions offered were strictly within the policies of apartheid at home. There was no compromising on that crucial point.

South Africa missed its first Olympic games in 1964. The blame for this went directly to SAN-ROC (the organization that had taken over from SASA), and, by the end of 1964, Dennis Brutus and John Harris, who had become SAN-ROC's leader after Brutus's banning, were both imprisoned. The relative calm in the South African international sports scene in 1965 reflected, perhaps more than anything else, the dynamic leadership that SASA and SAN-ROC had given to the protest movement.

Under Prime Minister Verwoerd, the extension of apartheid into sport was made complete, and loopholes were eliminated. His often-quoted Loskop Dam speech ensured that nonwhite athletes from outside South Africa would never be allowed to enter South Africa to compete with whites. To be sure, more concessions to nonwhites were offered but, once again, these concessions always reaffirmed internal apartheid in sports.

It was in this atmosphere that Chris de Broglio and Reg Hlongwane, in exile in London in 1966, re-established SAN-ROC. They were joined there in midyear by Dennis Brutus. By the end of 1966, the Supreme Council for Sport in Africa (SCSA) was formed, and Brutus and de Broglio had left an indelible and crucial stamp on its essence; the Supreme Council came to reflect African nationalism in its stand against apartheid in general and against apartheid in sport in particular.

Under the new prime minister, Mr. Vorster, the South Africans realized that their increasingly rigid stand in the face of growing international protest would soon lead to their complete sports isolation. Vorster made his famous April 11 (1967) speech in Parliament, which contained what later became known as the Tehran concessions; however, no matter how much of a breakthrough these concessions seemed to be, the ultimate reality remained: apartheid in sport inside South Africa was stronger than ever.

The concessions, however, were significant enough in terms of international sport for the IOC to vote to allow South Africa to compete in the Mexico games (the vote was taken at the IOC's Grenoble meeting in February 1968 after the release of the IOC commission's report on South Africa). The ensuing chaos almost devoured the Olympic movement as more than fifty nations, led by the African bloc and almost all nonwhite nations, threatened to boycott the games if South Africa was allowed to compete. The racial factor in international sport was never more clear than it was during this period that, finally, saw South Africa again excluded from the games.

Later in 1968, when the South African government refused to allow the former Cape Colored cricketer, Basil D'Oliveira, to come to South Africa as part of the British team, the British cancelled the tour.

The D'Oliveira affair also set the stage for the final period under study in which militant international opposition to sports apartheid grew and resulted in South Africa's eventual isolation in international sport. However, the MCC (the body responsible for cricket in Britain) fatefully decided to go ahead with plans for the 1970 cricket tour. "Stop the Seventy Tour," at first a murmur, became a deafening roar as more than fifty thousand demonstrators, not all of them peaceful, turned out for the warm-up during the 1969-1970 South African rugby tour of Britain and Ireland. This was a major turning point as the issue changed from what the effects a sporting relationship might have on supporting apartheid in South Africa to what effects such a relationship might have on domestic relations within the country competing against South Africa. All indications were that such effects would irrevocably damage race relations in Britain and in the entire Commonwealth. These factors led to the Prime Minister Wilson's government forcing the MCC to cancel the tour in May 1970.

This decision came only two months after the United States had been made to take a position against South Africa as a result of South Africa's refusal to admit black American tennis star Arthur Ashe to compete in South Africa. The result of this new United States opposition was that South Africa was forced out of the Davis cup in March 1970.

The British decision came only days after South Africa was excluded from the Olympic movement itself (as opposed to previously being banned from specific games). The IOC was, again, led by strong pressure from the African bloc to achieve this as a means to finally get South African sports integrated.

It was at this point—the end of May 1970—that a spontaneous outburst of opposition to South African sports policy was heard inside South Africa. It was led by white sportsmen and administrators for the first time. With South Africa excluded from competing in twelve international sports as well as from the Olympic movement, these people had been forced into a corner, and their survival as international sportsmen depended on a significant series of changes on the part of the government—a series that was not forthcoming. But the fact that such changes are now being called for by both whites and nonwhites in South Africa is significant in and of itself.

CONCLUSIONS

Sport is, indeed, a supportive and integral part of the apartheid system in South Africa. This is frequently attested to by the degree to which sport has become so important in South Africa and the stress that the press and government leaders place on sport and sporting relations with other nations. Although the day-to-day undertakings of sport may be administered by sports officials, any meaningful decision that could affect apartheid in sport or South Africa's sporting relations with the outside world is absolutely controlled by the government. There is no pretension in South Africa that sports officials are independent agents (even though they were so during the early stage of National party control until sports apartheid was challenged); the government, led by the prime minister, makes the decisions.

Any compromises made to nonwhites have always been made within the framework of apartheid. These compromises have been quite effective in terms of splitting up the nonracial movement in South Africa and yielding enough nonwhites who accepted such compromises to allow white South African officials to make the claim that the people support the existing social and sports structure, which is the equivalent of saying that the people accept apartheid. White South African officials have been able to claim that leaders of the nonracial movement were not representative of nonwhite opinion and that their radicalism actually alienated most nonwhites in South Africa.

Internationally, when nations agree to compete with South Africa, South Africans view that as an acceptance of their political system. This was best represented in the *Die Volksblad* [Bloemfontein] editorial of October 28, 1969: "Every international success of South Africa is a blow against our sport and political enemies."

The second conclusion is that the major factor in the politics of international sport has become the racial and not the ideological factor. While ideology has not been eliminated as an influence (witness Soviet-American competition in sports), it is no longer the cause celebre in international sports circles. Nations are not added to or excluded from international sports competition because of their political systems. South Africa, however, has been excluded from competition because of the way race affects both its domestic and international competition. This explains why such enormous pressure has been brought to bear against South Africa in international competition. This pressure has increased in direct proportion to the spread of non-Western nationalism and, especially, to the spread of African nationalism as embodied in the Supreme Council.

A reflection of the racial factor has been shown through the NOC survey in which 98 percent of the nonwhite nations were opposed to South Africa's international competition, while 68 percent of the white nations represented did not oppose such competition. (See the appendix.)

It has also been seen that when pressure groups such as CABTA, CARDS, CARE, AAM, and the ACOA operate without direct action to protest their nation's competition with South Africa, they serve primarily to bring the issue of apartheid before the public. However, without direct-action campaigns, no important tours have ever been cancelled (this, of course, does not apply to the more broadly based pressure groups, SAN-ROC and the Supreme Council). It was only with STST's direct action approach that a white nation cancelled a major tour in the period under study. This strengthens the belief that white nations will not end sports relations with South Africa except when their own domestic peace has been threatened.

The threat to the peace in the case of England in 1970 was largely the result of increasingly bad race relations within the country. More than for a concern over the moral issue involved with South Africa, Wilson's action in cancelling the tour was a result of the strain to race relations and the possible effect that a breach of the public peace would have had on the upcoming election in England. It should be carefully noted here that direct action undertaken in situations where race relations are at a breaking point would almost surely become counterproductive. The most obvious example would be South Africa itself, where direct action would undoubtedly result in suppression.

Finally, South Africans have made sport so important in their country that they have allowed themselves to become quite vulnerable to domestic and international pressure. The South Africans reaction to such pressure has been consistently hard-lined.

When nonwhites have refused to compete within the framework of apartheid sport, white South African officials have generally reacted with the kind of overkill that serves to increase the potential of movements founded on a moral basis, such as the movement for nonracial sport in South Africa.

There were several possible fates for nonwhites who refused to cooperate with apartheid sport: sports facilities were withdrawn to the point of yielding an effective end of that sport on a nonracial basis (such was the case in football); nonwhite athletes were denied the possibility of international competition without affiliating to the segregated bodies; travel documents were withdrawn from officials who represented nonracial sport; banning orders were issued for some nonracial leaders (Wilfred Brutus, Dennis Brutus, and George Singh); some leaders were arrested (Wilfred Brutus, Dennis Brutus, and John Harris) and imprisoned (Dennis

Brutus and John Harris) or were forced into exile (Wilfred Brutus, Dennis Brutus, Omar Cassem, Chris de Broglio, and Reg Hlongwane, not to mention the numerous outstanding South African athletes who were forced to compete overseas as a result of not being able to compete at home). Also, after nonwhite spectators began to show their approval of *any* foreign team competing against the South African teams, they were systematically banned as spectators unless they received a government permit to attend a specific event.

Thus, nonwhites did not, in fact, have the option to protest apartheid sport without serious personal and collective repercussions. A knowledge of such repercussions severely diminishes and, perhaps, destroys the argument of the South African officials that the nonwhites who do cooperate with the system are the ones who are representative of the nonwhite population in South Africa.

Internationally, no fewer than eighty-nine nations have become actively involved in the dispute over South Africa's international competition. In many of these countries, decisions on whether to compete against South Africa have been made at the very highest levels of government. Just as international competition has meant success for South Africa, a rejection of such competition has the opposite effect. This can be judged, in part, by the severity of the verbal attacks levied against those who rejected South Africa in international competition, such as the attacks on the IOC in 1963-1964, 1968, and 1970 and those on the British government after the cancellation of the 1970 cricket tour. In part, it can be judged by the clamor for change in policy by South African whites after their isolation was almost complete in 1970.

The latter point speaks directly to the controversy over the bridge building versus the isolationist approaches described in chapter 1. During all the years under study, there were, perhaps, five incidents where white sportsmen or white sports officials spoke up in favor of a change in the apartheid sports policy. This was during a period of considerable international competition for the South Africans when, presumably, they would have been witnessing the merits of multiracial societies through the bridge-building approach. The meager results do not uphold this approach.

Beginning in December 1969, with total sports isolation in sight, three important South African officials called for major policy changes in sport. When isolation was not only in sight but a fact in May 1970, the calls from white sportsmen and officials were not only for reform but for sports integration. But it took isolation to get these sportsmen to talk about multiracial sport. This bore out what the leaders of SAN-ROC had said all along, but most sportsmen refused to believe. These sportsmen were left with no alternative as a result of the actions of the international sports bodies: if they wanted to resume competition, the cost would clearly be the elimination of apartheid from sport.

Whether these calls for change yielded significant change is open to serious debate. Certainly there is importance in the calls themselves. However, even now, integration in sport in South Africa is far from reality. Until there is multiracialism at the club level in sports, any breakthroughs at the national level are only gestures–no matter how important they may seem. The new term, "multinationalism," means little as long as the system itself is still based on apartheid. The reality of life in South African society in general, and sport in particular, remains unchanged.

There is no small degree of irony in the fact that as South Africa was progressively eliminated from sport after sport, its leaders claimed that a small minority of people had caused all of the country's problems. Someday those same leaders will have to face, in one way or another, those same charges. It can only be hoped that day comes before George Orwell's "war minus the shooting" becomes an all-out racial war.

Epilogue

More than four years have passed since South Africa was excluded from the Olympic movement. While certain changes have been made, sports apartheid has remained intact within South Africa itself. As the international opposition to sports apartheid has grown, there has been increasing opposition to segregated sport inside South Africa.

In fact, for the first time the South African cabinet has begun to seriously weigh a move that would make all South Africans eligible to represent the country in all international competition. This would mean that the coveted Springbok colors would be worn by nonwhites.

A brief look at South African sport from 1970 through 1974 will show how this has come about.

MULTINATIONALISM VS. MULTIRACIALISM

On April 22, 1971 Prime Minister Vorster announced what appeared to be a new sports policy for South Africa. It was clearly designed to convince the international sports bodies that South Africa's policy had changed, while a careful examination led only to the inevitable conclusion that the primary change was one of semantics.

Thus, instead of talking about multiracial sport, Vorster talked about "multinational sport." The policy was based on the fact that South Africa is made of up several nations rather than several racial groups. According to this policy, multiracial sport would not be allowed on the club, provincial, or national levels.

South African whites and nonwhites could compete against each other only at "open international events," not as members of a South African team but as individuals. Vorster made a distinction between open international events (such as the Davis cup and the Olympics) and normal international events. Thus, nonwhite South Africans could not compete together against a British touring team: to qualify as an open international, several nations would have to compete.

Another part of the policy was that countries with traditional ties with South Africa, such as Britain, New Zealand, and Australia, could send multiracial teams to South Africa to compete against separate white and nonwhite South African teams at segregated stadiums. Under this policy, no whites would be permitted to attend a match where an overseas team played against nonwhite South Africans. As a result, the touring British rugby team played against separate white, Colored, and African teams when they came to South Africa in May 1972.

Finally, South Africa would send integrated teams overseas in only four events: the Olympic Games, the Davis cup, the Federation cup, and the Canada cup golf tournament. Even in these four exceptions, apartheid was still to rule at home: there would be no mixed trials for selection and the Springbok colors would not be awarded for such competition.

As Dennis Brutus has frequently said of multinationalism, "It's a new name for the old game." Internal sports apartheid was the same.

The structure of nonwhite sport in South Africa also remained the same. There were nonracial federations in each sport. These federations refused to cooperate with the policy of multinationalism just as they refused to accept the compromises offered by the white sports bodies during the period covered by this book. Since these federations refuse to affiliate with the white bodies in their code of sport, their members are not eligible to compete in the open internationals. For example, Jasmat Dhiraj, South Africa's leading nonwhite tennis player, was not allowed to play in the South African Open–even though it was classified as an open international–because he was a member of the nonracial union.

Other nonwhite federations remained affiliated with the white bodies in their codes of sport as they had in the past. These federations are not open to all racial groups but are either Colored, African or Indian. They have cooperated with the policy of multinationalism and, as a result, their members have competed in open internationals. While these federations maintain that the government has been fair to the nonwhite sportsmen, one only has to look at the amount of money spent on white and nonwhite sport in South Africa between 1965 and 1972. While whites make up less than 25 percent of the population, R2,708,900 was spent on white sport; during the same period, only R102,150 was spent on nonwhite sport. On a per capita basis, this means that money spent on white sport was more than 120 times greater than that spent on nonwhite sport.

The nonracial organizations had met in September 1970 to attempt to coordinate their efforts in achieving international recognition and to affect closer cooperation with each other. An ad hoc Committee of National Non-Racial Sports Organizations grew out of this meeting. The ad hoc committee provided the international federations with material against South Africa's participation, and attempted to show why they were the true representatives of nonwhite South Africans. The committee called the nonwhite bodies that cooperated with multinationalism "stooges."

In March 1973, the South African Council on Sport (SACOS) took over for the ad hoc committee. It was headed by Norman Middleton and Hassan Howa, two of the leading figures in the nonracial movement inside South Africa for almost a decade. SACOS represented the nonracial bodies in swimming, soccer, table tennis, athletics, cycling, tennis, weightlifting, rugby, cricket, and hockey. Because of the new climate for change within South African sports circles, SACOS was able to criticize mildly the official policies and not fear the severe reprisals that Dennis Brutus and others had faced ten years before. However, later in 1973 Howa was refused an exit passport to go to an international meeting.

Examples of the climate for change are seen in two polls taken in 1971: in the first, 925 prominent South Africans were interviewed and a full 79 percent favored sports integration; in the second poll, 276 out of 292 top white cricketers said they were prepared to play with or against nonwhites at the league level. It can easily be recalled that prior to December 1969, only three or four leading white figures could be found who favored integrated sports. Isolation had definitely taken its toll on support for government sports policy.

For Americans, the most publicized international open events in South Africa were the 1971 Professional Golfers Association (PGA) Championships; the 1973 South African Games; the 1973 South African Open Tennis Championship; and the 1973 light-heavyweight boxing championship match.

Lee Elder became the first black American to compete in South Africa when he competed with sixteen nonwhite South African golfers in a field of more than one hundred in the 1971 PGA Championship.

The list of those who chose to participate in the 1973 South African Games reads very much like the list of those who said they would support South Africa's continued international participation in the 1970 survey referred to in chapter 5: West Germany, Britain, Ireland, the United States, Switzerland, France, Italy, Canada, Israel, Holland, Belgium, Austria, and Rhodesia. Malawi was the only African nation represented there as it was the only nonwhite nation to say it supported South Africa's continued participation in the 1970 survey.

Five Africans from South Africa won medals in boxing, athletics, and cycling. Of some significance was the soccer series in the Games. It did not qualify as an open international since the Federation of International Football Associations (FIFA) had refused to allow teams to play in South Africa due to the multinational nature of the games. Therefore, it came as a surprise when the new Minister of Sport, Dr. Piet Koornhof, allowed the series to go ahead with only teams representing the four "nations" of South Africa. Since the nonracial South African Soccer Federation did not allow its members to participate, the weakened nonwhite teams were defeated by the full white side.

The effect of the South African Games on international sports leaders, especially those from Europe, was exactly what the South Africans hoped for—praise for their progress. Typical of the European reaction was that of Baron Erik von Frenckell, a Finnish member of the International Olympic Committee. The *Washington Post* of April 5, 1973, reported that the Baron said, "I believe this means that it will be only a matter of time before South Africa will again be admitted to the Olympic Games." However, the militancy of South Africa's opponents has so far kept the question from being raised at the IOC.

Two other prominent black American athletes came to South Africa to compete at the end of 1973. Bob Foster, the light-heavyweight boxing champion, came to fight against Pierre Fourie. Foster stayed within his training compound and repeatedly told newsmen that he was there simply to make money. (He grossed more than $200,000 for the fight.) His trip was totally nonpolitical, a fact which the nonwhite South Africans resented deeply. A story in the December 10, 1973, issue of *Sports Illustrated* quoted Foster, "I don't know how they treat others around here. That's not my business. They treat me like a king."

The visit of Arthur Ashe to compete in the South African Open Tennis Championship was another matter entirely. It was a momentous occasion for Ashe, who had been denied a visa three consecutive times prior to 1973. This was the first time that Ashe had applied since South Africa had been readmitted to the Davis Cup series in 1972, and the government was not about to open itself up to the criticism it received when it banned Ashe in 1970 and was subsequently barred for the Davis cup.

Ashe went out to meet the people and to see for himself. While he was criticized by most of the international protest groups for even going there and, thus, seemingly accommodating apartheid sport, he became something of a hero to nonwhite South Africans.

While the world might have thought that a revolution had occurred in South Africa in that year of the Games, Foster, and Ashe the world of apartheid sport was still filled with insanity. Glen Popham won the gold medal in the South African Games in karate and had been the captain of the Springbok team. While Popham's teammates were awarded the Springbok colors for winning the silver and bronze medals in that competition, Popham was denied them because it was discovered after the Games that Popham had been classified as "Colored."

INTERNATIONAL OPPOSITION TO APARTHEID SPORT

With the exception of the Davis Cup, South Africa lost more ground in its move to end sports isolation. Its largest losses came in its relation to its former allies, Australia and New Zealand.

The year 1971 in Australia seemed to be a carbon copy of 1969-1970 in Britain. The 1971 South African rugby tour of Australia resulted in violence, between five hundred and seven hundred arrests, an 18-day state of emergency in the State of Queensland, a strike by 125,000 workers, and a cost for police estimated at R1,600,000. The 1971 tour of Australia was completed, just as the 1969-1970 rugby tour of Britain, but at a staggering cost not even measured in the statistics cited. By the time the tour ended, calls for the cancellation of the 1971 South African cricket tour of Australia had spread beyond the minority that had begun the disruptions during the rugby tour. The cricket tour was opposed by the Council of Churches, the Council of Trade Unions, most of the leading Australian newspapers, many leading citizens, as well as by the state governments of South and Western Australia. Estimates for the cost of police protection for the tour ran to R40,000,000. When the federal government refused to back the tour, the Australian Board of Cricket Control cancelled the tour shortly before it was to begin.

It was more of the same in New Zealand. In 1971, the anti-apartheid group HART (Halt All Racist Tours) successfully forced the cancellation of the South African women's hockey tour of New Zealand and got the New Zealand Golf Association to request the withdrawal of the South African golf team from an October tournament.

The 1973 South African rugby tour of New Zealand aroused more protests from HART and CARE (Citizens' Association for Racial Equality). Both promised not to disrupt the tour if South Africa chose its team on merit, but when the South African government refused, CARE and HART went ahead with plans to mobilize the anti-apartheid forces as early as in 1972. New Zealand's new prime minister, Norman Kirk, refused to cancel the tour but, at the same time, totally withdrew government support for it.

More than half of the Commonwealth nations, led by the Supreme Council for Sport in Africa (SCSA), threatened to boycot the 1974 Commonwealth Games scheduled in New Zealand if the tour went on as planned.

In February Prime Minister Kirk told the New Zealand Rugby Football Union that it was in the best interest of the country if it cancelled the tour. However, the NZRFU went ahead with its plans.

With violence threatening the tour, Kirk was forced to ask that the tour be cancelled six weeks later. Kirk continued his determined posture when he announced on November 1, 1973, that he would not allow the 1974 Federation Cup Tennis Tournament (the women's equivalent of the Davis cup) to be held in New Zealand because the ILTF insisted that South Africa be allowed to participate in spite of apartheid tennis in South Africa. South Africa won the 1974 Davis cup when India, the other finalist, refused to compete against South Africa because of apartheid. It was an empty title.

Protests in England continued. A new organization called Stop the Apartheid Rugby Tour (SART) was formed by a coalition of SAN-ROC leaders, including Dennis Brutus, and former STST leaders, including Peter Hain. SART was formed to try to stop the 1974 British Lions tour of South Africa–a much more difficult task than stopping a South African side from coming to Britain. In fact, the tour did take place and it was the result of this tour that the South African cabinet had begun considering whether or not to award Springbok colors to nonwhites, as was mentioned at the outset of this epilogue.

According to the July 15, 1974 issue of *Newsweek*, the South Africans were humiliated by the British team as a consequence of not being able to employ its nonwhite stars. This is why the cabinet had agreed to take up the matter. Such a change might also be used as a gesture to the world after Vorster's October 1974 speech in which he promised an end to racial discrimination. The liberation of Angola and Mozambique will serve to accelerate this change and/or need for gestures.

However, even if the South African cabinet decided to allow nonwhites to wear the Springbok colors in matches such as the British tour, the percentage of nonwhite players who would then escape the agony of apartheid–at least while on the playing field–would still be almost insignificant. Whether it will soften international opposition to South African sports teams is not known at this point. It certainly will not change the lot of more than 99 percent of the nonwhite South Africans who compete at the club, provincial, and national levels. For those individuals, the paralysis of life that comes with apartheid will be the same.

Appendices

RESULTS OF THE SURVEY OF PUBLIC OPINION IN THE UNITED STATES OF THE ISSUE OF POLITICS AND RACE IN SPORT

A total of 233 people were asked the following questions in the following cities: New York, Philadelphia, Washington, Norfolk, Denver, Los Angeles. Of the 233 respondants, 78 (34%) were black, 155 (66%) were white; 87 were women (37%), 146 were men (63%), 134 were over 30 (58%) and 99 were under 30 (42%).

	Yes			No			Don't Know		
	A	B	W	A	B	W	A	B	W*
				(percentages)					
1. Do you think that sport *should be* above politics, that is, that politics should have no influence in sport?	77	78	77	21	18	22	2	4	1
2. Do you feel that sport, as it functions today, is above politics in:									
a. national competition?	33	33	33	61	61	61	6	6	6
b. international competition?	32	39	29	61	58	63	7	3	8
3. Do you feel that race is a factor in sports that makes it political?	45.5	54	42	46	44	48	8.5	3	10
4. Do you feel that the gestures made by black U.S. athletes in the 1968 Olympic games were justifiable in terms of the Olympic ideals of politics playing no part in sports?	40.5	57	32	51	35	61	8.5	9	8

*A = all; B = black; W = white.

LETTER FROM OSCAR STATE TO T. RANGASAMY, MAY 13, 1946

C O P Y

OSCAR STATE, Dip. C.P.T.C., F.B.A.P.T.
6b King Street, Twickenham, Middlesex, England

13th May, 1946.

Mr. T. Rangasamy,
92 Commercial Road,
Sidwell,
Port Elizabeth,
South Africa.

Dear Mr. Rangasamy,

Please pardon my delay in replying to your letter but I had to wait until I placed the matter before our Central Council. They considered your request with sympathy but it is with regret that I have to inform you that we cannot bring ant [*sic*] pressure on the South African Weight Lifting Federation to force them to recognise you. Their rules, as with all national sporting associations in South Africa, will not permit of mixed contests between white and coloured athletes. This is also a condition of the South African Olympic Council, therefore no coloured man could be chosen to represent South Africa in the international contests. For these reasons we cannot support your claim against the South African Weight Lifting Federation.

However we can suggest an alternative method for you to secure recognition for your lifters. We advise you to form an association of your own with some such title as "The Indian (or Coloured) Amateur Weight-Lifters' Association of South Africa. If you can present us with a properly drawn up constitution and rules, we are prepared to grant you full recognition as an affiliated association. Your members would then be entitled to our assistance on all lifting matters, your records would be recognised as South African (coloured) and if high enough, as British Empire records. Please advise me as soon as possible of your intentions in this matter.

Yours faithfully,

Hon. Sec.

RESULTS OF SURVEY OF THE NATIONAL OLYMPIC COMMITTEES ON THE ISSUE OF SOUTH AFRICAN PARTICIPATION IN THE 1968 OLYMPICS

The NOCs were asked to check one of the following answers to the question:

Our committee took the following stand on South African participation in the 1968 Mexico Olympics:

a. ____ approved.
b. ____ approved on the condition of an integrated team.
c. ____ approved on the condition that an integrated team would have been selected on the basis of integrated trials in South Africa.
d. ____ did not approve without complete sports integration.

The following countries checked *a:* Australia*, Austria, Belgium*, Canada*, Denmark*, Finland*, Great Britain*, Greece*, Ireland*, Luxemburg*, Malawi*, Norway*, Portugal*, Sweden*, United States*. [Total of fifteen nations.]

New Zealand was the only country to check *b.*

The following countries checked *d:* Algeria, Saudia Arabia, Barbados, Bulgaria, Cameroons, Central Africa Republic, Ceylon*, Columbia, Congo Brazzaville, Congo D.R., Cuba, Czechoslovakia, Dahomey, Equador, Ethiopia, Gabon, Ghana, Guinea, Guyana, Hungary, India, Indonesia, Iran, Iraq, Ivory Coast, Jamaica, Jordan, Kenya, Kuwait, Lebanon*, Liberia, Libya, Madagascar*, Malaysia*, Mali, Mexico, Morocco*, Niger, Nigeria, Pakistan, Philippines, Poland, Rumania, Senegal, Sierra Leone, Singapore, Sudan, Syria*, Tanzania, Togo, Trinidad and Tobago, Tunisia*, Uganda, U.S.S.R., U.A.R., Uruguay*, Venezuela, Yugoslavia*, Chad, Gambia, Korea DPR, Upper Volta, Mauritania, Zambia, Somalia [sixty-six nations].

*Answer obtained from press reports or personal interview.

THE OLYMPIC MOVEMENT*

ORGANIZATION

The IOC consists of a number of coopted members (in 1972 it had seventy-four members); to use the words of its founder—it is "a self-recruiting body". In fact, Olympism can only flourish if it enjoys perfect independence in all respects: money, politics, religion, technology.

A general meeting known as a session is held once a year, (twice, in years when the Games are celebrated); at this session, members elect the board of directors, the Executive Board. At the head of the IOC is a President. There have been five presidents since 1894.

MEMBERS

A member of the IOC must be capable of dealing with any subject, without however specializing exclusively in any one to which he might become enslaved; he must be sufficiently international not to be influenced by national prejudices in any international question; he must be free from all ties and restraints. In short, members of the IOC are chosen for their knowledge of sport, their influence, their worth, their independence and their availability. When coopting members, the countries from which they come must also be taken into consideration so as to ensure a fair geographical distribution of the ambassadors of Olympism. Similarly, it is customary to favour nationals of countries with a long Olympic tradition behind them.

Let us also mention that there may be more than two members with the same nationality.

The method of recruitment has frequently been discussed and especially criticized. This being to, and after studying all possible ways of creating an international assembly capable of making decisions without appeal and in complete impartiality, the most ardent champions of election by universal, proportional or representative suffrage, are led to the conclusion that the present solution alone is viable and capable of ensuring the continuance of the IOC.

*From: Monique Berlioux, *Olympism* (Lausanne: IOC, 1972), pp. 8-9. Reproduced with permission.

How is a member elected? On the recommendation of the Executive Board, which proposes his name for the approval of the general meeting.

Once elected, the member of the IOC takes the oath:

> "Recognizing the responsibilities that go with the great honour of being elected a member of the International Olympic Committee and representing it in my country. I undertake to promote the Olympic Movement to the best of my ability, to respect and safeguard the fundamental principles of the Olympic Charter as conceived by Baron Pierre de Coubertin, and to remain free of any political or commercial pressures as well as of any considerations of race or religion."

He then becomes the ambassador of Olympism in his country of origin and not his country's spokesman to the Committee. This distinction is a vital one. Finally, the only precedence among members is their date of admission to the Committee.

Until 1966, members of the IOC were elected for life. At their request they could be elected to honorary membership, with the possibility of attending general meetings and taking part in discussions, but without the right to vote. Since 1966, members elected after this date must retire at the age of 72. A member may resign at any time.

Notes

INTRODUCTION

1. Monique Berlioux, ed., *Olympism* (Lausanne: International Olympic Committee, 1972) p. 1.
2. *New York Times,* October 4, 1959.
3. Speech to the fifty-fifth session of the IOC in Munich (May 23, 1959), from *The Speeches of President Avery Brundage, 1952 to 1968* (Lausanne: IOC, 1969), pp. 41–42.
4. Statement by the coach of the Soviet backetball team in a television interview before the fifth game of the series, May 7, 1973.
5. Speech to the fifty-third session of the IOC in Sofia, September 22, 1957, in *Speeches of Brundage,* p. 34.
6. Speech to the sixtieth session of the IOC in Baden-Baden, October 16, 1963, *Speeches of Brundage,* p. 65.
7. *New York Times,* May 7, 1936.
8. Ibid., October 5, 1935.
9. Speech to the sixtieth session of the IOC in Baden-Baden, October 16, 1963, in *Speeches of Brundage,* p. 67.
10. *New York Times,* May 29, 1959.
11. Ibid., June 3, 1959.
12. Ibid., June 4, 1959.
13. Ibid., August 1, 1959.
14. Ibid., September 17, 1959.
15. Ibid., February 7, 1960.
16. Ibid., March 17, 1961.
17. Ibid., May 29, 1962.
18. Ibid., September 3, 1962.
19. *The Times* [London], February 8, 1963.
20. Ibid., February 21, 1963.
21. *New York Times,* October 6, 1963.
22. *The Times* [London], October 29, 1963.
23. *New York Times,* May 23, 1966.
24. Speech to the forty-eighth session of the IOC in Mexico City, April 17, 1953, in *Speeches of Brundage,* p. 10

25. Speech to the fifty-first session of the IOC in Cortinna d' Ampezzo, January 23, 1956, *Speeches of Brundage,* p. 22.
26. Speech to the sixty-second session of the IOC in Tokyo, October 6, 1964, *Speeches of Brundage,* p. 80.
27. It should be noted that South Africa also has prohibited integrated teams from other countries to participate in South Africa. 1970 was the first time that an integrated team (the New Zealand All-Blacks) ever entered South Africa.
28. *New York Times,* October 4, 1959.
29. Leo Kuper, "The Heightening of Racial Tension," *Africa: Social Problems of Change and Conflict,* ed. Pierre L. Van Den Berghe (San Francisco: Chandler Publishing Co., 1965), pp. 239-241.
30. A distinction of definition is made between racism (racialism) and ethnocentrism. Racism (racialism) is defined as discrimination against a person or a group of people based on that person's (group's) physical characteristics (such as skin color). Ethnocentrism is defined as discrimination against a person or group of people based on that person's (group's) cultural or ethnic characteristics. The former is more applicable to South Africa (although ethnocentrism is also a factor there), while the latter applies to the treatment of the Jews in Nazi Germany.
31. A white nation is loosely defined here as a nation whose predominant racial group is white. A nonwhite nation is loosely defined here as a nation whose predominant racial group is nonwhite.
32. Survey conducted in August 1972 in the following cities: New York, Philadelphia, Washington, D.C., Norfolk, Denver, and Los Angeles. Seventy-eight blacks and 155 whites were interviewed. The full details of this survey are in the appendix.
33. See: Peter Hain, *Don't Play with Apartheid* (London: George Allen and Unwin Ltd., 1971); Basil D'Oliveira, *The D'Oliveira Affair* (London: Collins, 1969); Chris de Broglio, *South Africa: Racism in Sport* (London: Christian Action Publications Ltd., 1970); and Harry Edwards, *The Revolt of the Black Athlete* (New York: The Free Press, 1969).

CHAPTER 1

1. *New York Times,* May 29, 1933.
2. Prime Minister John Vorster, address to Parliament, April 11, 1967, from *Report of the IOC Commission on South Africa* (Lausanne: IOC, 1968), p. 68.

3. Richard D. Mandell, *The Nazi Olympics* (New York: Macmillan Co., 1971), pp. 164-65.
4. Speech to the fifty-fifth session of the IOC in Munich (May 23, 1959), from *The Speeches of President Avery Brundage, 1952 to 1968* (Lausanne: IOC, 1969), p. 42.
5. *The Times* [London], May 20, 1970.
6. *Rand Daily Mail* [Johannesburg], March 25, 1970.
7. Ibid., September 12, 1967.
8. Dennis Brutus, interview, February 3, 1970; Chris de Broglio, interview, March 18, 1970; Omar Cassem, interview, March 22, 1970; Peter Hain, interview, April 14, 1970.
9. *The Times* [London], September 19, 1969.
10. C. Legum and J. Drysdale, *Africa Contemporary Record, Annual Survey and Documents, 1969-70* (Exeter: Africa Research Ltd., 1970), p. B287.
11. Ibid.
12. *The Times* [London], December 6, 1935.
13. *New York Times,* August 6, 1933.
14. Ibid., September 30, 1934.
15. Ibid., April 23, 1936.
16. Ibid., May 31, 1936.
17. Ibid., July 18, 1936.
18. *The Times* [London], July 18, 1936.
19. Ibid., August 1, 1936.
20. *New York Times,* August 2, 1936; *The Times* [London], August 3, 1936.
21. *New York Times,* August 6, 1936.
22. Ibid., August 7, 1936.
23. *The Times* [London], September 2, 1955.
24. *The World* [Johannesburg], April 11, 1969.
25. Muriel Horrell, ed., *A Survey of Race Relations in South Africa, 1955-56,* (Johannesburg: South African Institute of Race Relations, 1956), p. 227. (The *Survey* is an annual, published by the South African Institute of Race Relations. Hereafter, references will be cited as: Horrell, ed., *Survey:* followed by year covered. For example, this citation would read: Horrell, ed., *Survey: 1955-56,* p. 227.)
26. Cassem, interview, April 1, 1970.
27. *New York Times,* June 13, August 27, 1933.
28. Ibid., November 23, 1933.
29. Ibid., August 12, 1935.

30. Mandell, *Nazi Olympics,* p. 59.
31. *Report of the IOC Commission on South Africa,* p. 9.
32. *The Times* [London], September 2, 1955.
33. *New York Times,* August 19, 1935.
34. Ibid., October 21, 1935.
35. Horrell, ed., *Survey: 1967,* p. 21.
36. Mandell, *Nazi Olympics,* pp. 62-63.
37. *New York Times,* December 18, 1933.
38. *The Times* [London], April 13, 1968.
39. *New York Times,* July 16, 1936.
40. Brutus, interview, February 3, 1970.
41. *New York Times,* April 4, 9, 1933.
42. Ibid., September 26, 1935.
43. Ibid., November 23, 1933.
44. *Report of the IOC Commission on South Africa,* p. 14.
45. De Broglio, interview, March 18, 1970.
46. De Broglio, interview, April 3, 1970.
47. See: *New York Times,* November 5, 22, 1933, August 26, December 8, 1934, March 18, October 4, November 12, 16, 1935, March 9, 13, 31, May 10, 17, June 16, 20, 1936.
48. *New York Times,* May 17, June 16, 1936.
49. Mandell, *Nazi Olympics,* p. 68.
50. *New York Times,* October 20, December 7, 1935.
51. Ibid., October 11, 1935.
52. See: *New York Times,* May 31, June 6, 1933, August 12, September 3, 27, 1934, July 22, 31, August 5, 23, September 1, October 4, 18, 16-27, November 26, 27, December 1-4, 1935, January 4, 25, 1936.
53. Ibid., November 21, 1933.
54. Ibid., November 23, 1933.
55. Ibid., December 4, 1935.
56. Ibid.
57. *The Times* [London], August 12, 1935.
58. *New York Times,* June 28, 1934.
59. Ibid., August 11, 1934.
60. Ibid., September 19, 1934.
61. Ibid., September 27, 1934.
62. Speech to the fifty-fifth session of the IOC in Munich, May 23, 1959, from *The Speeches of President Avery Brundage, 1952 to 1968* (Lausanne: IOC, 1969), p. 41.
63. Speech to the sixtieth session of the IOC in Baden-Baden, October 16, 1963, ibid., p. 67.

CHAPTER 2

1. *New Zealand Herald* [Aukland], January 30, 1970.
2. Chris de Broglio, interview, April 29, 1970.
3. Oscar State to T. Rangasamy, May 13, 1946.
4. Ibid. The full text of this letter is in the appendix.
5. Muriel Horrell, *A Survey of Race Relations in South Africa, 1951-52* (Johannesburg: South African Institute of Race Relations, 1952), p. 75. The *Survey* is an annual published by the South African Institute of Race Relations. Hereafter, references will be cited as: Horrell, ed., *Survey,* followed by year covered. For example, this citation would read: Horrell, ed., *Survey: 1951-52,* p. 75.
6. *The Times* [London], August 25, 1951.
7. Ms., *Sport and Politics in an Urban African Community,* 1963, pp. 4-5 (the author, living in South Africa, wished to remain anonymous for his own safety).
8. *The Times* [London], October 27, 1954.
9. *Sport and Politics,* p. 5.
10. *The Times* [London], July 8, 1955.
11. Ibid., October 13, 1955.
12. Horrell, ed., *Survey: 1955-56,* p. 226.
13. *The Times* [London], September 2, 1955.
14. Ibid., December 5, 1955.
15. *Sport and Politics,* p. 7.
16. Horrell, ed., *Survey: 1955-56,* pp. 226-27.
17. Dennis Brutus, interview, December 29, 1972.
18. Horrell, ed., *Survey: 1955-56,* p. 227.
19. Horrell, ed., *Survey: 1956-57,* p. 220.
20. Ibid.
21. Brutus, interview, December 29, 1972.
22. Horrell, ed., *Survey: 1955-56,* p. 227.
23. *The Times* [London], January 19, 1957.
24. Horrell, ed., *Survey: 1956-57,* p. 220.
25. Horrell, ed., *Survey: 1957-58,* p. 217.
26. Ibid.
27. *The Times* [London], December 28, 1957.
28. Ibid., February 1, 1958.
29. Horrell, ed., *Survey: 1957-58,* p. 217.
30. *The Times* [London], July 14, 1958.
31. Brutus, interview, December 29, 1972.
32. Opening address by Alan Paton to SASA conference, January 10-11,

1959, cited by Richard Thompson, *Race and Sport* (London: Oxford University Press, 1964), pp. 17-18.

33. Ibid.
34. Brutus, interview, December 29, 1972.
35. *The Times* [London], March 11, 1959.
36. Brutus, interview, December 29, 1972.
37. Basil D'Oliveira, *The D'Oliveira Affair* (London: Collins, 1969), p. 38.
38. Minutes of the fifty-fifth session of the IOC, Munich, 1959, in *Report of the IOC Commission of South Africa* (Lausanne: IOC 1968), p. 17.
39. Ibid., pp. 17-18.
40. De Broglio, interview, June 6, 1970.
41. Thompson, *Race and Sport,* p. 32.
42. *The Times* [London], June 13, 1959.
43. See: *The Times* [London]: June 13, 19, 30, July 21, August 13, 15, October 7, 1959; Thompson, *Race and Sport,* p. 43.
44. *The Times* [London], May 20, 1959.
45. Minutes of the meeting of the IOC executive board with the National Olympic Committees, Rome, 1959, in *Report of the IOC Commission on South Africa,* p. 16.
46. Minutes of the fifty-fifth session of the IOC, Munich, 1959, in *Report of the IOC Commission on South Africa,* p. 17.
47. Ibid.
48. *The Times* [London], February 24, 1959.
49. Thompson, *Race and Sport,* p. 22.
50. *The Times* [London], December 24, 1959.
51. Horrell, ed., *Survey: 1959-60,* pp. 57-60.
52. Thompson, *Race and Sport,* p. 45.
53. *The Times* [London], January 8, 1960.
54. Thompson, *Race and Sport,* pp. 48-49.
55. *The Times* [London], April 6, 1960.
56. D'Oliveira, *D'Oliveira Affair,* pp. 44-45.
57. *The Times* [London], April 7, 1960.
58. Ibid.
59. Ibid., April 12, 1960.
60. Ibid., April 14, 1960.
61. Ibid.
62. *The Times* [London], April 16, 1960.
63. Omar Cassem, interview, June 9, 1970.

64. *The Times* [London], April 14, 1960.
65. Brutus, interview, April 29, 1970.
66. Horrell, ed., *Survey: 1959-60,* p. 263.
67. See: *The Times* [London], August 22, 27, 1960, and Horrell, ed., *Survey: 1959-60,* p. 264.
68. Minutes of the meeting of the IOC executive board with the Commission on Amateurism, Lausanne, March 1962, in *Report of the IOC Commission on South Africa,* p. 19.
69. Horrell, ed., *Survey: 1961,* p. 273.
70. Ibid., p. 278.
71. Horrell, ed., *Survey: 1959-60,* p. 265.
72. *The Times* [London], February 5, 1960.
73. Horrell, ed., *Survey: 1959-60,* p. 264.
74. Ibid., p. 276.
75. Ibid., p. 277.
76. Ibid., p. 274.
77. *The Times* [London], July 19, 1961.
78. Ibid., July 21, 1961.
79. Horrell, ed., *Survey: 1961,* p. 278.
80. *The Times* [London], April 8, 1961.
81. Ibid., April 6, 1960.
82. Horrell, ed., *Survey: 1961,* pp. 273-74.
83. Ibid.
84. Ibid.
85. Ibid.
86. Ibid.
87. Ibid.
88. Ibid., p. 276.
89. Ibid., p. 275.
90. *The Times* [London], January 18, 1961.
91. Thompson, *Race and Sport,* pp. 57-58.
92. Horrell, ed., *Survey: 1961,* pp. 279-80.
93. Ibid., p. 280.
94. Horrell, ed., *Survey: 1962,* p. 68.
95. Ibid., p. 70.
96. Ibid., pp. 69-70.
97. *The Times* [London], February 1, 1962.
98. Ibid.
99. *Star* [Johannesburg], February 2, 1962.
100. Ibid., February 3, 1962.

101. Ibid., February 14, 1962.
102. Ibid., February 2, 1962.
103. Horrell, ed., *Survey: 1962,* p. 218.
104. Ibid., pp. 217-218.
105. *The Times* [London], May 8, 1962.
106. Horrell, ed., *Survey: 1962,* p. 219.
107. Ibid., p. 217.
108. *Star* [Johannesburg], May 28, 1962.
109. Horrell, ed., *Survey: 1962,* pp. 218-19.
110. *New York Times,* January 29, 1962.
111. *The Times* [London], February 14, 1962.
112. Minutes of the IOC executive board with the Commission on Amateurism, Lausanne, March 1962, in *Report of the IOC Commission on South Africa,* p. 19.
113. Horrell, ed., *Survey: 1962,* p. 213.
114. *Star* [Johannesburg], March 31, 1962.
115. Ibid., April 17, 1962.
116. Ibid.
117. See: *The Times* [London], April 19, 1962, and Horrell, ed., *Survey: 1962,* p. 221.
118. *Star* [Johannesburg], April 30, 1962.
119. *The Times* [London], April 26, 1962.
120. *New York Times,* May 13, 1962.
121. Minutes of the fifty-ninth session of the IOC, Moscow, June 1962, in *Report of the IOC Commission on South Africa,* p. 20.
122. *Star* [Johannesburg], June 8, 1962.
123. Ibid.
124. Thompson, *Race and Sport,* pp. 18-19.
125. *The Times* [London], July 19, 1962.
126. Horrell, ed., *Survey: 1962,* p. 215.
127. Ibid., pp. 222-23.
128. *New York Times,* October 21, 1935.
129. De Broglio, interview, March 18, 1970.
130. *The Times* [London], January 29, 1963.
131. Ibid.
132. Ibid.
133. *Sunday Express* [Johannesburg], August 25, 1963.
134. *The Times* [London], May 31, 1963.
135. Dennis Brutus and Chris de Broglio, joint interview, April 29, 1970.
136. Tex Maule, "A Flare in the Dark," *Sports Illustrated* (June 3, 1968), p. 70.

137. Brutus, interview, April 29, 1970.
138. *New York Times,* September 22, 1963.
139. Brutus, interview, April 29, 1970.
140. *New York Times,* September 23, 1963.
141. John Harris tape to the IOC Baden-Baden session, October 1963 (London: SAN-ROC files).
142. *New York Times,* August 21, 1963.
143. Ibid., October 11, 1963.
144. Ibid., October 15, 1963.
145. *Post* [Natal], October 20, 1963.
146. Minutes of the sixtieth session of the IOC, Baden-Baden, October 1963, in *Report of the IOC Commission on South Africa,* p. 21.
147. Ibid.
148. *The Times* [London], October 21, 1963.
149. *Evening Post* [Port Elizabeth], October 21, 1963.
150. Ibid.
151. Ibid.
152. *The Times* [London], October 22, 1963.
153. Horrell, ed., *Survey: 1963,* p. 284.
154. *The Times* [London], February 5, 1963.
155. Ibid.
156. Horrell, ed., *Survey: 1963,* pp. 295-96.
157. *Sunday Express* [Johannesburg], March 10, 1963.
158. Horrell, ed., *Survey: 1963,* p. 294.
159. De Broglio, interview, June 3, 1970.
160. Horrell, ed., *Survey: 1963,* p. 293.
161. *Star* [Johannesburg], August 19, 1963.
162. *Post* [Natal], August 25, 1963.
163. Ibid.
164. Horrell, ed., *Survey: 1963,* p. 290.
165. *Sunday Times* [Johannesburg], September 8, 1963.
166. Ibid., September 15, 1963.
167. *Star* [Johannesburg], December 17, 1963.
168. Horrell, ed., *Survey: 1963,* p. 288.
169. Ibid., p. 296.
170. Ibid., p. 288.
171. Chris de Broglio, *South Africa: Racism in Sport* (London: Christian Action Publications Ltd., 1970), p. 30.
172. *Star* [Johannesburg], January 9, 1963.
173. *Rand Daily Mail* [Johannesburg], January 11, 1963.
174. *The Times* [London], January 24, 1963.

175. *Star* [Johannesburg], January 24, 1963.
176. *Daily News* [Durban], January 25, 1963.
177. Ibid.
178. *The Times* [London], December 2, 1935.
179. Horrell, ed., *Survey: 1963,* p. 292.
180. *Post* [Natal], August 25, 1963.
181. *Star* [Johannesburg], December 17, 1963.

CHAPTER 3

1. *New York Times,* January 3, 1964.
2. *New York Times* and *The Times* [London], January 15, 1964.
3. Minutes of the meeting of the executive board of the IOC, January 25, 26, 1964, in *Report of the IOC Commission on South Africa* (Lausanne: IOC, 1968), p. 24.
4. Ibid.
5. Resolution voted at the Innsbruck session on the South African question, in *Report of the IOC Commission on South Africa,* p. 23.
6. *The Times* [London], January 28, 1964.
7. *New York Times,* January 29, 1964.
8. Ibid., January 24, 1964.
9. John Harris, open letter, February 10, 1964 (London: SAN-ROC files).
10. *The Times* [London], February 14, 15, 1964.
11. Muriel Horrell, ed., *A Survey of Race Relations in South Africa: 1964* (Johannesburg: South African Institute of Race Relations, 1965), p. 333. The *Survey* is an annual published by the South African Institute of Race Relations. Hereafter references will be cited as: Horrell, ed., *Survey,* followed by the year covered. For example, this citation would read: Horrell, ed., *Survey: 1964,* p. 333.
12. *The Times* [London], June 27, 1964.
13. *New York Times,* June 27, 1964.
14. *The Times* [London], June 27, 1964.
15. Ibid., June 29, 1964.
16. Horrell, ed., *Survey: 1964,* p. 334.
17. Ibid., p. 32.
18. Dennis Brutus, interview, March 27, 1973.
19. Ibid.
20. Horrell, ed., *Survey: 1964,* pp. 93-94.

21. Brutus, interview, March 27, 1973.
22. Peter Hain, interview, April 14, 1970.
23. Ibid.
24. Ibid.
25. *The Times* [London], June 27, 1964.
26. Horrell, ed., *Survey: 1964,* p. 343.
27. Ibid.
28. *The Times* [London], June 27, 1964.
29. Horrell, ed., *Survey: 1964,* pp. 336-38.
30. Ibid., p. 341.
31. *Star* [Johannesburg], January 20, 1964.
32. *Sunday Express* [Johannesburg], March 9, 1964.
33. *Rand Daily Mail* [Johannesburg], March 13, 1964.
34. Ibid., June 15, 1964.
35. *Sunday Express* [Johannesburg], August 28, 1964.
36. Minutes of the thirty-fourth Ordinary Congress of FIFA, October 8, 1964, p. 10, FIFA collection.
37. Ibid., pp. 11-12.
38. Ibid., p. 12.
39. Horrell, ed., *Survey: 1964,* p. 344.
40. Ibid.
41. *New York Times,* December 13, 1964.
42. Horrell, ed., *Survey: 1964,* p. 343.
43. Ibid., p. 344.
44. *New York Times,* June 28, 1964.
45. Ibid., November 5, 1964.
46. See: *Report of the IOC Commission on South Africa,* p. 9 and Horrell, ed., *Survey: 1965,* p. 303.
47. See: *Sunday Times* [London], March 16, 1965; Horrell, ed., *Survey: 1965,* p. 307; John Laurence, *The Seeds of Disaster* (London: Victor Golanz Ltd., 1968), p. 247.
48. Laurence, *Seeds,* p. 253.
49. *Sunday Tribune* [Durban], April 16, 1967.
50. Laurence, *Seeds,* pp. 254-55.
51. Ibid., pp. 258-60.
52. Ibid., p. 263.
53. Ibid., p. 260.
54. Horrell, ed., *Survey: 1965,* p. 99.
55. Horrell, ed., *Survey: 1966,* p. 297.
56. *New York Times,* April 13, 1965.

57. Ibid., October 7, 1965.
58. *The Times* [London], October 11, 1965.
59. *New York Times,* October 1, 1965.
60. *Sunday Times* [London], August 19, 1965.
61. Horrell, ed., *Survey: 1965,* p. 312.
62. Brutus, interview, March 27, 1973.
63. Chris de Broglio, interview, March 27, 1973.
64. Ibid.
65. Horrell, ed., *Survey: 1966,* p. 298.
66. *The Times* [London], January 13, 1966.
67. *Daily News* [Durban], February 8, 1966.
68. *The Times* [London], February 18, 1966.
69. *Star* [Johannesburg], April 23, 1966.
70. Chris de Broglio, *South Africa: Racism in Sport* (London: Christian Action Publications Ltd., 1970), p. 16.
71. See: *Star* [Johannesburg], April 20, 22, 23, 1966.
72. Minutes of the IOC executive board, April 21-24, 1966, in *Report of the IOC Commission on South Africa,* p. 26.
73. Minutes of the sixty-fourth session of the IOC, Rome, April 25-28, 1966, in *Report of the IOC Commission on South Africa,* p. 27.
74. *Cape Times* [Cape Town], April 28, 1966.
75. *Star* [Johannesburg], April 28, 1966.
76. SAN-ROC to the African and Asian members of the IOC, memorandum, November 22, 1966, SAN-ROC collection.
77. Ibid.
78. *New York Times,* August 11, 1934.
79. Horrell, ed., *Survey: 1966,* p. 297.
80. *Star* [Johannesburg], July 7, 1966.
81. Ibid., July 8, 1966.
82. Ibid.
83. Ibid., August 18, 1966.
84. Ibid.
85. Ibid., September 7, 1966.
86. Brutus, interview, March 27, 1973.
87. Chris de Broglio to J. Thorpe, July 18, 1966, SAN-ROC collection.
88. *Guardian* [Manchester], August 3, 1966.
89. *Star* [Johannesburg], April 23, 1966.
90. SAN-ROC, memorandum on discrimination in SAAAU, July 27, 1966, SAN-ROC collection.
91. Sierra Leone National Sports Council to IAAF, August 24, 1966, SAN-ROC collection.

92. IAAF, official agenda, 1966, pp. 2-4, IAAF collection.
93. SAN-ROC, memorandum, September 5, 1966, SAN-ROC collection.
94. SAN-ROC to all national weightlifting federations, June 21, 1966, SAN-ROC collection.
95. SAN-ROC to all provincial weightlifting associations, June 21, 1966, SAN-ROC collection.
96. SAN-ROC, memorandum, November 22, 1966, SAN-ROC collection.
97. *Golden City Post,* October 23, 1966.
98. Brutus, interview, March 27, 1973.
99. *The World* [Johannesburg], August 5, 1966.
100. Ibid., August 29, 1966.
101. *Star* [Johannesburg], November 19, 1966.
102. Ibid., July 13, 1966.
103. *The World* [Johannesburg], August 5, 1966.
104. Horrell, ed., *Survey: 1966,* p. 297.
105. *Star* [Johannesburg], July 27, 1966.
106. Brutus, interview, March 27, 1973
107. SCSA, "Resolution Concerning South Africa," Bamako, December 1966, SCSA collection.
108. *Sunday Express* [Johannesburg], January 22, 1967.
109. *Guardian* [Manchester], January 23, 1967.
110. Ibid.
111. Horrell, ed., *Survey: 1967,* p. 325.
112. See: *Evening Post* [Port Elizabeth] and *Rand Daily Mail* [Johannesburg], as reported in *The Times* [London], January 28, 1967; *Sunday Times* [Johannesburg], January 29, 1966; *Sunday Tribune* [Durban], January 29, 1966.
113. *The Times* [London], March 4, 1967.
114. Ibid., January 31, 1967.
115. Ibid., February 2, 1967.
116. Ibid., February 1, 1967.
117. Horrell, ed., *Survey: 1967,* p. 323.
118. *The Times* [London], February 10, 1967.
119. *New York Times,* February 21, 1967.
120. *Evening Post* [Port Elizabeth], March 6, 1967.
121. Laurence, *Seeds,* p. 241.
122. *The Times* [London], March 6, 1967.
123. *Evening Post* [Port Elizabeth], March 6, 1967.
124. *Evening News* [London], March 16, 1967.

125. *Star* [Johannesburg], March 22, 1967.
126. Ibid.
127. SAN-ROC, press release, March 23, 1967, SAN-ROC collection.
128. *Star* [Johannesburg], March 30, 1967.
129. *The People* [Kampala], April 1, 1967.
130. Ibid.
131. *Star* [Johannesburg], March 30, 1967.
132. Ibid., April 4, 1967.
133. *The Times* [London], April 10, 1967.
134. Hansard Report, April 11, 1967 in *Report of the IOC Commission on South Africa*, pp. 67-69.
135. Ibid., p. 70.
136. Ibid., pp. 71-72.
137. *The Times* [London], April 12, 1967.
138. *Evening Post* [Port Elizabeth], April 12, 1967.
139. *New York Times*, April 12, 1967.
140. *The Times* [London], April 13, 1967.
141. Ibid.
142. *Evening Post* [Port Elizabeth], April 13, 1967.
143. *The Times* [London], April 14, 1967.
144. *Sunday Times* [Johannesburg], April 16, 1967.
145. SAN-ROC, press release, April 17, 1967, SAN-ROC collection.
146. De Broglio, interview, June 3, 1970.
147. *Sunday Times* [Johannesburg], April 16, 1967.
148. Ibid.
149. Ibid.
150. *Sunday Tribune* [Durban], April 16, 1967.
151. *Sunday Express* [Johannesburg], April 16, 1967.
152. Ibid.
153. *Star* [Johannesburg], April 19, 20, 1967.
154. Ibid., April 20, 1967.
155. Tex Maule, "A Flare in the Dark," *Sports Illustrated* (June 3, 1968), p. 70.
156. Ibid.
157. *Rand Daily Mail* [Johannesburg], April 17, 1967.
158. *Star* [Johannesburg], April 19, 1967.
159. Dennis Brutus to Avery Brundage, April 19, 1967, SAN-ROC collection.
160. Motion on the South African problem, presented by the African NOCs, May 3, 1967, in *Report of the IOC Commission on South Africa*, pp. 37-38.

161. Minutes of the IOC executive board meeting with the NOCs, May 3, 1967, in *Report of the IOC Commission on South Africa,* pp. 35-36
162. Ibid.
163. Minutes of the IOC executive board meeting, February 11, 12, 1967, Copenhagen, in *Report of the IOC Commission on South Africa,* pp. 2, 30.
164. SAOGA delegation to the IOC Executive, May 4, 1967, SAN-ROC collection.
165. Ibid.
166. Ibid.
167. Brutus, interview, March 27, 1973.
168. SAN-ROC, press release, May 5, 1967, SAN-ROC collection.
169. Minutes of the sixty-fifth session of the IOC, Tehran, May 6-9, 1967, in *Report of the IOC Commission on South Africa,* p. 32.
170. Ibid.
171. *Eastern Province Herald* [Port Elizabeth], May 6, 1967.
172. Ibid.
173. *Cape Argus* [Cape Town], May 6, 1967.
174. *Star* [Johannesburg], May 8, 1967.
175. See: *New York Times,* May 8, 1967, and ACOA to USOC, May 8, 1967.
176. Dennis Brutus to Avery Brundage, May 7, 1967, SAN-ROC collection.
177. SAN-ROC, press release, June 28, 1967, SAN-ROC collection.
178. Horrell, ed., *Survey: 1967,* p. 323.
179. Dennis Brutus, address to the U.N. International Seminar on Apartheid, Racial Discrimination and Colonialism in Southern Africa, Lusaka, July 24-August 4, 1967.
180. *Star* [Johannesburg], July 17, 1967.
181. Horrell, ed., *Survey: 1967,* p. 325.
182. Brutus, to the U.N. International Seminar.
183. Ibid.
184. *New York Times,* July 24, 1967.
185. Avery Brundage to Lord Killanin, August 8, 31, 1967, in *Report of the IOC Commission on South Africa,* pp. 48-50.
186. *The Times* [London], August 17, 1967.
187. See: *Cape Times* [Cape Town] and *Evening Standard* [London], September 9, 1967.
188. *Sunday Express* [Johannesburg], August 27, 1967.
189. *Daily News* [Durban], September 9, 1967.

190. *Cape Times* [Cape Town], September 13, 1967.
191. Ibid.
192. *Report of the IOC Commission on South Africa,* pp. 6-7.
193. *The Times* [London], September 12, 1967.
194. *Cape Argus* [Cape Town], September 16, 1967.
195. Brutus, interview, March 27, 1973.
196. *Cape Argus* [Cape Town], September 16, 1967.
197. *Eastern Province Herald* [Port Elizabeth], September 14, 1967.
198. Ibid.
199. *The Times* [London], September 18, 1967.
200. *Sunday Tribune* [Durban], September 17, 1967.
201. *Eastern Province Herald* [Port Elizabeth], October 17, 1967.
202. Transcript of the testimony of the SAN-ROC delegation to the IOC Commission in Lausanne, November 1967, SAN-ROC collection.
203. Ibid.
204. Ibid.
205. Brutus, interview, March 27, 1973.
206. *Report of the IOC Commission on South Africa,* p. 14.
207. Dennis Brutus to Dan Kunene, cable, November 21, 1967, SAN-ROC collection.
208. *Los Angeles Times,* November 23, 1967.
209. Ibid., November 24, 1967.
210. Ibid.
211. *New York Times,* December 15, 1967.
212. Ibid.
213. Ibid.
214. Ibid., December 16, 1967.
215. Ibid.
216. *Star* [Johannesburg], December 18, 1967.
217. *The Times* [London], December 18, 1967.
218. Brutus, interview, March 27, 1973.
219. *Star* [Johannesburg], December 14, 1967.
220. SCSA, Lagos resolution on South Africa, December 12, 1967, SCSA collection.
221. *Star* [Johannesburg], December 15, 1967.
222. Ibid., December 16, 1967.
223. *The Times* [London], December 22, 1967.
224. *Post* [Natal], December 24, 1967.
225. African Football Confederation, memorandum, November 1, 1967, SAN-ROC collection.

226. *Post* [Natal], November 26, 1967.
227. SAN-ROC, private draft strategy, January 26, 1968, SAN-ROC collection.
228. SAN-ROC to the Afro-Asian Solidarity Committee, January 16, 1968, SAN-ROC collection.
229. SAN-ROC to Harry Edwards, January 16, 1968, SAN-ROC collection.
230. SAN-ROC, private draft strategy, January 26, 1968.
231. *Sunday Tribune* [Durban], January 28, 1968.
232. *The Times* [London], January 29, 1968.
233. Ibid., January 30, 1968.
234. ANC, *Commentary #12,* January 30, 1968, SAN-ROC collection.
235. See: *The Times* [London] and *New York Times,* January 3, 1968.
236. *Report of the IOC Commission on South Africa,* pp. 14-15.
237. Ibid.
238. Dennis Brutus to Avery Brundage, January 31, 1968, SAN-ROC collection.
239. Harry Edwards, statement on South Africa and the Olympics, February 8, 1968, ACOA collection.
240. *New York Post,* February 8, 1968.
241. *Post* [Natal], February 11, 1968.
242. IOC, resolution on South Africa, February 15, 1968, IOC collection.
243. IOC, *Olympic Rules and Regulations* (Lausanne: IOC, 1972), p. 20.
244. SAOGA delegation to the IOC Executive, Tehran, May 4, 1967, SAN-ROC collection.
245. IOC, *Newsletter #5* (February 1968): 53. (The IOC publishes the *Newsletter* each month from Lausanne.)
246. *Eastern Province Herald* [Port Elizabeth], February 16, 1968.
247. Ibid.
248. Ibid.
249. *Sunday Times* [Johannesburg], February 18, 1968.
250. IOC, *Newsletter* #5 (February 1968): 69.
251. *The Times* [London], February 17, 1968.
252. *Daily Telegraph* [London], February 17, 1968.
253. *New York Times,* February 22, 1968.
254. *Observer* [London], February 18, 1968.
255. *Eastern Province Herald* [Port Elizabeth], February 16, 1968.
256. *Morning Star* [London], February 16, 1968.
257. Avery Brundage to Dennis Brutus, February 16, 1968, SAN-ROC collection.

258. *The Times* [London], February 17, 1968.
259. Ibid.
260. *New York Times,* February 18, 1968.
261. *Sunday Times* [London], February 18, 1968.
262. *Guardian* [Manchester], February 19, 1968.
263. Ibid.
264. *Sunday Times* [London], February 18, 1968.
265. *The Times* [London], February 19, 1968.
266. Ibid.
267. Ibid.
268. *The Times* [London], February 21, 1968.
269. *Daily Mirror* [London], February 23, 1968.
270. *The Times* [London], February 22, 1968.
271. Ibid.,February,21, 22, 1968.
272. *New York Times,* February 25, 1968.
273. IOC, *Newsletter #5* (February 1968): 67.
274. *The Times* [London], February 27, 1968.
275. *New York Herald Tribune,* February 27, 1968.
276. Ibid.
277. Ibid.
278. *The Times* [London], February 29, 1968.
279. Ibid.
280. Ibid., March 1, 1968.
281. Ibid.
282. *New York Times,* March 2, 1968.
283. *Observer* [London], March 3, 1968.
284. See: *Observer* [London], March 3, 1968, and *The Times* [London], March 5, 1968.
285. *The Times* [London], March 6, 1968.
286. Ibid., March 8, 1968.
287. Brutus, interview, April 29, 1970.
288. *New York Times,* March 10, 1968.
289. Ibid., March 12, 1968.
290. *The Times* [London], March 13, 1968.
291. *SAN-ROC News and Views* (March 20, 1968), SAN-ROC collection.
292. *Eastern Province Herald* [Port Elizabeth], April 3, 1968.
293. ACOA, press release, April 10, 1968, ACOA collection.
294. Steve Mokone, ACOA press conference, April 10, 1968, ACOA collection.
295. *New York Post,* April 12, 1968.

296. *The Times* [London], April 11, 1968.
297. SCSA to all related to the IOC, April 11, 1968, SCSA collection.
298. *New York Times,* April 15, 1968.
299. *The Times* [London], April 13, 1968.
300. *Eastern Province Herald* [Port Elizabeth], April 16, 1968.
301. Ibid.
302. Maule, "Flare," pp. 66, 69.
303. Ibid., April 19, 1968.
304. IOC, *Newsletter #8* (May 1968): 147-48.
305. Ibid., p. 151.
306. *The Times* [London], April 22, 23, 1968.
307. *The Times* [London], April 23, 1968.
308. Ibid.
309. Ibid., April 22, 1968.
310. IOC, *Newsletter #8*, pp. 149-50
311. Speech to the sixty-third IOC session in Madrid, October 1965, in *The Speeches of President Avery Brundage, 1952 to 1968* (Lausanne: IOC, 1960), p. 85.
312. Ibid.
313. IOC, *Newsletter #8*, pp. 149-50.
314. *New York Times,* May 29, 1959.
315. Ibid., February 9, 1963.
316. Maule, "Flare," pp. 66, 69.
317. IOC, *Newsletter #8,* p. 150.
318. *The Times* [London], April 25, 1968.
319. *Sunday Express* [Johannesburg], April 28, 1968.
320. *Sunday Times* [Johannesburg], April 28, 1968.
321. *Sunday Express* [Johannesburg], April 28, 1968.
322. Ibid.
323. Ibid.
324. *The Times* [London], May 4, 1968.
325. *Star* [Johannesburg], May 17, 1968.
326. Ibid.
327. Ibid., May 15, 1968.
328. Ibid., August 12, 1968.
329. Horrell, ed., *Survey: 1968,* p. 301.
330. *The World* [Johannesburg], May 30, 1968.
331. Brutus, interview, March 27, 1973.
332. *Evening News* [London], May 5, 1968.
333. *New York Times,* June 8, 1968.

334. *Star* [Johannesburg], May 15, 1968.
335. Dennis Brutus to the ILTF, June 1968, SAN-ROC collection.
336. SAN-ROC, "The Fight Against Racialism in International Tennis," June 6, 1968, SAN-ROC collection.
337. Horrell, ed., *Survey: 1968,* p. 299.
338. Dennis Brutus to Queen Elizabeth, July 11, 1968, SAN-ROC collection.
339. *The Times* [London], July 6, 1968.
340. SAN-ROC, document on Mexican games activities, October 1968, SAN-ROC collection.
341. *Star* [Johannesburg], October 28, 1968.
342. *Sunday Express* [Johannesburg], October 27, 1968.
343. Horrell, ed., *Survey: 1968,* p. 299.
344. SAN-ROC/ACOA, transcript of press conference, October 10, 1968, ACOA collection.
345. SAN-ROC to Charles de Gaulle, cable, September 18, 1968, and SAN-ROC to French Minister of Sports, December 11, 1968, SAN-ROC collection.
346. *Sunday Times* [London], September 30, 1969.
347. Anti-Apartheid Movement of Ireland, *Annual Report,* September 1968 (Dublin: Irish AAM), p. 9.
348. *Cape Argus* [Cape Town], August 26, 1968.
349. *The Times* [London], August 29, 1968.
350. Ibid.
351. Ibid., August 30, 1968.
352. Ibid., September 9, 1968.
353. Ibid.
354. Ibid., September 10, 1968.
355. Ibid., September 13, 1968.
356. Ibid., September 12, 1968.
357. Ibid.
358. Ibid., September 17, 1968.
359. *Evening News* [London], September 18, 1968.
360. *The Times* [London], September 18, 1968.
361. Ibid.
362. Ibid., September 19, 1968.
363. *Sunday Express* [Johannesburg], September 22, 1968.
364. *The Times* [London], September 20, 1968.
365. Ibid., September 21, 1968.

366. Ibid., September 24, 1968.
367. Ibid., September 25, 1968.
368. Ibid.
369. *Guardian* [Manchester], December 6, 1968.
370. Ibid., December 5, 1968.
371. *Star* [Johannesburg], July 31, 1968.
372. *The Times* [London], September 26, 1968.
373. *New York Times,* September 1, 1968.
374. Harry Edwards, *The Revolt of the Black Athlete* (New York: Free Press, 1968), pp. 98-99.
375. Ibid.
376. Ibid., pp. 102-3.
377. *The Times* [London], September 26, 1968.
378. *New York Times,* October 16, 1968.
379. Edwards, *Revolt,* p. 104.
380. *The Times* [London], October 18, 1968.
381. *New York Times,* October 17, 1968.
382. Edwards, *Revolt,* pp. 103-104.
383. *The Times* [London], October 19, 1968.
384. Edwards, *Revolt,* p. 105.
385. *The Times* [London], October 20, 1968.
386. Ibid.
387. Ibid.
388. Edwards, *Revolt,* p. 107.
389. Survey conducted in August 1972 in the following cities: New York, Philadelphia, Washington, D.C., Denver, Norfolk, and Los Angeles. Seventy-eight blacks and 155 whites were interviewed (results are included in the appendix).
390. IOC, *Newsletter #15* (December 1968): 577.
391. Maule, *Flare,* p. 62.
392. IOC, *Newsletter #15*, p. 577.
393. Ibid., p. 578.
394. Motion on the South Africa problem presented by the NOCs of Africa during the sixty-seventh session at Mexico, October 2, 1968, SAN-ROC collection.
395. SAN-ROC to the federations of wrestling, weightlifting, shooting, swimming, canoeing, and boxing, October 1, 1968, SAN-ROC collection.
396. *The Times* [London], October 12, 1968.

CHAPTER 4

1. *Sunday Tribune* [Durban], March 16, 1969.
2. Ibid.
3. *Star* [Johannesburg], January 4, 1969.
4. Ibid.
5. Ibid., January 9, 1969.
6. Ibid., January 4, 1969.
7. *Cape Argus* [Cape Town], January 11, 1969.
8. SAN-ROC, press release, January 10, 1969, SAN-ROC collection.
9. *Morning Star* [London], January 14, 1969.
10. Dennis Brutus to the manager of the West German Athletic team, January 30, 1969, SAN-ROC collection.
11. *Star* [Johannesburg], January 28, 1969.
12. Ibid.
13. *News/Check* [Johannesburg], February 7, 1969.
14. Dennis Brutus, interview, March 27, 1973.
15. *Sunday Express* [Johannesburg], February 9, 1969.
16. Ibid.
17. IOC, *Newsletter #19* (April 1969), p. 226. (This is a monthly publication issued by the IOC in Lausanne.)
18. *Eastern Province Herald* [Port Elizabeth], March 24, 1969.
19. *Guardian* [Manchester], February 5, 1969.
20. *Star* [Johannesburg], February 21, 1969.
21. *Eastern Province Herald* [Port Elizabeth], March 9, 1969.
22. *The South African Sportsman* [Johannesburg], March 1969.
23. *Evening News* [London], March 3, 1969.
24. *Morning Star* [London], March 4, 1969.
25. *Star* [Johannesburg], March 5, 1969.
26. *Eastern Province Herald* [Port Elizabeth], March 8, 1969.
27. *Evening News* [London], March 11, 1969.
28. Ibid.
29. *Rand Daily Mail* [Johannesburg], March 13, 1969.
30. See: *Eastern Province Herald* [Port Elizabeth], March 13, 1969, and *Morning Star* [London], March 17, 1969.
31. *The Times* [London], March 18, 1969.
32. *Zealandia* [Dunedin], March 27, 1969.
33. *Natal Mercury* [Durban], March 21, 1969.
34. *Eastern Province Herald* [Port Elizabeth], March 25, 1969.
35. Ibid.

36. *Zealandia* [Dunedin], March 27, 1969.
37. *The Times* [London], March 24, 1969.
38. Ibid.
39. SCSA, press release Yaounde, March 26, 1969, SCSA collection.
40. *Aukland Star,* March 28, 1969.
41. *World* [Johannesburg], April 9-16, 1969.
42. *Sunday Times* [Durban], June 1, 1969.
43. *Sunday Times* [Johannesburg], June 1, 1969.
44. *The Times* [London], June 9, 1969.
45. *Aukland Star,* October 24, 1969.
46. *Cape Argus* [Cape Town], March 1, 1969.
47. *The Times* [London], August 20, 1969.
48. Ibid.
49. *Sunday Tribune* [Durban], September 7, 1969.
50. Muriel Horrell, ed., *A Survey of Race Relations in South Africa, 1969* (Johannesburg: South African Institute of Race Relations, 1970), p. 250. *A Survey* is an annual published by the South African Institute of Race Relations. Hereafter, references will be cited as: Horrell, ed., *Survey:* followed by the year covered. For example, this citation would read: Horrell, ed., *Survey: 1969,* p. 250.
51. *Morning Star* [London], March 17, 1969.
52. SAN-ROC to Oscar State, June 14, 1969, SAN-ROC collection.
53. *Post* [Natal], July 13, 1969.
54. FIH, official report, Mexico, 1968, FIH collection.
55. Horrell, ed., *Survey: 1969,* p. 252.
56. Ibid.
57. *Morning Star* [London], November 20, 1969.
58. *The Times* [London], March 31, 1969.
59. *Post* [Natal], April 20, 1969.
60. Ibid.
61. *Sunday Tribune* [Durban], April 13, 1969.
62. *Star* [Johannesburg], May 7, 1969.
63. *Sunday Tribune* [Durban], April 13, 1969.
64. *Star* [Johannesburg], May 13, 1969.
65. *The Times* [London], May 20, 27, 1969.
66. Ibid., May 14, 1969.
67. *Sunday Times* [Johannesburg], June 1, 1969.
68. *The Times* [London], June 30, 1969.
69. SAN-ROC to all ILTF members, July 1, 1969, SAN-ROC collection.
70. *Star* [Johannesburg], July 1, 1969.

71. *Daily News* [Durban], July 7, 1969.
72. *Sunday Express* [Johannesburg], July 27, 1969.
73. Brutus, interview, March 27, 1973.
74. Horrell, ed., *Survey: 1969,* p. 250.
75. *Eight O'Clock* [Aukland], July 5, 1969.
76. SAN-ROC, press release, August 16, 1969, SAN-ROC collection.
77. *Outlook* [Melbourne], April 1969.
78. Ibid.
79. Horrell, ed., *Survey: 1969,* p. 252.
80. *Star* [Johannesburg], March 12, 1969.
81. Horrell, ed., *Survey: 1969,* p. 255.
82. CARE, *An ABC of Racial Sport* (Aukland: CARE, 1969).
83. *Listener* [New Zealand], April 3, 1969.
84. Horrell, ed., *Survey: 1969,* p. 255.
85. Colin Legum and John Drysdale, *Africa Contemporary Record, Annual Survey and Documents, 1969-70* (Exeter: Africa Research Ltd., 1970), p. B273.
86. *The Times* [London], September 19, 1969.
87. *Star* [Johannesburg], September 21, 1969.
88. Ibid., September 23, 1969.
89. *The Times* [London], September 26, 1969.
90. Horrell, ed., *Survey: 1969,* p. 255.
91. Legum and Drysdale, *Africa Record,* p. B287.
92. *Sunday Times* [Johannesburg], October 26, 1969.
93. *The Times* [London], November 22, 1969.
94. Te Ragatahi, to Maori council, transcript of presentation, December 6, 1969, CARE collection.
95. *Guardian* [Manchester], December 10, 1969.
96. SAN-ROC, November 20, 1969.
97. *Guardian* [Manchester], November 22, 1969.
98. Ibid.
99. Horrell, ed., *Survey: 1969,* p. 254.
100. Ibid.
101. *The Times* [London], January 23, 1969.
102. Ibid.
103. *Guardian* [Manchester], January 23, 1969.
104. *The Times* [London], April 7, 1969.
105. Ibid.
106. Ibid., April 8, 1969.
107. *Evening Post* [Port Elizabeth], April 7, 1969.
108. *The Times* [London], April 9, 1969.

109. See: *Sunday Times* [London], April 13, 1969, and *The Times* [London], April 14, 1969.
110. *Guardian* [Manchester], April 11, 1969.
111. *Daily Sketch* [London], April 21, 1969.
112. *The Times* [London], April 25, 1969.
113. Ibid., April 26, 1969.
114. Ibid., May 2, 1969.
115. Brutus, interview, March 27, 1973.
116. *The Times* [London], June 9, 1969.
117. Ibid., July 8, 1969.
118. *Guardian* [Manchester], July 10, 1969.
119. *The Times* [London], July 10, 1969.
120. *Evening News* [London], July 17, 1969.
121. *Evening Post* [Port Elizabeth], July 17, 1960.
122. *Eastern Province Herald* [Port Elizabeth], August 12, 1969.
123. Ibid.
124. *The Times* [London], August 11, 1969.
125. *Rand Daily Mail* [Johannesburg], September 9, 1969.
126. STST, transcript of press conference, September 10, 1969, STST collection.
127. *The Times* [London], September 11, 1969.
128. *Guardian* [Manchester], September 11, 1969.
129. *The Times* [London], September 22, 1969.
130. *Christian Science Monitor* [Boston], September 27, 1969.
131. Peter Hain, *Don't Play with Apartheid* (London: George Allen and Unwin, 1971), p. 126.
132. *The Times* [London], October 11, 1969.
133. Ibid., October 20, 1969.
134. Ibid., October 25, 1969.
135. Hain, *Don't Play with Apartheid,* p. 127.
136. Legum and Drysdale, *Africa Record,* p. B287.
137. Ibid.
138. *Star* [Johannesburg], October 29, 1969.
139. *The Times* [London], October 29, 1969.
140. *Rand Daily Mail* [Johannesburg], October 31, 1969.
141. *The Times* [London], October 31, 1969.
142. Ibid.
143. *AMANDLA* [bulletin of the Irish AAM] (October 1969): 3.
144. Irish AAM, various documents, November 4, 1969, AAM collection.
145. *The Times* [London], November 4, 1969.
146. Ibid.
147. *Guardian* [Manchester], November 7, 1969.

148. "Apartheid Is Not a Game," *New Statesman* [London] (November 7, 1969): 1-2.
149. See: *Evening News* [London], November 11, 1969, and Hain, *Don't Play with Apartheid,* p. 132.
150. *Guardian* [Manchester], November 10, 1969.
151. Horrell, ed., *Survey: 1969,* p. 248.
152. *The Times* [London], November 11, 1969.
153. Ibid.
154. Ibid., November 13, 1969.
155. Horrell, ed., *Survey: 1969,* p. 248.
156. See: *The Times* [London], November 17, 18, 1969; *Observer* [London], November 16, 1969; *Sunday Mirror* [London], November 16, 1969; *Daily Express* [Johannesburg], November 18, 1969.
157. *The Times* [London], November 17, 1969.
158. Peter Hain, interview, April 14, 1970.
159. *Guardian* [Manchester], November 20, 1969.
160. Ibid., November 21, 1969.
161. Administrative Council of the Irish Labour party, resolution on the South African tour, November 14, 1969, AAM collection.
162. *The Times* [London], November 26, 1969.
163. *Guardian* [Manchester], November 22, 1969.
164. STST, confidential briefing on Twickenham, November 22, 1969, STST collection.
165. *Guardian* [Manchester], November 24, 1969.
166. *The Times* [London], November 27, 1969.
167. Ibid., November 28, 1969.
168. Ibid., December 3, 1969.
169. Hain, *Don't Play with Apartheid,* p. 139.
170. *Guardian* [Manchester], December 5, 1969.
171. *The Times* [London], December 6, 1969.
172. Hain, *Don't Play with Apartheid,* p. 140.
173. *The Times* [London], December 8, 1969.
174. Irish AAM, press conference transcript, December 10, 1969, AAM collection.
175. *The Times* [London], December 12, 1969.
176. *Sunday Times* [Johannesburg], December 14, 1969.
177. *Natal Mercury* [Durban], December 16, 1969.
178. *Guardian* [Manchester], December 19, 1969.
179. Ibid., December 23, 1969.
180. Hain, *Don't Play with Apartheid,* p. 142.

181. *Sunday Telegraph* [London], December 21, 1969.
182. *Guardian* [Manchester], December 24, 1969.
183. Ibid.
184. *The Times* [London], December 22, 1969.
185. *AMANDLA* (December 1969).
186. *Guardian* [Manchester], January 2, 1970.
187. Ibid.
188. SAN-ROC to the East African nations re MCC, December 31, 1969, SAN-ROC collection.
189. *The Times* [London], January 3, 8, 9, 1970.
190. Ibid., January 8, 1970.
191. Ibid., January 9, 1970.
192. Irish AAM, declaration on rugby tour of Ireland, Irish AAM collection.
193. *Irish Press* [Dublin], January 8, 1970.
194. *Irish Independent* [Dublin], January 10, 1970.
195. *Irish Press* [Dublin], January 10, 1970.
196. Ibid.
197. *Sunday Independent* [Dublin], January 11, 1970.
198. *The Times* [London], January 12, 1970.
199. *Irish Times* [Dublin], January 12, 1970.
200. *Guardian* [Manchester], January 14, 1970.
201. *Morning Star* [London], January 14, 1970.
202. *Evening Post* [Port Elizabeth], January 17, 1970.
203. *Guardian* [Manchester], January 21, 1970.
204. *The Times* [London], January 21, 1970.
205. Ibid., January 30, 1970.
206. Ibid., January 29, 1970.
207. Ibid.
208. *Guardian* [Manchester], January 31, 1970.
209. Ibid.
210. *Daily Mirror* [London], February 3, 1970.
211. *The Times* [London], February 2, 1970.
212. Ibid., February 3, 1970.
213. *Morning Star* [London], February 4, 1970.
214. *Evening Standard* [London], February 9, 1970.
215. Hain, *Don't Play with Apartheid,* p. 168.
216. *Daily Telegraph* [London], February 23, 1970.
217. Hain, *Don't Play with Apartheid,* p. 169.
218. *The Times* [London], February 23, 1970.

219. Ibid.
220. Ibid.
221. *Guardian* [Manchester], February 20, 1970.
222. Information gathered by personal attendance at March 7, 1970, STST conference in London.
223. *The Times* [London], March 23, 1970.
224. *Star* [Johannesburg], March 28, 1970.
225. *The Times* [London], March 25, 1970.
226. Ibid., April 5, 1970.
227. Hain, *Don't Play with Apartheid,* p. 176.
228. *Observer* [London], April 12, 1970.
229. *Guardian* [Manchester], April 17, 1970.
230. Ibid.
231. Ibid., April 21, 1970.
232. *Observer* [London], April 26, 1970.
233. Ibid.
234. *Guardian* [Manchester], April 28, 1970.
235. Ibid., April 21, 1970.
236. Ibid., April 22, 1970.
237. Ibid.
238. Ibid., April 23, 1970.
239. Ibid., April 24, 1970.
240. Ibid.
241. Ibid., April 30, 1970.
242. *Sunday Times* [London], April 26, 1970.
243. *Guardian* [Manchester], April 30, 1970.
244. Ibid., April 27, 1970.
245. Ibid., April 30, 1970.
246. Ibid., April 29, 1970.
247. Ibid., May 1, 1970.
248. *Observer* [London], May 3, 1970.
249. *Sunday Times* [London], May 3, 1970.
250. *Guardian* [Manchester], May 4, 1970.
251. See: *Sunday Times* [London], May 3, 1970, and *Observer* [London], May 3, 1970.
252. *Guardian* [Manchester], May 4, 1970.
253. Ibid., May 6, 12, 1970.
254. Ibid., May 13, 1970.
255. Ibid., May 15, 1970.
256. Ibid., May 13, 1970.

257. *Observer* [London], May 10, 1970.
258. *Guardian* [Manchester], May 7, 1970.
259. *The Times* [London], May 9, 1970.
260. *Guardian* [Manchester], May 15, 1970.
261. Ibid.
262. Ibid.
263. Ibid.
264. Ibid.
265. Ibid.
266. *Star* [Johannesburg], May 15, 1970.
267. *Rand Daily Mail* [Johannesburg], May 16, 1970.
268. *The Times* [London], May 16, 1970.
269. Ibid.
270. *Sunday Times* [London], May 17, 1970.
271. *Observer* [London], May 17, 1970.
272. *The Times* [London], May 16, 1970.
273. *Guardian* [Manchester], May 18, 1970.
274. *Evening Standard* [London], May 19, 1970.
275. *Guardian* [Manchester], May 20, 1970.
276. Ibid.
277. *The Times* [London], May 20, 1970.
278. See: *Evening News* [London], May 20, 1970, and *Guardian* [Manchester], May 20, 1970.
279. *Evening Standard* [London], May 20, 1970.
280. *Guardian* [Manchester], May 22, 1970.
281. Ibid.
282. Ibid.
283. Ibid., May 23, 1970.
284. *The Times* [London], May 23, 1970.
285. *Guardian* [Manchester], May 22, 1970.
286. *Sunday Times* [London], May 24, 1970.
287. *Evening Standard* [London], May 23, 1970.
288. *Guardian* [Manchester], May 25, 1970.
289. *Star* [Johannesburg], May 23, 1970.
290. *Rand Daily Mail* [Johannesburg], May 23, 1970.
291. *The Times* [London], May 23, 1970.
292. *Sunday Times* [London], May 24, 1970.
293. *Guardian* [Manchester], May 23, 1970.
294. Ibid.
295. *The Times* [London], May 23, 1970.

296. Ibid.
297. Ibid.
298. *Star* [Johannesburg], January 28, 1970.
299. See: *Star* [Johannesburg], *The Times* [London], *Guardian* [Manchester], *Daily Express* [Johannesburg], *Daily Telegraph* [London], and *San Francisco Chronicle,* all January 29, 1970.
300. *Star* [Johannesburg], January 29, 1970.
301. Ibid.
302. *Rand Daily Mail* [Johannesburg], January 29, 1970.
303. *Star* [Johannesburg], January 29, 1970.
304. *San Francisco Chronicle,* January 29, 1970.
305. Ibid.
306. Ibid.
307. See: *The Times* [London], January 29, 1970, and *Guardian* [Manchester], January 29, 1970.
308. *Sunday Tribune* [Durban], February 1, 1970.
309. *New Zealand Herald* [Aukland], January 30, 1970.
310. Ibid.
311. *The Times* [London], January 17, 1970.
312. Ibid.
313. *San Francisco Chronicle,* February 2, 1970.
314. *The Times* [London], March 21, 1970.
315. *International Herald Tribune* [Paris], April 27, 1970.
316. Oliver S. Crosby, testimony to the Subcommittee on African Affairs of the House Committee on Foreign Affairs, February 4, 1970 (Mimeographed) London: SAN-ROC files.
317. Based on Dennis Brutus' Testimony to the Subcommittee on African Affairs of the House Committee on Foreign Affairs, February 5, 1970 (Mimeographed) London: SAN-ROC files.
318. *Morning Star* [London], February 3, 1970.
319. U.N. Special Committee on Apartheid, press release #GA/AP/187, March 23, 1970.
320. Ibid., press release #GA/AP/190, April 14, 1970.
321. *Rand Daily Mail* [Johannesburg], March 24, 1970.
322. Horrell, ed., *Survey: 1970,* p. 279.
323. See: *Australian* [Sydney], January 14, 1970, *Melbourne Age,* January 21, 1970.
324. *New York Times,* March 24, 1970.
325. *Rand Daily Mail* [Johannesburg], March 25, 1970.
326. Ibid.

327. *Star* [Johannesburg], March 25, 1970.
328. See: ibid., March 24, 1970, and *Rand Daily Mail* [Johannesburg], March 25, 1970.
329. *Rand Daily Mail* [Johannesburg], March 25, 1970.
330. *The Times* [London], April 6, 1970.
331. Horrell, ed., *Survey: 1970,* p. 279.
332. U.N. Special Committee on Apartheid, press release #GA/AP/190.
333. *Guardian* [Manchester], May 19, 1970.
334. Horrell, ed., *Survey: 1970,* p. 280.
335. IOC, *Olympic Review #30-31,* p. 207 (Lausanne: IOC).
336. *Sunday Times* [London], March 29, 1970.
337. *Star* [Johannesburg], March 28, 1970.
338. Ibid.
339. *The Times* [London], January 29, 1970.
340. Horrell, ed., *Survey: 1970,* p. 280.
341. *Sunday Times* [London], March 29, 1970.
342. Horrell, ed., *Survey: 1970,* p. 279.
343. *Guardian* [Manchester], May 14, 1970.
344. *New Zealand Herald* [Aukland], January 28, 1970.
345. Tom Newnham to Masinde Muliro, March 16, 1970, CARE collection.
346. *The Times* [London], March 20, 1970.
347. *Guardian* [Manchester], May 8, 1970.
348. Ibid., May 14, 1970.
349. Ibid., May 15, 1970.
350. Ibid., April 24, 1970.
351. Ibid., May 25, 1970.
352. Ibid.
353. Horrell, ed., *Survey: 1970,* pp. 275-76.
354. *Rand Daily Mail* [Johannesburg], May 16, 1970.
355. Ibid.
356. *Star* [Johannesburg], May 14, 1970.
357. SAN-ROC, report on the Cairo meeting of the SCSA, SAN-ROC collection.
358. African NOCs' charges against SANOC, addressed to the IOC Amsterdam session, May 1970, SAN-ROC collection.
359. South African delegation to the IOC, May 15, 1970, p. 1, SAN-ROC collection.
360. Ibid.
361. Ibid., p. 2.

362. Ibid., p. 4.
363. Ibid., p. 5.
364. Ibid., pp. 5-7.
365. Ibid., pp. 7-8.
366. See: *The Times* [London], May 16, 1970, *Guardian* [Manchester], May 16, 1970, *Sunday Times* [London], May 17, 1970, and *Observer* [London], May 17, 1970.
367. *Rand Daily Mail* [Johannesburg], May 16, 1970.
368. *The Times* [London], May 16, 1970.
369. *Newsweek* (May 25, 1970): 18.
370. *The Times* [London], May 16, 1970.
371. *Observer* [London], May 17, 1970.
372. *The Times* [London], May 16, 1970.
373. Monique Berlioux, *Olympism* (Lausanne: IOC, 1972), p. 8.
374. Ibid., p. 10.
375. Ibid., p. 2.
376. All figures were compiled from the official *Olympic Directory, 1969* (Lausanne: IOC, 1969).
377. *Guardian* [Manchester], May 25, 1970.
378. Ibid., June 1, 1970.
379. *Rand Daily Mail* [Johannesburg], May 25, 1970.
380. Ibid.
381. Ibid., May 26, 1970.
382. Ibid., May 27, 1970.
383. Ibid., May 28, 1970.
384. Ibid., May 30, 1970.
385. *Guardian* [Manchester], June 1, 1970.

Bibliography

MANUSCRIPTS AND BOOKS

Manuscripts

"Sport and Politics in an Urban African Community." Johannesburg, 1967 (anonymous).

Books

Berlioux, Monique, *Olympism.* Lausanne: IOC, 1972.

Brundage, Avery. *The Speeches of President Avery Brundage, 1952 to 1968.* Lausanne: IOC, 1969.

Bunting, Brian. *The Rise of the South African Reich.* New York: Penguin, 1969.

De Broglio, Chris. *South Africa: Racism in Sport.* London: Christian Action Publications Ltd., 1970.

D'Oliveira, Basil. *The D'Oliveira Affair.* London: Collins, 1969.

Drysdale, John, and Legum, Colin, eds. *Africa Contemporary Record, Annual Survey and Documents, 1968-69.* London: Africa Research Ltd., 1969.

_____. *Africa Contemporary Record, Annual Survey and Documents, 1969-70.* Exeter: Africa Research Ltd., 1970.

Edwards, Harry. *The Revolt of the Black Athlete.* New York: Free Press, 1969.

Hain, Peter. *Don't Play with Apartheid.* London: George Allen and Unwin, 1971.

Horrell, Muriel, ed. *A Survey of Race Relations in South Africa.* Johannesburg: South African Institute of Race Relations, 1949-1973.

Mandell, Richard D. *The Nazi Olympics.* New York: Macmillan, 1971.

Morse, Arthur D. *While Six Million Died.* London: Secker and Warburg, 1968.

Owens, Jesse. *Blackthink: My Life as a Black Man and White Man.* New York: William Morrow, 1970.

Schobel, Heinz. *The Four Dimensions of Avery Brundage.* Leipzig: Edition Leipzig, 1968.

Thompson, Richard. *Race and Sport.* London: Oxford University Press, 1964.

Van den Berghe, Pierre, ed. *Africa: Social Problems of Change and Conflict.* San Francisco: Chandler Publishing Co., 1965.

PERIODICALS AND NEWSPAPERS

Periodicals

"Apartheid Is Not a Game." *New Statesman* (November 7, 1969): 1-2.

"Dennis Brutus Interviewed." *Outlook* (April 1969): 1-6.

"England in Danger." *New Statesman* (May 1, 1970): 1-2.

Lureman, Steyn. "The South African Games Will Succeed." *South African Sportsman* (March 1969): 12-15.

Maule, Tex. "A Flare in the Dark." *Sports Illustrated* (June 3, 1968): 60-74.

"NCAA." *Newsweek* (January 5, 1970): 35.

Olsen, Jack. "The Black Athlete: A Shameful Story." *Sports Illustrated* (July 1, 1968): 15-27.

Olympic Review. 1968-1972 (Numbers 1 through 61). The first twenty-seven issues of this monthly publication of the IOC were called *Newsletter.*

"South Africa: A Losing Game." *Newsweek* (May 25, 1970): 18.

Newspapers

Aukland Star.

Australian [Sydney].

Cape Argus [Cape Town].

Cape Times [Cape Town].

Christian Science Monitor [Boston].

Daily Express [Johannesburg].

Daily Mirror [London].

Daily News [Durban].

Daily Sketch [London].

Daily Telegraph [London].

Eastern Province Herald [Port Elizabeth].

Eight O'Clock [Aukland].

Evening News [London].

Evening Post [Port Elizabeth].

Evening Standard [London].

Guardian [Manchester].
Golden City Post.
International Herald Tribune [Paris].
Irish Independent [Dublin].
Irish Press [Dublin].
Irish Times [Dublin].
Los Angeles Times.
Melbourne Age.
Morning Star [London].
Natal Mercury [Durban].
News/Check [Johannesburg].
New York Herald Tribune.
New York Post
New York Times.
New Zealand Herald [Aukland].
New Zealand Listener.
Observer [London].
People [Kampala].
Post [Natal].
Press [Christchurch].
Rand Daily Mail [Johannesburg].
San Francisco Chronicle.
Star [Johannesburg].
Sunday Express [Johannesburg].
Sunday Independent [Dublin].
Sunday Mirror [London].
Sunday Telegraph [London].
Sunday Times [Johannesburg].
Sunday Times [London].
Sunday Tribune [Durban].
The Times [London].
World [Johannesburg].

COLLECTIONS

Note: All documents listed in the text and in the footnotes are available from the organizations listed below. The most significant collection is that of SAN-ROC, which has a tremendous library of the history of the extension of apartheid into sport. Other crucial collections are located at the offices of the International Olympic Committee, the American Committee on Africa, the Stop the

Seventy Tour Committee, and the Supreme Council for Sport in Africa. The remaining organizations listed, the Irish Anti-Apartheid Movement and the Citizens Association for Racial Equality (New Zealand), have collections relevant to their nations' relations with South Africa. The addresses of the organizations and their collections are:

1. American Committee on Africa (ACOA)
   164 Madison Avenue
   New York, N.Y. 10016
   (212) 532-3700

2. Citizens Association for Racial Equality (CARE)
   Box 2794
   Aukland, New Zealand

3. International Olympic Committee (IOC)
   Chateau de Vidy
   1007 Lausanne
   Switzerland

4. Irish Anti-Apartheid Movement
   173 Barton Road East
   Dundrum, Dublin 14
   Ireland

5. South African Non-Racial Open Committee (SAN-ROC)
   28 Seymour Street
   Portman Court Hotel
   London W1, England

6. Stop The Seventy Tour Committee (STST)
   c/o Peter Hain
   21a Gwendolyn Avenue
   London SW15, England

7. Supreme Council for Sport in Africa (SCSA)
   Box 2065
   Yaounde, Cameroon
   West Africa

Index